AF480837

Crack the SAT Math Code:
Proven Techniques and Exercises
Edition: I

Succeed on the SAT Math Test: Easy Techniques

Dr. Summiya Parveen

Dr. Aruna Tomar

Copyright © Dr. Summiya Parveen
All Rights Reserved.

This book has been self-published with all reasonable efforts taken to make the material error-free by the author. No part of this book shall be used, reproduced in any manner whatsoever without written permission from the author, except in the case of brief quotations embodied in critical articles and reviews.

The Author of this book is solely responsible and liable for its content including but not limited to the views, representations, descriptions, statements, information, opinions and references ["Content"]. The Content of this book shall not constitute or be construed or deemed to reflect the opinion or expression of the Publisher or Editor. Neither the Publisher nor Editor endorse or approve the Content of this book or guarantee the reliability, accuracy or completeness of the Content published herein and do not make any representations or warranties of any kind, express or implied, including but not limited to the implied warranties of merchantability, fitness for a particular purpose. The Publisher and Editor shall not be liable whatsoever for any errors, omissions, whether such errors or omissions result from negligence, accident, or any other cause or claims for loss or damages of any kind, including without limitation, indirect or consequential loss or damage arising out of use, inability to use, or about the reliability, accuracy or sufficiency of the information contained in this book.

Made with ❤ on the Notion Press Platform
www.notionpress.com

Preface

Welcome to "Crack the SAT Math Code: Proven Techniques and Exercises." This book is designed to be your comprehensive guide to mastering the mathematics section of the SAT exam. Whether you're a high school student preparing to take the test for the first time or an experienced test-taker looking to improve your score, the strategies and exercises in this book are tailored to help you succeed.

The SAT math section can be daunting, but it doesn't have to be. With the right approach and plenty of practice, you can develop the skills and confidence needed to tackle even the most challenging math problems. In this book, you'll find a wealth of proven techniques, comprehensive content coverage, and effective exercises to help you crack the SAT math code and achieve your target score.

Throughout these pages, you'll discover strategies for approaching different types of math questions, clear explanations of key concepts, and ample opportunities to practice your skills. Whether you're struggling with algebraic equations, geometry theorems, or data analysis, this book is here to guide you every step of the way.

Remember, success on the SAT math section is not just about memorizing formulas—it's about understanding the underlying concepts, applying effective problem-solving strategies, and practicing consistently. I encourage you to approach your study with dedication and perseverance, and to use this book as a valuable tool on your journey to SAT math mastery.

I wish you the best of luck as you prepare for the SAT exam. Remember, you have the knowledge and skills within you to succeed—you just need to unlock them. Let "Crack the SAT Math Code" be your guide as you embark on this exciting journey.

Warm regards,
Dr Summiya Parveen
Assistant Professor
COER University
Roorkee, Haridwar
Uttarakhand 247667
India
Email Id: summiyaparveen82@gmail.com

Book Description:

Unlock the secrets to SAT math success with "Crack the SAT Math Code: Proven Techniques and Exercises." This comprehensive guide is your key to mastering the mathematical concepts and problem-solving strategies needed to conquer the SAT math section.

Inside this book, you'll discover:

- **Proven Techniques:** Learn time-tested strategies for approaching SAT math questions with confidence and precision. From tackling algebraic equations to dissecting complex geometry problems, "Crack the SAT Math Code" equips you with the tools you need to decode even the most challenging math puzzles.

- **Comprehensive Content Coverage:** Dive deep into the core mathematical concepts tested on the SAT. With clear explanations and illustrative examples, this book covers everything from arithmetic and algebra to geometry, trigonometry, and data analysis, ensuring you have a solid foundation to tackle any question that comes your way.

- **Effective Exercises:** Put your skills to the test with a variety of carefully crafted exercises designed to reinforce your understanding of key concepts and hone your problem-solving abilities. Detailed solutions and explanations accompany each exercise, guiding you through the thought process behind each solution and helping you learn from your mistakes.

- **Test-Taking Strategies:** Gain valuable insights into the structure of the SAT math section and discover expert tips for maximizing your score. Whether you're struggling with time management, uncertain about which questions to prioritize, or seeking ways to minimize errors, "Crack the SAT Math Code" provides the guidance you need to succeed on test day.

- **Full-Length Practice Tests:** Put your skills to the ultimate test with multiple full-length practice tests modeled after the SAT math section. These tests simulate the actual exam experience, allowing you to assess your progress, identify areas for improvement, and build confidence as you work towards achieving your target score.

Unlock the door to SAT math success with "Crack the SAT Math Code: Proven Techniques and Exercises" and pave your way to academic excellence and future opportunities.

TABLE OF CONTENTS

INTRODUCTION

Part (I) Heart Algebra

1. Linear Equations in One Variable
2. Linear Equations in Two Variables
3. Linear Equations - Word Problems
4. Systems of Linear Equations
5. Linear Inequalities
6. Linear Systems and Inequalities

Part (II) Advance Algebra

1. Absolute Value Equations, Inequalities and Graphs
2. Quadratic Equations, Polynomial Equations and Rational Equations
3. Exponential Equations, Radicals
4. Equivalent expressions, Isolating Quantities
5. Nonlinear equations and non-linear functions
6. Linear, Quadratic and Exponential Equations
7. Quadratic, Exponential, and Polynomial

Part (III) Problem Solving and Data Analysis

1. Ratios, Rates, Proportional Relationships, and Units/Conversions
2. Percentages
3. Two-Variable Data - Models and Scatterplots
4. Probability and Conditional Probability
5. Distributions and Measures of Center and Spread
6. Data Inferences - Inference from Sample Statistics and Margin of Error, Evaluating Statistical Claims - Observational Studies and Experiments

Part (IV) Geometry and Trigonometry

1. Area and Volume Formulas; Word Problems
2. Lines, Angles, and Triangles, Congruent and Similar Triangles
3. Right Triangles and Trigonometry
4. Circles - Unit Circles, Angles/Arc, Equation

Part (V) Math Formula/ Key Notes

INTRODUCTION TO MATH

Welcome to the college entrance exam test!

Recent Changes

Here we will be looking at the Math section of the test. In the past, Math was separated into two sections (No-Calculator and Calculator), but the new test will have Math in one section.

Additionally, the new test is shorter. Instead of 3 hours and 15 minutes, it is now 2 hours and 15 minutes.

One of the biggest changes, however, is the test is now *digital.*

Yes, you will be taking it all on a computer! Not to worry, it's quite normal. Most assessment tests these days are done on a computer. If you have used strategies in the past that used pencil to paper, you can still use those same strategies.

Format: The test will have 2 "modules" for the Math section. Before the beginning of the "regular" test questions, the computer will give 2 "pretest" questions, which will determine what the rest of the questions will look like.

So here's how it's going to go step-by-step for the Math section:

1. Module 1 will begin

2. Two pretest questions

3. "Operational" questions. These questions are the "real" test questions, so to speak. There will be 20 operational questions. These will be a mix of four-option multiple choice ($\approx75\%$) and student produced response (SPR) ($\approx25\%$) in the classic ABCD/four option format type of questions. You have 35 minutes to do this.

4. Module 1 will end

5. Module 2 will begin

6. Two pretest questions

7. "Operational" questions. Same thing as in the first module. These are the "real" test questions. You will again have 35 minutes to do this.

8. Module 2 will end

Common Questions

1. How will I go back to (a) question(s)? The test assessment software will give you the ability to flag a question for you to look back at it later.

2. How will I keep track of my time? Thankfully, there will be a timer right on your computer that you can look at.

3. How can I leave notes for myself? The software has the ability to let you highlight things as well as write notes for yourselves. It is still very annotation-friendly.

4. Which computer will I be using? Yours! Most computers are compatible with the test, but if you don't have one, you can register for one.

5. Will there be charging stations? Yes, but you still need to have your computer fully charged when you arrive.

6. How will I receive internet connectivity? The internet connectivity will be available at the testing center.

7. Can I take the test at home? No. You will still have to take it at a testing center.

8. Why are there 2 modules? Glad you asked! The 1st module will actually determine the level of difficulty of the 2nd module. This is called adaptive testing.

9. Can I use a calculator? Yes! A built-in graphing calculator is available throughout the Math section. (Students can also bring their own approved calculator)

10. Will I have access to a reference sheet for formulas? Yes!

Contents: The Math section of the test has 4 main domains:

1. Algebra: ≈35% of entire test / 13-15 questions, and covers linear equations, inequalities, and systems of equations.

2. Advanced Math: ≈35% of entire test / 13-15 questions, and measures skills and understanding of absolute value, quadratic, exponential, polynomial, rational, radical, and other nonlinear equations.

3. Problem-Solving and Data Analysis: ≈15% of entire test / 5-7 questions, and includes the topics of ratios, rates, proportions and unit rate.

4. Geometry and Trigonometry: ≈15% of entire test / 5-7 questions, and focuses on area and volume, angles, triangles, trigonometry, and circles.

Scoring

The scoring is still on a 1600-point scale.

Verbal: 200-800

Math: 200-800

A common misconception from students is that each question is worth a certain amount of points. It makes sense since most tests are like this, but there is no way to "tally" the test like this. Some questions are worth more than others based on which test and modules you're taking. This is because harder questions can sometimes be worth less points. So unfortunately, there's not a hard and fast rule.

Timing: Since you have 35 minutes for each module, and you have 22 questions per module, you'll have a little over 1.5 minutes to do each question. So you will have to work fairly fast, but watch your pace too. The way you can work fast while still getting questions right is to become highly familiar with question types, concepts, strategies and the formatting of the test. All of this will be discussed.

Part (I)
Heart Algebra

1. Linear Equations in One Variable
2. Linear Equations in Two Variables
3. Linear Equations - Word Problems
4. Systems of Linear Equations
5. Linear Inequalities
6. Linear Systems and Inequalities

Lesson 1 - Linear Equations in One Variable

Introduction to Linear Equations:

- A linear equation represents a straight-line relationship between variables.

- The general form of a linear equation is $\mathbf{ax + b = c}$, where:

    - $\mathbf{a}$ is the coefficient of the variable.

    - $\mathbf{x}$ is the variable you're trying to solve for.

    - $\mathbf{b}$ is a constant.

    - $\mathbf{c}$ is another constant.

Components of a Linear Equation:

- In a linear equation, you'll find variables (like $\mathbf{x}$), coefficients (like $\mathbf{a}$), constants (like $\mathbf{b}$ and $\mathbf{c}$), and equal signs.

- **Variables** are the unknowns you're trying to solve for.

- **Coefficients** are the numbers multiplied by the variable.

- **Constants** are the numbers without variables.

- The **equal sign** signifies that the expression on the left side is equal to the expression on the right side.

Solving Linear Equations:

- The goal is to isolate the variable (usually $\mathbf{x}$) on one side of the equation.

- You can do the same operation to both sides while maintaining equality.

- **Steps:**

    1. Simplify both sides by combining like terms.

    2. Move constants to one side and variable terms to the other side.

    3. Perform inverse operations to isolate the variable.

    4. Check your solution by substituting it back into the equation.

Solving Multi-Step Equations:

- Some linear equations require multiple steps to solve.

- Follow the order of operations (PEMDAS) to simplify the equation.

- Example: Solve $3x - 5 = 7$.

    1. Start by adding 5 to both sides to isolate the term with $\mathbf{x}$.

    2. Now, you have $3x = 12$.

3. Divide both sides by 3 to find x = **4**.

Solving Equations with Fractions and Decimals:

- Handle equations with fractional or decimal coefficients similarly to whole numbers.

- Example: Solve $(1/2)x - 0.5 = 2$.

  1. First, add 0.5 to both sides.

  2. You get $(1/2)x = 2.5$.

  3. Multiply both sides by 2 to find $x = 5$.

Linear Equations with Fractional Coefficients:

- Example: Solve $\frac{1}{2}x - 3 = 2$.

  $$\frac{1}{2}x = 2 + 3$$
  $$\frac{1}{2}x = 5$$

  To clear the fraction, multiply both sides by 2 to get $2 * \frac{1}{2}x = 5 * 2$
  then solve $x = 10$

- Example : Solve for x: $\frac{3}{2}x - \frac{1}{2}x = 4$.

  LCM is 2 : $\frac{(3-1)}{2}x = 4$.

  $$\frac{2}{2}x = 4.$$

  Simplify: $x = 4$

  SO $x = 4$

Linear Equations with Irrational Coefficients:

- Example: Solve $\sqrt{2x} + 4 = 8$.
  Subtract 4 from both sides to get $\sqrt{2x} = 4$, then square both sides to isolate x:
  $2x = 16$
  so $x = 8$.

Linear Equations with Variables in Both the Numerator and Denominator:

- Example: Solve
  $$\frac{(2x + 1)}{(3x - 2)} = 4.$$
  Cross-multiply to get $2x + 1 = 4(3x - 2)$, then solve for x.

Word Problems with Linear Equations:

- In real-world scenarios, you can translate problems into linear equations.

- Define variables to represent unknowns.

- Solve the equation for the variable.

    Example: If **x** represents the number of apples, and you know you have 3 more than twice the number of apples, you can write an equation: $x = 2x + 3$.

Example 1: Solving a Basic Linear Equation

Equation: $2x - 5 = 11$

Steps:

1. Start by adding 5 to both sides to isolate the term with **x**.

    - $2x - 5 + 5 = 11 + 5$
    - $2x = 16$

2. Now, to find **x**, divide both sides by 2.

    - $(2x)/2 = 16/2$
    - $x = 8$

Solution: $x = 8$

Example 2: Solving a Multi-Step Linear Equation

Equation: $2(x - 3) = 4x + 1$

Steps:

1. Distribute the 2 on the left side by multiplying it by both terms in the parentheses.

    - $2x - 6 = 4x + 1$

2. Move all terms with **x** to one side and constants to the other side. Let's subtract 2x from both sides and subtract 1 from both sides.

    - $2x - 4x - 6 - 1$

3. Simplify both sides.

    - $-2x - 7 = 0$

4. To isolate **x**, add 7 to both sides.

    - $-2x = 7$

5. Finally, divide by -2 to find **x**.

    - $(-2x)/(-2) = 7/(-2)$
    - $x = -7/2 \, or -3.5$

Solution: $x = -7/2 \, or -3.5$

Example 3: A Word Problem: You have $30, and you want to buy some notebooks for $5 each. Write an equation to represent the situation and find how many notebooks you can buy.

Solution:

- Let **x** represent the number of notebooks.

- The cost of each notebook is $5, so the total cost is $5x$.

- You have $30 to spend, so you can write the equation: $5x = 30$.

Steps to Solve:

1. Divide both sides by 5 to isolate **x**.

    - $(5x)/5 = 30/5$

    - $x = 6$

Solution: You can buy 6 notebooks with $30.

Practice questions:

Adding or Subtracting Fractions with Different Denominators

1. $\frac{3}{2} + \frac{13}{7}$
2. $\frac{1}{2} + \frac{1}{5}$
3. $\frac{5}{3} - \frac{2}{7}$
4. $3 - \frac{3}{7}$
5. $\frac{7}{4} - \frac{5}{8}$
6. $\frac{5}{8} - \frac{1}{7}$

Solve the Multi-Step Equations - Fractions

7. $\frac{x}{2} + \frac{1}{3} = \frac{x}{3} + \frac{1}{2}$
8. $\frac{2x+4}{3x-1} = \frac{1}{2}$
9. $\frac{x+3}{2} + (x - 1) = \frac{4}{5}$
10. $\frac{2}{3}(x + 5) = \frac{4}{9}$
11. $\frac{1}{5}\left(\frac{x}{2} + \frac{3}{4}\right) = \frac{1}{4}$

One Step Equations

12. $2 + x = 10$
13. $21 - x = 20$
14. $15 = 3x + 9$
15. $\frac{5}{2}x = 20$
16. $2x = 10$

Multi-Step Equations and Word Problems

17. Solve for x: $\frac{3x}{4} - 2 = \frac{x}{2} + 3$
18. Solve for x: $\sqrt{x + 5} = 2$
19. Solve for x: $\frac{x}{(x-1)} + \frac{x}{(x+2)} = 2$
20. Solve for x: $4(x - 3) = 2x + 10$
21. You have $50, and you want to buy a toy that costs $18. Write an equation to represent this situation and find out how much money you'll have left.
22. The sum of two consecutive odd integers is 44. Write an equation to represent this situation and find the two integers.
23. Solve for x: $3(2x - 1) + 4 = 2(x + 3) - 1$.
24. You want to buy tickets for a concert. Each ticket costs $25, and you have a budget of $200. Write an equation to represent this situation and find how many tickets you can buy
25. Solve for x: $\frac{1}{4}x - 5 = 7$.
26. Solve for x: $2(3x - 2) + 4 = 3(x + 1) - 2$.

27. Solve for x: $\frac{2}{3}x + 6 = 4$.

28. You want to paint a room. You need 3 gallons of paint, and each gallon costs \$12. Write an equation to represent the cost of painting the room and find the total cost.

Answer

1. $\dfrac{47}{14}$

2. $\dfrac{7}{10}$

3. $\dfrac{29}{21}$

4. $\dfrac{18}{7}$

5. $\dfrac{9}{8}$

6. $\dfrac{27}{56}$

7. $x = 1$

8. $x = -9$

9. $x = \dfrac{1}{5}$

10. $x = -\dfrac{13}{3}$

11. $x = 1$

12. $x = 8$

13. $x = 1$

14. $x = 2$

15. $x = 8$

16. $x = 5$

17. $x = 20$

18. $x = -1$

19. $x = 4$

20. $x = 11$

21. You'll have $32 left after buying the toy.

22. The equation representing this situation is: $n + (n + 2) = 44$

    The two consecutive odd integers are 21 and 23.

23. $x = 1$

24. You can buy 8 tickets for the concert.

25. $x = 48$

26. $x = 1/3$

27. -3

28. The total cost of painting the room is $36.

Lesson 2-Linear Equations in Two Variables

Linear Equations in Two Variables

- A linear equation in two variables, often denoted as **ax + by = c**, represents a relationship between two variables, x and y, such that the highest exponent of each variable is 1.

- The equation can be used to model and solve various real-world problems involving two related quantities.

Representing Linear Equations Graphically

Graphing Linear Equations/Functions

Graphing Linear Equations on the Coordinate Plane

- The coordinate plane consists of the x-axis (horizontal) and the y-axis (vertical).

- A linear equation can be graphically represented as a straight line on this plane.

  Example: Graph the equation $2x - y = 1$ on the coordinate plane.

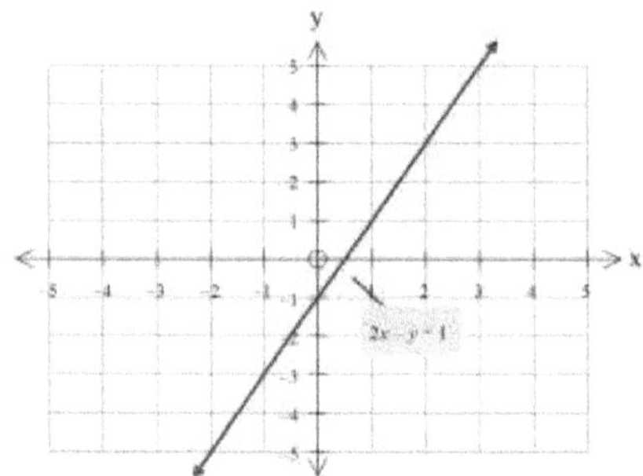

Intercepts and Slope

- The x-intercept is where the line crosses the x-axis, and the y-coordinate is 0.

- The y-intercept is where the line crosses the y-axis, and the x-coordinate is 0.

- Example: For the equation 3x + 4y = 12:

  For x-intercept put $y = 0$ in the given equation $3x + 4(0) = 12 \Rightarrow 3x = 12 \Rightarrow x = 4$

  The x-intercept is (4, 0), and

  For y-intercept put $x = 0$ in the given equation $3(0) + 4y = 12 \Rightarrow 4y = 12 \Rightarrow y = 3$

  the y-intercept is (0, 3).

The slope is -3/4, which means that for every 1-unit increase in x, y decreases by 3/4 units.

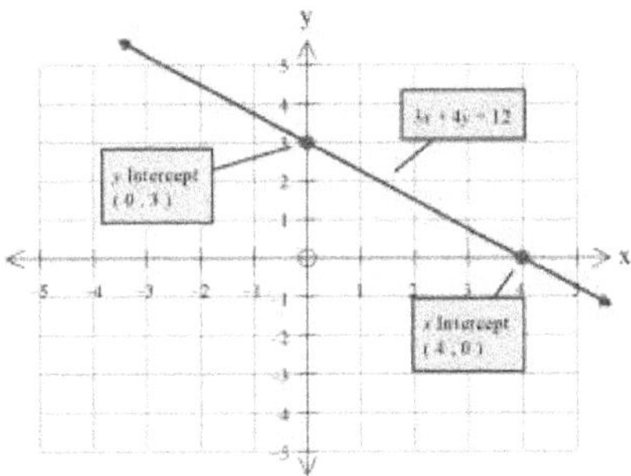

Characteristics of Linear Graphs/Functions

- Linear graphs are straight lines, and their slope and intercepts provide valuable information about the relationship between the variables.

- A slope of 0 indicates a horizontal line, and a slope of 1/0 or undefined slope represents a vertical line

Function Notation

- Linear equations can be written in function notation as **y = mx + c**, where **m** is the slope and **c** is the y-intercept.

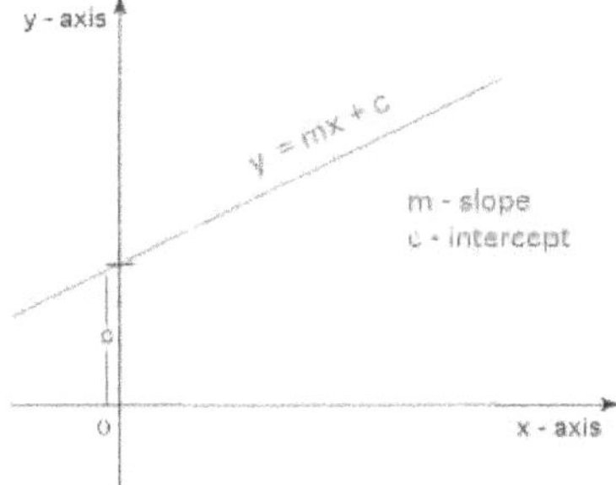

Finding Slope and Y-Intercept

Understanding Slope and Y-Intercept

- The slope (**m**) represents the rate of change of the line, indicating how much y changes for a given change in x.

- The y-intercept (**c**) is the point where the line crosses the y-axis.

Example: For the equation $y = -2x + 5$:

- The slope is -2, indicating that for every 1 unit increase in x, y decreases by 2 units.
- The y-intercept is 5, which is the point (0, 5) where the line crosses the y-axis.

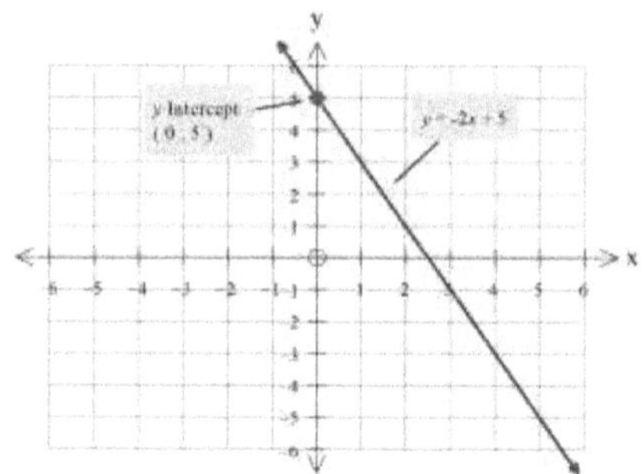

Understanding Slope as a Rate of Change

- The slope measures the change in y for each unit change in x. It can be positive, negative, or zero, depending on the direction of the line.

Calculating Slope from Two Points

- The slope can be calculated using the formula:

- $$m = \frac{(y_2 - y_1)}{(x_2 - x_1)}$$

  where (x_1, y_1) and (x_2, y_2) are two points on the line.

- **Example:** Given points (2, 3) and (5, 1), calculate the slope:

  $$\text{Slope, } m = \frac{(1 - 3)}{(5 - 2)} = -\frac{2}{3}$$

Writing Equations in Slope-Intercept Form

- The slope-intercept form is $y = mx + c$, where **m** is the slope and **c** is the y-intercept.
- **Example:** Convert the equation $3y + 6x = 12$
- Divide by 3 : $3y + 6x = 12 \Rightarrow \frac{3y + 6x}{3} = \frac{12}{3} \Rightarrow y + 2x = 4$
- slope-intercept form: $y = -2x + 4$

Extracting Slope, X-Intercept, and Y-Intercept from Linear Equations

- From the equation, you can identify the slope, x-intercept, and y-intercept directly.
- **Example:** For the equation $4y = -8x + 16$

Divide by 4 : $4y = -8x + 16 \Rightarrow \frac{4y}{4} = \frac{-8x+16}{4} \Rightarrow y = -2x = 4$

slope-intercept form: $y = -2x + 4$

Slope: -2 (from the coefficient of x)

X-intercept: plug $y = 0$, in the given equation $(2, 0)$

Y-intercept: plug $x = 0$, in the given equation $(0, 4)$

Identifying the Slope, X-Intercept, and Y-Intercept from Graphs

- The slope is determined by the steepness of the line, while the intercepts are the points where the line crosses the axes.

- **Example:** Analyze the graph and find the slope, x-intercept, and y-intercept.

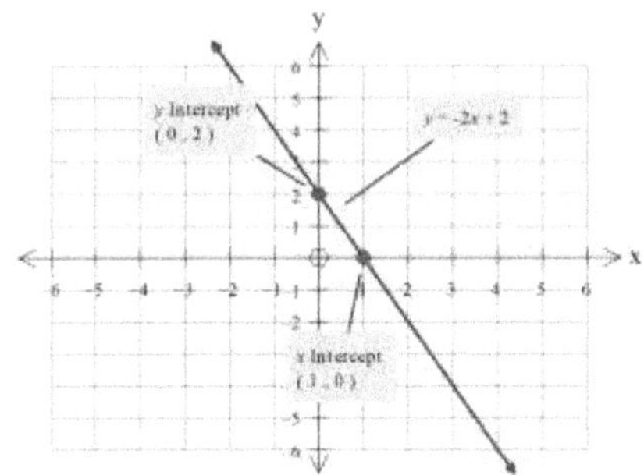

- Slope: -2
- X-intercept: (1, 0)
- Y-intercept: (0, 2)

Interpreting Slope in Real-World Contexts

- In real-world applications, the slope represents the rate of change between the two variables, making it a useful tool for analyzing relationships.

- **Example:** In a business context, if **y** represents profit and **x** represents the number of products sold, a slope of -3 means that for each additional product sold, profit decreases by $3.

Writing Equations of Lines/Functions

Writing Equations Given Slope and a Point

- Given a slope and a point on the line, you can write the equation in slope-intercept form.

$$(y - y_1) = m(x - x_1)$$

- **Example:** Given a slope of 2 and a point $(3, 4)$, write the equation of the line:

$$y - 4 = 2(x - 3)$$

Writing Equations Given Two Points

- With two points on the line, you can calculate the slope and use one of the points to write the equation in point-slope form.

- **Example:** Given points (1, 2) and (3, 6), write the equation of the line:

  Calculate the slope: $m = \dfrac{(6-2)}{(3-1)} = 2$

  Using point-slope form: $y - 2 = 2(x - 1)$

Point-Slope Form of a Linear Function Equation

- The point-slope form is **y - y₁ = m(x - x₁)**, where (x_1, y_1) is a point on the line, and **m** is the slope.

- **Example:** For the equation $y - 5 = 3(x - 2)$:

  Point (2, 5) is on the line, and the slope is 3.

Standard Form of a Linear Equation

- The standard form is **Ax + By = C**, where A, B, and C are constants, and A should be a positive integer.

- **Example:** Convert the equation $y = \dfrac{2}{3}x - 4$ and translate to standard form: y =2x/3 - 4

  $$y = \frac{2x - 12}{3}$$
  $$3y = 2x - 12$$
  $$2x - 3y = 12 \quad \text{(A, B, and C are constants, and A should be positive)}$$

Writing Equations Given a Graph

- Analyzing the graph allows you to find the equation for a linear function.

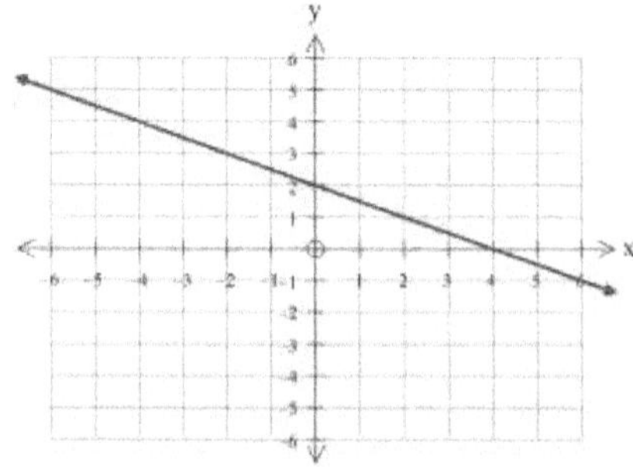

Equation: $y = -0.5x + 2$

Converting Between Different Forms of Linear Equations

- You can convert between the point-slope form, slope-intercept form, and standard form as needed.

- Example: Convert the equation $y = 3x + 1$ from slope-intercept form to standard form:

$$-3x + y = 1$$

Midpoint and Distance, Given Two Points

- The midpoint of two points is the average of their x and y coordinates, while the distance between them can be calculated using the distance formula.

- **Example:** Find the midpoint and distance between points $(1, 3)$ and $(5, 7)$.

Midpoint: $\frac{(1 + 5)}{2}, \frac{(3 + 7)}{2} = (3, 5)$

Distance: $\sqrt{((5 - 1)^2 + (7 - 3)^2)} = \sqrt{16 + 16} = \sqrt{32}$

Parallel and Perpendicular Lines

Understanding Parallel Lines

- Parallel lines have the same slope and never intersect.

- **Example:** The lines $y = 2x + 3$ and $y = 2x - 1$ are parallel because they have the same slope (2)

-

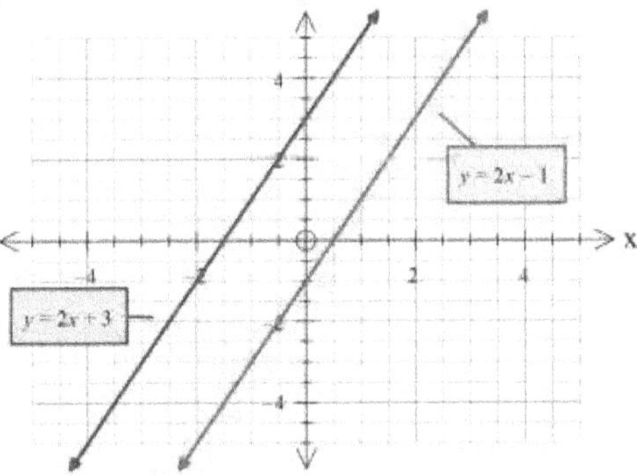

Understanding Perpendicular Lines

- Perpendicular lines have negative reciprocal slopes and intersect at a right angle.

- **Example:** The lines $y = 3x - 2$ and $y = -\frac{1}{3}x + 4$ are perpendicular because their slopes are negative reciprocals of each other.

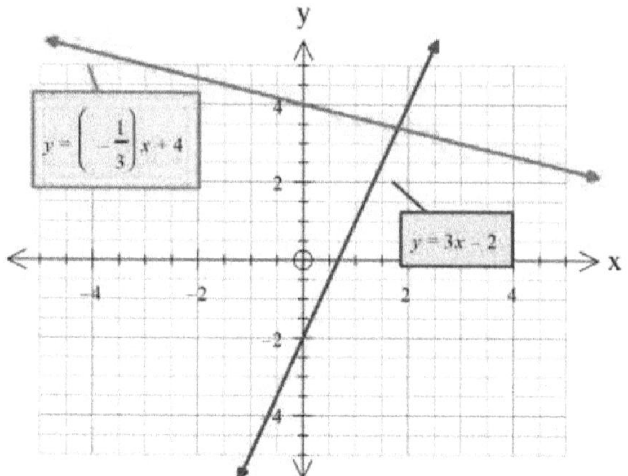

Equations of Parallel and Perpendicular Lines

- Parallel lines have equations with the same slope but different y-intercepts.

- Perpendicular lines have equations with negative reciprocal slopes and different y-intercepts.

Practices Question

1.Find the equation of a line perpendicular to the one passing through (2, 3) and (5, 1), and that passes through the point (4, -2).

2. Write the equation of a line in standard form, given the slope is 5/7 and it passes through the point (−2, 3).

3. Graph the equation of a line that has a slope of -3/2 and a y-intercept of 4.

4. Find the x-intercept of the line represented by the equation $2x - 3y = 12$.

5. Given the equation $4y - 2x = 8$, express it in slope-intercept form.

6. Determine the equation of a line passing through (1, 4) and parallel to the line $3x + 2y = 7$.

7. Calculate the distance between the points (3, -2) and (5, 6).

8. A line has a slope of -1/3 and passes through the point (6, 9). Find the equation of this line.

9. Write the equation of a line in point-slope form that passes through (3, 1) and is perpendicular to the line $2x - 4y = 8$.

10. Given the equation $3x + 4y = 5$, convert it to the point-slope form and graph it on the coordinate plane.

11. Write the slope-intercept form of the equation of the line through the given points.

(i) through: (4, −2) and (−4, −4)

(ii) through: (5, −2) and (−4, −3)

12. Write the point-slope form of the equation of the line described.

(i) through: (1, − 2), perpendicular to $-x + 2y = 2$

(ii) through: (5, 2), perpendicular to $5x + y = -3$

13. All tickets for a concert are the same price. The ticket agency adds a fixed fee to every order. A person who orders 5 tickets pays $93. A person who orders 3 tickets pays $57.

(i). Write an equation relating the total cost to the number of tickets purchased.

(ii). How much do 4 tickets cost?

14. Find the midpoint of each line segment.

(i) (2, −1), (−6, 0)

(ii) (−3.1, −2.8), (−4.92, −3.3)

15. Find the distance between each pair of points.

(i) (5, −8), (−8, 6)

(ii) (4, 6), (−4, −3)

Find the other endpoint of the line segment with the given endpoint and midpoint.

16. Endpoint: (−1, 9), midpoint: (−9, −10)

17. Endpoint: (2, 5), midpoint: (5, 1)

18. Endpoint: (5, 2), midpoint: (−10, −2)

19. Endpoint: (9, −10), midpoint: (4, 8)

20. Find the point that is one-fourth of the way from (2, 4) to (10, 8).

Answer:

1. The equation of the line is $y + 2 = (3/2)(x - 4)$.

2. The equation in standard form is $5x - 7y = -31$.

3. The line has a slope of -3/2 and a y-intercept at $(0, 4)$.

4. The x-intercept is $(6, 0)$.

5. The equation in slope-intercept form is $y = (1/2)x + 2$.

6. The equation of the parallel line is $y - 4 = (-3/2)(x - 1)$.

7. The distance between the points is $\sqrt{68}$.

8. The equation of the line is $y - 9 = (-1/3)(x - 6)$.

9. The equation of the perpendicular line is $y - 1 = -2(x - 3)$.

10. In point-slope form, the equation is $y - 5/4 = (-3/4)(x - 0)$.

11. (i) $y = \frac{1}{4}x - 3$ (ii) slope-intercept form is: $y = \frac{1}{9}x - \frac{23}{9}$

12. (i) The point-slope form: $y + 2 = -2x + 2$ (ii) The point-slope form: $y - 2 = \frac{1}{5}x - 1$

13 (i) The equation relating the total cost (C) to the number of tickets purchased (n) is: $C = pn + f$

where p is the price of each ticket and f is the fixed fee added to every order.

(ii) Four tickets cost $75.

14.(i) $(-2, -0.5)$ (ii) $(-4.01, -3.05)$

15.(i) $\sqrt{365}$ (ii) $\sqrt{145}$

16. The other endpoint is (-17, -29).

17. The other endpoint is (8, -3).

18. The other endpoint is (-25, -6).

19. The other endpoint is (-1, 26).

20. The point that is one-fourth of the way from $(2, 4)$ to $(10, 8)$ is $(4, 5)$.

Lesson 3 - Linear Equations - Word Problems

Translating Word Problems into Equations

Understanding Word Problem Structures

Word problems come in various formats, but they often have common structures. Recognizing these structures is crucial for solving them effectively. Key structures include problems involving proportions, rates, distances, and work.

Defining Variables

In word problems, variables represent unknown quantities that need to be determined. Assign clear and meaningful variables to unknowns where possible, especially when handling multiple variables in same question. For instance, besides the standard unknown notations of "x" and "y", you could use "d" for distance, "r" for rate, and so on. This will ensure you don't lose sight of the question and variable being focused on.

Setting Up Equations from Word Problems

To translate a word problem into an equation:

1. Identify what the problem is asking.

2. Define your variables.

3. Write an equation that represents the given situation.

4. Solve the equation to find the unknown.

Interpreting the Parts of an Equation

In a linear equation, you have terms representing constants and variables. Understand which part of the equation corresponds to which element in the word problem. Be mindful of coefficients, operations, and units of measurement.

Example 1: Proportion Word Problem

Problem: You have a recipe that makes 4 servings of a dish. If you want to make 8 servings, how much of each ingredient do you need?

Translation and Equation: Let "x" be the amount of each ingredient needed for 8 servings. The proportion is 4 servings / x = 8 servings / y, where "y" is the amount of each ingredient for 4 servings. This can be written as: $4/x = 8/y$.

Example 2: Distance Word Problem

Problem: You drive at a constant speed for 3 hours and travel 180 miles. What is your speed?

Translation and Equation: Speed = Distance/time. Let "s" be the speed, "d" be the distance, "t" be the time. $s = \frac{d}{t}$

The equation is: $s * 3 = 180$.

$$s = \frac{180}{3}$$

$$s = 60$$

Speed 60 miles per hour

Solving Word Problems with Linear Equations

Strategies for Solving Word Problems

1. Read the problem carefully.

2. Identify the unknowns and define variables.

3. Translate the problem into an equation.

4. Solve the equation using appropriate methods.

5. Check your solution to ensure it makes sense in the context of the problem.

Solving for Age and Rate

Word problems frequently involve determining someone's age or a rate of change. Use linear equations to set up and solve for these unknowns.

Solving for Speed, Distance, and Time

Problems related to speed, distance, and time are common. You can use linear equations to relate these three variables. Ensure consistency in units when setting up equations.

Analyzing Scenarios Involving Multiple Entities

In more complex problems, multiple entities or variables interact. Construct equations that describe the relationships between these entities and solve for the desired unknowns.

Example 3: Age Word Problem

Problem: Alice is 5 years older than Bob. The sum of their ages is 35. How old is each of them?

Translation and Equation: Let "B" be Bob's age and "A" be Alice's age. We have the equations:

$A = B + 5$ (Alice is 5 years older than Bob) and

$B + A = 35$ (the sum of their ages is 35).

$B + (B + 5) = 35$

$2B = 35 - 5$

$2B = 30$

$B = 15$

$A = B + 5 \Rightarrow 15 + 5 \Rightarrow 20$

"15" be Bob's age and "20" be Alice's age.

Example 4: Speed, Distance, and Time Word Problem

Problem: You drive at a speed of 60 mph. How long does it take you to travel 150 miles?

Translation and Equation: Speed = Distance/time. Let "s" be the speed, "d" be the distance, "t" be the time.

Let "t" be the time in hours.

$$s = \frac{d}{t}$$

$$60 = \frac{150}{t}$$

The equation is: $60t = 150$.

$$t = \frac{150}{60} = \frac{5}{2}$$

Work and Money

Work-Related Word Problems: Word problems involving work often concern the concept of work rates. Identify the work rate for each entity and set up equations accordingly.

Problems Involving Money

Money-related word problems can be about budgets, investments, or savings. Use linear equations to represent income, expenses, and savings. Keep track of time and interest rates when applicable

Example 5: Work Rate Word Problem

Problem: If it takes you 4 hours to complete a project, and your friend can complete the same project in 6 hours, how long will it take both of you working together?

Translation and Equation: Let "t" be the time in hours it takes to complete the project when working together. The work rate is defined as work done per hour.
So work rate is 1/4 for you and 1/6 for your friend. So network rate equation is given by ...

The equation is:

$$\frac{1}{4} + \frac{1}{6} = \frac{1}{t}$$

$$\frac{3 + 2}{12} = \frac{1}{t} \Rightarrow \frac{5}{12} = \frac{1}{t}$$

$$5t = 12$$

$$t = \frac{12}{5}$$

Example 6: Money Budget Word Problem

Problem: You want to save $500 in 6 months by saving the same amount each month. How much should you save each month?

Translation and Equation: Let "x" be the amount you need to save each month.

The equation is: $6x = 500$.

$$x = \frac{500}{6} = 83.3 ,$$

Answer $83.3

Practice Questions:

1. **Age Problem:** Sarah is 12 years older than her sister. The sum of their ages is 44. How old is Sarah's sister?

2. **Money Problem:** John wants to save $500 in 8 months by saving the same amount each month. How much should he save each month?

3. **Work Rate Problem:** If it takes Mark 5 hours to complete a project, and his friend can complete the same project in 3 hours, how long will it take both of them working together?

4. **Distance Problem:** A train travels at a speed of 60 mph. How long will it take to travel 120 miles?

5. **Age Problem:** The sum of Tom's age and Jane's age is 50. If Tom is 10 years older than Jane, how old is each of them?

6. **Money Problem:** You receive your paycheck and find out that 20% of it was deducted for taxes. If your net pay is $800, what was your gross income before taxes?

7. **Work Rate Problem:** If it takes 4 workers 6 hours to build a house, how long would it take 6 workers to build the same house?

8. **Speed Problem:** A cyclist covers 30 miles in 2 hours. What is the average speed of the cyclist?

9. **Age Problem:** The sum of a father's age and his son's age is 48. If the father is three times as old as his son, how old is each of them?

10. **Distance Problem:** If a car travels at a constant speed of 55 mph, how far will it travel in 4.5 hours?

11. **Money Problem:** A toy store has a sale with a 20% discount on all items. If a toy originally costs $25, how much will it cost during the sale?

12. **Work Rate Problem:** If a machine can produce 12 widgets in 4 hours, how long will it take the machine to produce 18 widgets?

13. **Speed Problem:** A boat can travel 120 miles downstream in 3 hours. If the current is 20 mph, what is the speed of the boat in still water?

14. **Money Problem:** Sarah earned $150 this week, and she saved 25% of her earnings. How much money did she save?

15. **Distance Problem:** A plane flies at a constant speed of 500 mph. How long does it take to fly 1,000 miles?

Word problems in Slope-intercept form

16. Biologists have found that the number of chirps some crickets make per minute is related to temperature. The relationship is very close to being linear. When crickets chirp 124 times a minute, it is about 68°F. When they chirp 172 times a minute, it is about 80°F.

(i). Find an equation for the line that models this situation.

(ii). How warm is it when the crickets are chirping 150 times a minute?

17. An internet service provider charges $18 per month plus an initial set –up fee. One customer paid a total of $81 after 2 months of service.

(i). Write an equation modeling this situation.

(ii). What is the initial set-up fee?

(iii). How much does it cost after 5 months of service?

18. All tickets for a concert are the same price. The ticket agency adds a fixed fee to every order. A person who orders 5 tickets pays $93. A person who orders 3 tickets pays $57.

(i). Write an equation relating the total cost to the number of tickets purchased.

(ii). How much do 4 tickets cost?

19. An airplane 30,000 feet above the ground begins descending at the rate of 2000 feet per minute. Assume the plane continues at the same rate of descent. The plane's height and minutes above the ground are related to each other.
(i). Write an equation to model the situation.
(ii). Find the altitude of the plane after 5 minutes.

20. The math department sponsors a Math Family Fun Night each year. In the first year, there were 35 participants. In the third year, there were 57 participants.
(i). Write an equation to predict how many participants at any given year.
(ii). How many participants are predicted for the 5th year?

Answer:

1. Sarah's sister is 16 years old.

2. John should save $62.50 each month.

3. It will take them 1.875 hours (1 hour and 52.5 minutes) when working together.

4. It will take 2 hours to travel 120 miles.

5. Tom is 30 years old, and Jane is 20 years old.

6. Your gross income before taxes was $1,000.

7. It will take 4 hours to build the house with 6 workers.

8. The cyclist's average speed is 15 mph.

9. The father is 36 years old, and his son is 12 years old.

10. The car will travel 247.5 miles in 4.5 hours.

11. During the sale, the toy will cost $20.

12. It will take the machine 4.5 hours to produce 18 widgets.

13. The speed of the boat in still water is 100 mph.

14. Sarah saved $37.50.

15. The plane will take 2 hours to fly 1,000 miles.

16. (i) The equation that models the relationship is: $y = \frac{1}{4}x + 37$

    (ii) when the crickets are chirping 150 times a minute, it is approximately 74.5°F.

17. (i) $cost = 18x + 45$ (ii). $45 (iii). $135

18. (i) $y = 18x + 3$ (ii) Four tickets cost $75.

19. (i) $h = 30,000 - 2,000t$, where h is the height & t is the time in minutes.

    (ii) The altitude of the plane after 5 minutes is 20,000 feet above the ground.

20. (i) the equation to predict the number of participants at any given year is
    $P = 11y + 24$, Where P represent the number of participants, and y represent the year.
    (ii) The predicted number of participants for the 5th year is 79.

Lesson 4 - Systems Equations of Linear

Introduction to Systems of Equations

Defining Systems of Equations: A system of two linear equations in two variables is a set of equations that involve the same variables. Solving the system means finding values for the variables that satisfy both equations simultaneously.

Graphical Representation of Solutions: The solutions to a system of equations are the points where the graphs of the equations intersect. These points represent values that make both equations true.

Methods for Solving Systems: Various methods are used to solve systems of equations, including graphing, elimination, and substitution. The preferred choice of method is elimination method.

Example 1: Defining Systems of Equations

Write a system of equations to represent the following situations:

- You have $50 in your wallet, and you have 4 $5 bills and some $10 bills.

- You are buying apples for $2 each and oranges for $3 each, and you spend a total of $17.

Solution:
Let x represent the number of $10 bills and y represent the number of $5 bills.
Equation 1: $\$10x + \$5y = \$50$ (total money in the wallet)
Equation 2: $2x + 3y = \$17$ (total spent on fruits)

Let's use the elimination method to find the values of x and y.

Equation 1: $\$10x + \$5y = \$50$

Equation 2: $2x + 3y = \$17$

We can start by multiplying Equation 2 by -5 to make the coefficients of x in both equations equal:

Modified Equation 2: $-10x - 15y = -85$
Now add equation 1 and equation 2 to eliminate x
$-10y = -35 \implies y = 3.5$

Substituting back in original equation 2,

$-6x + y = -\$16$

$-6x + \$3.5 = -\$16$

$-6x = -\$16 - \$3.5$

Add $19.50 to both sides to isolate y:

$-6x = -\$19.50$

$x = \$3.25$

So, the solution to the system is:

x = \$3.25 (number of \$10 bills) y = \$3.50 (number of \$5 bills)

Example 2: Graphical Representation of Solutions

Graph the following system of equations and find the solution:

- $2x - 3y = 9$
- $x + y = 2$

Solution:
Graph the two equations on the same coordinate plane. The solution is the point of intersection where the graphs cross.

Graph:
A a graph here showing the lines intersecting at a point.

- The first equation, $2x - 3y = 9$, represents a line on the coordinate plane.

- The second equation, $x + y = 2$, represents another line.

- The point (3, -1) is the solution because it is the point where both lines intersect, making both equations true.

Explanation:

Equation 1: $2x - 3y = 9$

Equation 2: $x + y = 2$

We can start by finding some key points for each equation and then graphing them on a coordinate plane.

For Equation 1: Let's find two points.

When $x = 0$:

$2(0) - 3y = 9$

$-3y = 9$

$y = -3$ So, one point is (0, -3).

When $y = 0$:

$2x - 3(0) = 9$

$2x = 9$

x = 9/2

Another point is (4.5, 0).

For Equation 2: Let's find two points.

When $x = 0$:

$0 + y = 2$

$y = 2$

So, one point is (0, 2).

When $y = 0$:

$x + 0 = 2$

$x = 2$

Another point is (2, 0).

Now, let's graph these two lines:

The two lines intersect at the point (3, -1). This point is the solution to the system of equations because it satisfies both Equation 1 and Equation 2. So, the solution is:

$x = 3 \; y = -1$

The solution is (3, -1), which is the point of intersection.

Solving Systems by Graphing

Graphical Approach to Solving Systems: Graph both equations on the same coordinate plane. The point(s) where the graphs intersect are the solutions to the system.

Identifying Solution Points on Graphs: Solution points are the coordinates of the intersection(s) of the graphs. These points make both equations true.

Example 3: Identifying Solution Points on Graphs

For the system of equations, find the solution point:

- $3x + 2y = 10$
- $2x - y = 2$

Solution:
Graph the two equations on the same coordinate plane, and identify the point where the graphs intersect.

Graph: A a graph here showing the lines intersecting at a point. The solution point is (2, 2).

Explanation:

- The graphs of both equations intersect at the point (2, 2), making both equations true for these values of x and y.

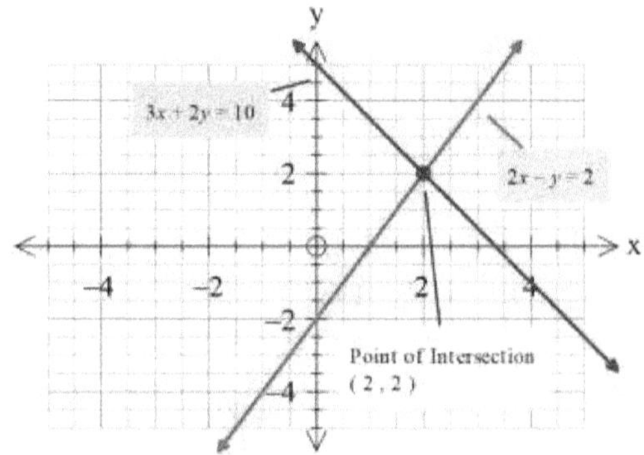

Solving Systems by Elimination

Elimination Method for Solving Systems: Combine the equations to eliminate one variable, making it easier to solve for the other. Add or subtract the equations so that one variable cancels out.

Transforming Equations for Elimination: Manipulate the equations to ensure they have the same coefficient for one of the variables before adding or subtracting them.

Example 4: Elimination Method for Solving Systems

Solve the system of equations using the elimination method:

- $3x + 2y = 10$
- $2x - y = 4$

Solution:

Step 1: Multiply both sides of Equation 2 by 2 to make the coefficients of y in both equations equal:

Modified Equation 2: $4x - 2y = 8$

Now, the system becomes:

- $3x + 2y = 10$
- $4x - 2y = 8$

Step 2: Add Equation 1 and the modified Equation 2 to eliminate y:

$(3x + 2y) + (4x - 2y) = 10 + 8$

Simplifying this:

$7x = 18$

Step 3: Now, solve for x by dividing both sides by 7:

$$x = \frac{18}{7}$$

Step 4: Substitute the value of x back into one of the original equations, Equation 2 is a bit simpler for this:

$$2x - y = 4$$

$$2\left(\frac{18}{7}\right) - y = 4$$

Now, solve for y:

$$\frac{36}{7} - y = 4$$

Subtract (36 / 7) from both sides:

$$y = 4 - \frac{36}{7}$$

To make the denominators the same, convert 4 to 28/7:

$$y = \frac{28}{7} - \frac{36}{7}$$

Now, subtract the fractions:

$$y = -\frac{8}{7}$$

So, the solution to the system is:

$$x = \frac{18}{7}, y = -\frac{8}{7}$$

Example 5: Cases of No Solution and Infinitely Many Solutions

No Solution => Lines are parallel and have the same slope

For Example $y = 2x + 7, y = 2x - 3$
Slope = 2

Problem1: : Find 'a' if equations have no solution
$$ax + 3y = 8$$
$$-3x + 10y = 12$$
Rearrange -
$$y = -\frac{ax}{3} + \frac{8}{3}, \quad slope = -\frac{a}{3}$$
$$y = \frac{3x}{10} + \frac{12}{10}, \quad slope = \frac{3}{10}$$
since slopes have to be the same$-\frac{a}{3} = \frac{3}{10} \Rightarrow a = -\frac{9}{10}$

Infinite Solution => Lines are same or multiples, and therefore coefficients are always in proportion

For Example: : $x + 2y = 5, 2x + 4y = 10$

Problem 2:

Find 'a', 'b' if equations have infinite solutions

$x + 2y = a$

$-3x + by = -8$

Coefficients have to be in proportion; so $\frac{1}{-3} = \frac{2}{b} = \frac{a}{-8}$

solving,

$a = \frac{8}{3}, b = -6$

Solving Systems by Substitution

Substitution Method for Solving Systems: Solve one equation for one variable and substitute this expression into the other equation. This reduces the system to one equation with one variable.

Finding Exact Solutions: Substitution provides exact solutions that satisfy both equations in the system.

Example 6: Substitution Method for Solving Systems

Solve the system of equations using the substitution method:

- $2x + 3y = 8$

- $x = 2$

Solution: From the second equation $x = 2$

Now, substitute this expression for x into the first equation: $2(2) + 3y = 8$

Simplify and solve for y:

$4 + 3y = 8$

$3y = 8 - 4$

$3y = 4$

$y = \frac{4}{3}$

So, the solution is: $x = 2, y = \frac{4}{3}$

Word Problems Involving Systems

Translating Real-World Scenarios into Systems of Equations: Word problems can be modeled as systems of equations by defining variables and setting up equations based on the problem's context.

Solving Systems in Context: Solve the systems of equations derived from word problems using the methods discussed earlier. This helps find real-world solutions.

Interpreting Solutions in Practical Terms: Interpret the solutions in the context of the problem. What do they represent? How do they relate to the real-world scenario? Understand the practical implications of the solutions.

Example 7: Translating Real-World Scenarios into Systems of Equations

You have two types of candies, Type A and Type B. Type A costs $1 per piece, and Type B costs $2 per piece. You want to buy 10 candies for $15. Write a system of equations to represent this situation.

Solution: This problem involves two unknowns: the number of Type A candies (A) and the number of Type B candies (B). To set up a system of equations, we need to express the given information mathematically.

1. The total number of candies you want to buy is 10. So, we have the equation:

   Equation 1: $A + B = 10$ (total number of candies)

2. The total cost of the candies is $15. Type A candies cost $1 each, and Type B candies cost $2 each. So, we can express the total cost as:

   Equation 2: $A + 2B = 15$ (total cost)

These two equations represent the constraints of the problem, where Equation 1 ensures that you buy a total of 10 candies, and Equation 2 ensures that the total cost does not exceed $15.

Now, you can use various methods (substitution, elimination) to solve this system and find the values of A and B that satisfy both equations.

Example 8: Solving Systems in Context

You have $200 to spend on textbooks and calculators. Textbooks cost $20 each, and calculators cost $40 each. You want to buy a total of 8 items. Write a system of equations to represent this situation and solve it.

Solution: This problem involves two types of items: textbooks (x) and calculators (y), and you have budget and quantity constraints. Here's how we can set up a system of equations to represent this:

1. The total number of items you want to buy is 8. So, we have the equation: Equation 1: $x + y = 8$ (total number of items)

2. You have a budget of $200, and textbooks cost $20 each, while calculators cost $40 each. So, we can express the total cost as: Equation 2: $20x + 40y = 200$ (total cost)

These two equations represent the constraints of the problem. Equation 1 ensures that you buy a total of 8 items, and Equation 2 ensures that the total cost does not exceed your budget of $200.

Practice Questions: Systems of 2 Linear Equations in 2 Variables:

Solve each system by elimination.

1. $3x - 2y = 8$

    $2x + y = 4$

2. $2x + 3y = 13$

    $3x - 4y = 2$

3. $2x + y = 7$

    $3x - 2y = 8$

4. $x + 2y = 6$

    $3x + y = 8$

5. $3x + 2y = 10$

    $2x + y = 4$

6. $-7x + y = -19$

    $-2x + 3y = -19$

7. $3x + 2y = 11$

    $x - 2y = 1$

8. $2x + 8y = 6$

    $-5x + 20y = -15$

9. $3 + 2x - y = 0$

    $-3 - 7y = 10x$

Infinite solutions. Find a, b

10. $-2p - 3q = 12$
    $ap + 16q = b$
    $2s + 7r = a$
    $-8s + br = 9$
11. $m - an = 8$
    $bm - 9n = 36$

No Solutions: Find a, b

12. $ax + 3y = 8$
    $-3x + 10y = 12$
13. $br + 7s = 8$
    $-3r + 8s = 15$
14. $x - 2y = 7$
    $ax - 3y = 8$

15. $p + 3q = 52$

$-5p + bq = 71$

17. The Fruit Stand Problem:

You are buying apples and oranges at a fruit stand. Apples cost \$2 each, and oranges cost \$3 each. You buy a total of 10 fruits for \$22. How many apples and oranges did you purchase?

18. The Ticket Problem:

You want to buy tickets for a movie. Adult tickets cost \$8 each, and child tickets cost \$5 each. You buy a total of 5 tickets for \$36. How many adult and child tickets did you purchase?

19. The Coffee Shop Problem:

At a coffee shop, a small coffee costs \$2, and a large coffee costs \$4. You order a total of 5 coffees and pay \$16. How many small and large coffees did you order?

20. The Bookstore Problem:

You visit a bookstore and buy two types of books: paperback books that cost \$10 each and hardcover books that cost \$20 each. You purchase a total of 6 books for \$100. How many paperback and hardcover books did you buy?

Answer

1. $x = 16/7, y = -4/7$
2. $x = 2, y = 3$
3. $x = 22/7, y = 5/7$
4. $x = 2, y = 2$
5. $x = -2, y = 8$
6. $x = 2, y = -5$
7. $x = 3, y = 1$
8. $x = 3, y = 0$
9. $x = -1, y = 1$
10. $a = 32/3$ and $b = -192/3$
11. $a = -9/4$ and $b = -28$
12. $a = 2$ and $b = 9/2$
13. $a = -9/10$
14. $b = -21/8$
15. $a = 3/2$
16. $b = -15$
17. **The Fruit Stand Problem:**
    - Let's use x for the number of apples and y for the number of oranges.
    - The equations are: $x + y = 10$ (total fruits) and $2x + 3y = 22$ (total cost).
    - The solution is $x = 8$ apples and $y = 2$ oranges.
18. **The Ticket Problem:**
    - Let x be the number of adult tickets and y be the number of child tickets.
    - The equations are: $x + y = 5$ (total tickets) and $8x + 5y = 36$ (total cost).
    - The solution is $x = 11/3$ adult tickets and $y = 4/3$ child tickets.
19. **The Coffee Shop Problem:**
    - Use x for the number of small coffees and y for the number of large coffees.
    - The equations are: $x + y = 5$ (total coffees) and $2x + 4y = 16$ (total cost).
    - The solution is $x = 2$ small coffees and $y = 3$ large coffees.

20. **The Bookstore Problem:**

- Let x represent the number of paperback books and y for hardcover books.

- The equations are: $x + y = 6$ (total books) and $10x+20y=100$ (total cost).

- The solution is $x=2$ paperback books and $y=4$ hardcover books.

Lesson 5 - Linear Inequalities

Introduction to Linear Inequalities

Linear inequalities are mathematical expressions that compare two algebraic expressions using inequality symbols, such as < (less than), > (greater than), ≤ (less than or equal to), or ≥ (greater than or equal to). These inequalities play a crucial role in expressing and analyzing relationships between variables. Understanding them is fundamental to solving problems in various fields, from economics to physics.

Linear Inequalities in One Variable: Linear inequalities in one variable involve expressions where a variable is compared to a constant using inequality symbols. The goal is to find the set of values for the variable that satisfy the inequality. Here's an overview of the process:

Representation: A linear inequality in one variable can be expressed as:

$$ax + b < c$$

Where:

- a, b, and c are constants.
- x is the variable.

Solving Steps:

A. Isolate the Variable:

Collect all terms involving the variable on one side of the inequality.

Use inverse operations to isolate the variable on one side.

Example 1: Solve the inequality $2x - 3 > 5$.

1. **Setup:** $2x - 3 > 5$
2. **Isolate the variable:** $2x > 8$
3. **Solve for x:** $x > 4$

So, x must be greater than 4 for the inequality to hold true.

Example 2: Solve the inequality $-3y + 7 \leq 4$.

1. **Setup:** $-3y + 7 \leq 4$
2. **Isolate the variable:** $-3y \leq -3$.

Common Mistakes to Avoid:

1. **Sign Flipping:** Be cautious when multiplying or dividing by a negative number. The inequality sign should flip.

   For Example: If $-3x < 9$, dividing by -3 requires flipping the sign: $x > -3$.

2. **Combining Like Terms:** Simplify both sides of the inequality correctly before isolating the variable.

   For Example: In $3x - 2 + 4 > 7$, combine like terms before isolating x.

Linear inequalities in two variables involve expressions where two variables are compared using inequality symbols. The solution to a linear inequality in two variables is a region in the coordinate plane. Let's explore the representation, solution, and application of linear inequalities in two variables:

Representation: A linear inequality in two variables can be expressed as:

$$ax + by < c$$

Where:

- a, b, and c are constants.

- x and y are the variables.

Graphical Representation: Representing a linear inequality in two variables involves graphing the corresponding linear equation and shading the region that satisfies the inequality.

1. **Graph the Linear Equation:**

    - Consider the equality $ax + by = c$.

    - Graph the line represented by this equation.

2. **Determine the Shaded Region:**

    - Identify the side of the line that satisfies the inequality.

    - Use a test point (usually the origin) to determine which side to shade.

Solution:

The solution to a linear inequality in two variables is the shaded region on the coordinate plane.

- If the inequality is strict ($<$, $>$), use a dashed line.

- If the inequality is non-strict ($\leq$, $\geq$), use a solid line

Linear Inequalities in Two Variables

Example 3: Consider the inequality $3x - 2y \leq 12$.

Method 1:

Graph the Linear Equation: $3x - 2y = 12$

Find two points and connect them to form the line.

Determine the Shaded Region:

- Choose a test point, say $(0,0)$.

- Substitute the coordinates into the inequality: $3(0) - 2(0) \leq 12$.

- Since $0 \leq 12$ is true, shade the side containing the origin.

This shaded region represents all points (x, y) that satisfy the given linear inequality.

Method 2:
Rearrange to shift y to one side

$$3x - 2y \leq 12$$
$$-2y \leq -3x + 12$$
$$2y \geq 3x - 12$$

$$y \geq \left(\frac{3}{2}\right)x - 6$$

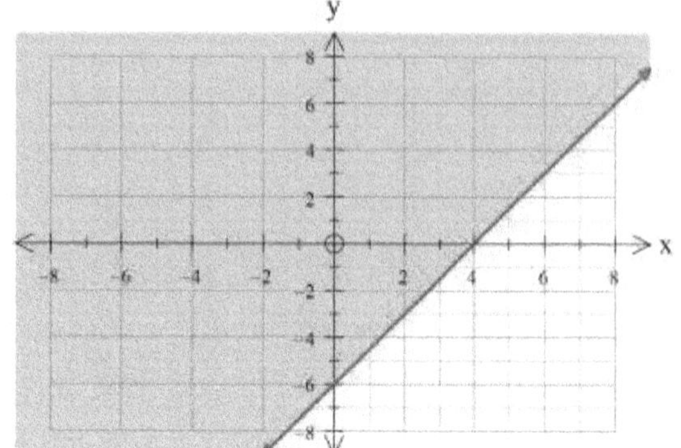

Inequality side following a positive

y in the equation,

Determines the shaded region
$y \geq$ *shade above the line*
$y \leq$ *shade below the line*

Linear Inequality Word Problems

Translating real-world scenarios into mathematical expressions is an essential skill. This section guides you through the process of writing linear inequalities based on word problems, enabling you to model and solve practical situations.

Let's break down the process of translating word problems into linear inequalities.

Example 4: You have $500 to spend on clothes, and each shirt costs $25. Write a linear inequality to represent the situation.

1. **Identify the unknown:** Let x be the number of shirts to buy.

2. **Establish the relationship:** The total cost ($25x$) should be less than or equal to the budget (500).

$$25x \leq 500$$

3. **Finalize the inequality:** 25 times the number of shirts should be less than or equal to $500.

Example 5: A company charges $30 per hour for consulting services and wants to earn at least $1500 in a week. Write a linear inequality to represent the weekly earnings.

1. **Identify the unknown:** Let x be the number of consulting hours.

2. **Establish the relationship:** The total earnings ($30x$) should be greater than or equal to $1500.

$$30x \geq 1500$$

3. **Finalize the inequality:** 30 times the number of consulting hours should be greater than or equal to $1500.

Key Phrases and Translations in Linear Inequality Word Problems

Understanding key phrases is crucial for identifying when to use linear inequalities in problem-solving. This section highlights common phrases that indicate the need for inequalities in mathematical modeling.

Key Phrase	Translation into Inequality	Example
More than c, Greater than c, or Higher than c	$> c$	"More than 10" translates to $x > 10$
Less than c or Lower than c	$< c$	"Less than 5" translates to $y < 5$
Greater than or equal to c or At least c	$\geq c$	"At least 20" translates to $z \geq 20$
Less than or equal to c or At most c	$\leq c$	"At most \$30" translates to $w \leq 30$
No less than c	$\geq c$	"No less than 15" translates to $a \geq 15$
No more than c	$\leq c$	"No more than 8" translates to $b \leq 8$

Additional Phrases:

- **"Least," "lowest," or "minimum" value:** The smallest value that satisfies the inequality.

- **"Greatest," "highest," or "maximum" value:** The largest value that satisfies the inequality.

- **"A possible" value:** Implies the existence of a solution without specifying a range. This may require further information to form a specific inequality.

Examples 6:

(a) If the temperature is no less than 20 degrees Celsius, the translation is $T \geq 20$.

(b) If the speed must be at most 60 km/h, the translation is $S \leq 60$.

(c) If the minimum number of participants required is 50, the translation is $N \geq 50$.

Practice Problems:

Linear Inequalities in One Variable:

1. Solve the inequality $2x + 1 \leq 5$.
2. Solve for x in the inequality: $-2x + 5 > 7$.
3. If $3y - 2 \leq 10$, find the possible values for y.
4. Graph the solution set for the inequality: $4 - 3x \geq 1$.
5. Solve the inequality $3x + 2 < 5$
6. Solve the inequality $\frac{1}{2}x - 3 > 4$.
7. If $2a + 1 \geq 5$, what is the range of values for a?
8. Express the phrase "at least 15" as a linear inequality.
9. $4x + 2 > 10$, solve for x.
10. Graph the solution set for the inequality: $-2x + 3 < 9$.
11. Solve the inequality $2x - 7 \leq 5$

Linear Inequalities in Two Variables:

12. Solve for y in the inequality: $3x - 2y \leq 12$.
13. Express the inequality $2x + 4y > 8$ in slope-intercept form $(y = mx + b)$.
14. If the point $(2, -1)$ is in the solution set of $ax + by < 5$, find the possible values for a and b.
15. Determine the shaded region for the inequality: $4x + 3y < 5$.
16. Find the maximum and minimum values of the expression $2x + y$ in the region that satisfies both of the inequalities:
$$0 \leq x \leq 1$$
$$0 \leq y \leq 2$$

Word problem on Linear Inequalities in One Variable:

17. Your budget for a trip is $300. If you plan to spend at most $40 per day, write and solve a linear inequality to find the maximum number of days you can stay.
18. A factory produces at least 100 units of a product each day. Write a linear inequality to represent this situation, where x is the number of units produced.
19. A car rental company charges $25 per day and wants to make at least $500 in a month. Write a linear inequality to represent the number of days a car must be rented.

Word problem on Linear Inequalities in Two Variables:

20. A rectangular garden has a length twice its width. The perimeter should not exceed 60 meters. Write a system of linear inequalities to represent the length (l) and width (w).
21. A company sells two types of products, x and y. The company must sell at least 50 units of each product. Write a system of linear inequalities to represent this situation.
22. A basketball team scored at least 60 points in each game. Write a system of linear inequalities for the number of points scored in two consecutive games.
23. A company produces two types of products, A and B. Product A costs $2 per unit to produce and product B costs $3 per unit to produce. The company has a budget of $1000 per day. The company must produce at least 100 units of product A and 50 units of product B per day.

Answer:

1. $x \le 2$
2. $x < -1$.
3. $y \le 4$.
4. Shaded region to the left of $x = \frac{1}{3}$ on a number line.
5. $x < 1$
6. $x > 14$.
7. $a \ge 2$.
8. $x \ge 15$.
9. $x > 2$.
10. Shaded region to the right of $x = 3$ on a number line.
11. $x \le 6$
12. $y \ge \frac{3}{2}x - 6$.
13. $y > -\frac{1}{2}x + 2$.
14. $2a - b < 5$
15.

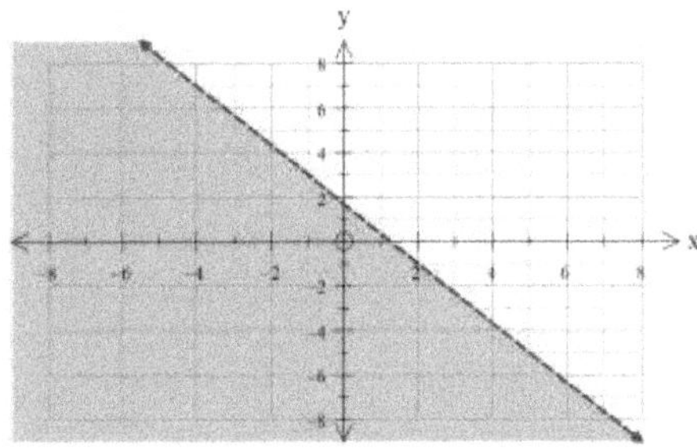

16. The maximum value of the function is 4 and the minimum value of the function is 0.
17. $40d \le 300, d \le 7.5$.
18. $x \ge 100$
19. $25d \ge 500, d \ge 20$
20. $l = 2w, 2l + 2w \le 60$.
21. $x \ge 50, y \ge 50$.
22. $x \ge 60, y \ge 60$.
23. $2x + 3y \le 1000$
    $\quad x \ge 100$
    $\quad y \ge 50$

Lesson 6 - Linear Systems and Inequalities

Graphing Linear Systems

A linear system is a collection of two or more linear equations in the same variables. The solution to a linear system is the set of all values of the variables that satisfy all of the equations in the system.

To graph a linear system, you can graph each of the equations in the system on the same coordinate plane. The solution to the system is the points of intersection of the lines.

Example 1: The system of equations

$$y = 2x + 1$$

$$y = x + 2$$

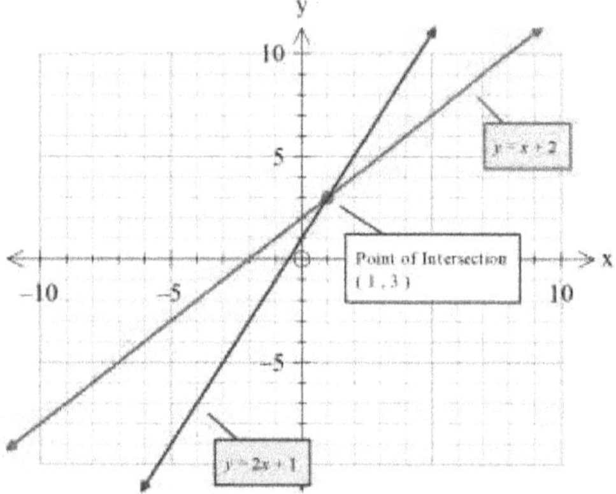

The system of equations can be graphed by plotting the lines $y = 2x + 1$ and $y = x + 2$ on the same coordinate plane. The solution to the system is the point $(1, 3)$, which is the point of intersection of the two lines.

Graphing Linear Inequalities

A linear inequality is a mathematical statement that compares two expressions using one of the following symbols:

- $<$ (less than)
- $>$ (greater than)
- $\leq$ (less than or equal to)
- $\geq$ (greater than or equal to)

These inequalities can be expressed in one or two variables.

To graph a linear inequality in two variables, you can shade the region of the coordinate plane that satisfies the inequality. The boundary line is included in the solution if the inequality includes an equality sign ($\leq$ or $\geq$).

Example 2: the inequality $2x + 3y < 6$ can be graphed by shading the region of the coordinate plane below the line

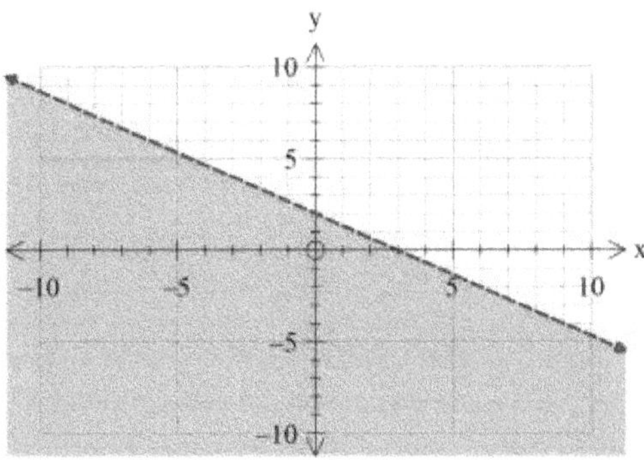

$$y < -\left(\frac{2}{3}\right)x + 2$$

Graphing Linear Systems of Inequalities

A linear system of inequalities is a collection of two or more linear inequalities in the same variables. The solution to a linear system of inequalities is the set of all points that satisfy all of the inequalities in the system.

To graph a linear system of inequalities, you can shade the region of the coordinate plane that satisfies all of the inequalities in the system. The solution to the system is the region that is shaded by all of the inequalities.

Representing solutions with shaded areas

- **Graph the Boundary:**

    - Begin by graphing the corresponding linear equation without the inequality symbol.

    - For example, for $ax + by \leq c$, graph the line $ax + by = c$.

- **Identify Shaded Side:**

    - Choose a test point not on the line, usually the origin $(0,0)$.

    - Substitute the coordinates into the inequality.

    - If the inequality is true for the test point, shade the side that contains the test point. If false, shade the opposite side

- **Solid or Dashed Line:**

    - If the inequality includes or equals ($\leq$ or $\geq$), use a solid line.

    - If the inequality is strict ($<$ or $>$), use a dashed line.

- **Shade the Region:**

    - Once the line is drawn, shade the appropriate side based on the test point

Example 3: Consider the inequality $2x + y \leq 5$:

1. **Graph the Boundary:**

- Graph the line $2x + y = 5$.

- Plot points $(0, 5)$ and $\left(\frac{5}{2}, 0\right)$ and draw a solid line through them.

2. **Identify Shaded Side:**

   - Use the test point (0,0) and substitute into the inequality: $2(0) + 0 \leq 5$.

   - Since $0 \leq 5$ is true, shade the side containing the origin.

3. **Solid or Dashed Line:**
   - Use a solid line because the inequality includes or equals.
4. **Shade the Region:**
   - Shade the side containing the origin.

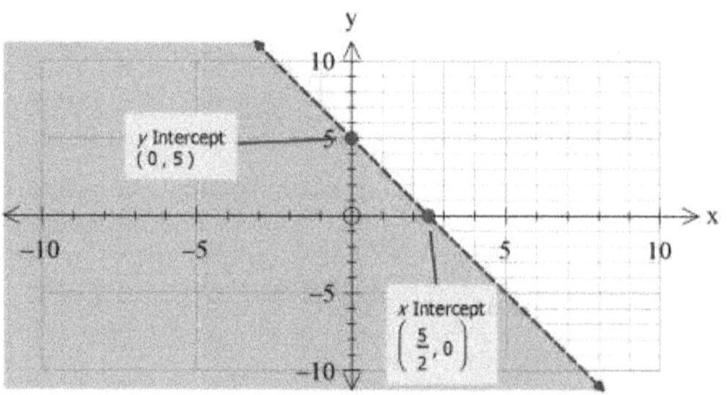

Example 4 : The system of inequalities $x + y \leq 3, x \geq 0, and\ y \geq 0$ can be graphed by shading the region of the coordinate plane that is shaded by all three inequalities. The solution to the system is

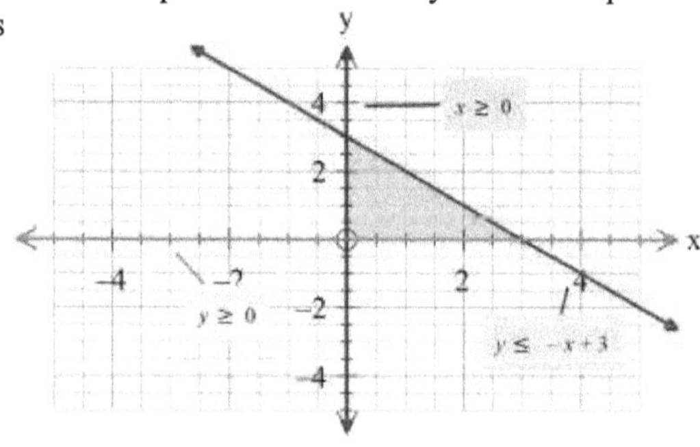

Example 5: Solve the following system of linear inequalities:

$$x + y \leq 6$$
$$y - 2x \geq 0$$
$$x \geq 0$$
$$y \geq 0$$

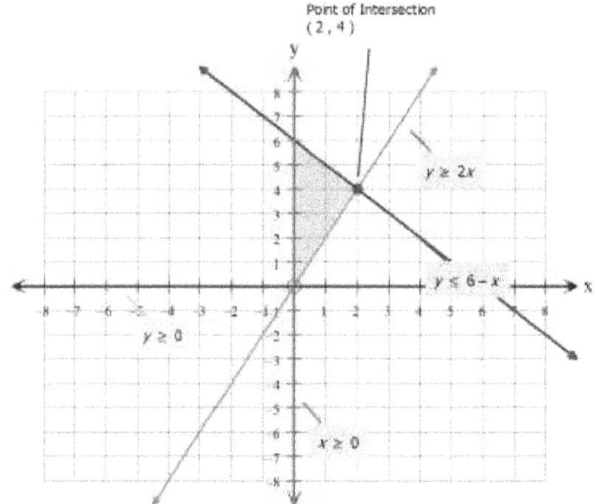

The blue line represents $x + y = 6$, the green line represents $y - 2x = 0$, the red line represents $x = 0$, and the black line represents $y = 0$.

By observing the graph, we can see that the solution to the system of inequalities is the shaded region above the green line and to the right of the red line. However, we also need to consider the fact that x and y must be non-negative. Therefore, the solution to the system of inequalities is the

shaded region above the green line, to the right of the red line, and below the black line and to the right of the black line.

In mathematical notation, the solution to the system of inequalities is:

$$0 \leq x \leq 2$$

$$0 \leq y \leq 6$$

Result:

$$y \leq 6 - x$$
$$y \geq 2x$$
$$x \geq 0$$
$$y \geq 0$$

Practice Questions:

1. **Linear Systems:** Solve the system of equations graphically:
$$2x + y = 4$$
$$x - y = 2$$

2. **Graphing Inequalities:** Graph the inequality $3x + 2y \leq 6$ on the coordinate plane.
3. **Intersection Points:** Find the intersection points of the lines $y = 2x - 3$ *and* $y = -x + 4$.
4. **System of Inequalities:** Represent the solution to the system of inequalities graphically:
$$2x + y \geq 3$$
$$x - y \leq 2$$

5. **Graphical Solution:** Graphically determine the solution to the system:
$$y \leq x + 2$$
$$2x - y \geq 1$$

6. Graph the system of linear inequalities:
$$x + y \leq 4$$
$$x \geq 0$$
$$y \geq 0$$

7. Solve the system of linear inequalities:
$$2x + 3y > 6$$
$$x \geq 0$$
$$y \geq 0$$

8. Find the region that satisfies all of the following inequalities:
$$x + y \leq 4$$
$$x \geq 1$$
$$y \geq 2$$

9. Write a system of linear inequalities that represents the following situation:
A company produces two types of products, A and B. Product A costs $2 per unit to produce and product B costs $3 per unit to produce. The company has a budget of $1000 per day. The company must produce at least 100 units of product A and 50 units of product B per day.

10. Graph the region that satisfies all of the following inequalities:

$$x + y \leq 2$$
$$2x - y \geq -1$$
$$x \geq 0$$
$$y \geq 0$$

11. Graph the region that satisfies all of the following inequalities:
$$x \leq 2$$
$$y \leq 3$$
$$x + y \leq 5$$

12. Graph the region that satisfies all of the following inequalities:
$$x \leq 1$$
$$y \leq 2$$

$$x - y \leq 5$$

13. **System of Inequalities:** Represent the solution to the system of inequalities graphically:

$$x + 2y \leq 6$$
$$3x - y \geq 4$$
$$x \geq 0$$
$$y \geq 0$$

14. **System of Inequalities:** Represent the solution to the system of inequalities graphically:

$$2x + y \leq 4$$
$$x - 2y \leq 2$$
$$x \geq 0$$
$$y \geq 0$$

15. **System of Inequalities:** Represent the solution to the system of inequalities graphically:

$$x + y \leq 3$$
$$2x - y \geq 1$$
$$x \geq 0$$
$$y \geq 0$$

16. **System of Inequalities:** Represent the solution to the system of inequalities graphically:

$$4x + 2y \leq 8$$
$$2x - y \geq -1$$
$$x \geq 0$$
$$y \geq 0$$

17. **System of Inequalities:** Represent the solution to the system of inequalities graphically:

$$2x + 3y \geq 6$$
$$x - 2y \leq 2$$
$$x \geq 0$$
$$y \geq 0$$

18. A store sells two types of smartphones, A and B. Each type A smartphone costs $200, and each type B smartphone costs $250. The store wants to sell at least 30 smartphones and make a profit of at least $3000. If x represents the number of type A smartphones and y represents the number of type B smartphones sold, write a system of linear inequalities to represent this situation.

19. A company manufactures two models of laptops, X and Y. Each X model requires 4 hours of assembly time and 2 hours of testing time, while each Y model requires 3 hours of assembly time and 3 hours of testing time. The company has a total of 40 hours for assembly and 24 hours for testing each day. If the profit from each X model is $200 and from each Y model is $150, write a system of linear inequalities to maximize the profit.

20. A landscaping company offers two types of services: lawn mowing and hedge trimming. The company charges $30 for each lawn mowing service and $20 for each hedge trimming service. The company wants to earn at least $150 per day and spend no more than 5 hours on each type of service. On average, a lawn mowing service takes 1 hour, while a hedge trimming service takes 2 hours. How many lawn mowing services and hedge trimming services should the company offer to meet its financial goal and time constraint?

Answer:

1. $x = 2, y = 0$
2. Shaded region below the line $3x + 2y = 6$.
3. Intersection points: $\left(\frac{7}{3}, \frac{5}{3}\right)$
4. Shaded region above the line $2x + y = 3$ and below the line $x - y = 2$.
5. Shaded region below $y = x + 2$ and above $2x - y = 1$.
6. To graph the system of linear inequalities $x + y \leq 4$, $x \geq 0$, $and\ y \geq 0$, first graph the line $x + y = 4$. This line will have a slope of -1 and a y-intercept of 4. Shade the region below the line. Then, shade the region to the right of the line $x = 0$ and the region above the line $y = 0$. The solution to the system of inequalities is the shaded region

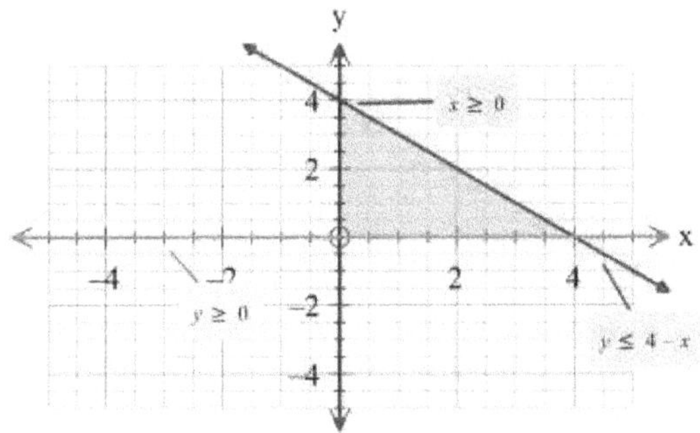

7. For $2x + 3y > 6$,We can rewrite this inequality as $y > -\frac{2}{3}x + 2$. We can represent this by plotting the points (0,2) and (3,0) and connecting them with a line and shading the region above the line.
   For x ≥ 0, it means that x values are non-negative, so we shade the part of the graph where x is greater than or equal to 0, which is to the right of the y-axis.
   For y ≥ 0, it means that y values are non-negative, so we shade the part of the graph where y is greater than or equal to 0, which is above the x-axis.
   As a result, the solution to the system of inequalities is the shaded region above the orange line, to the right of the y-axis, and above the x-axis.

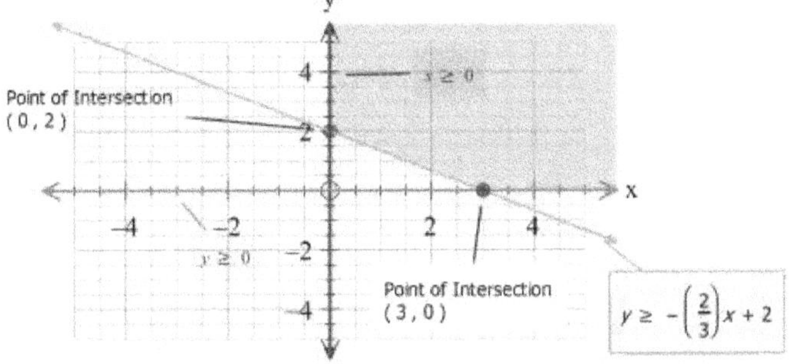

8. The region that satisfies all of the following inequalities is the shaded triangle below.

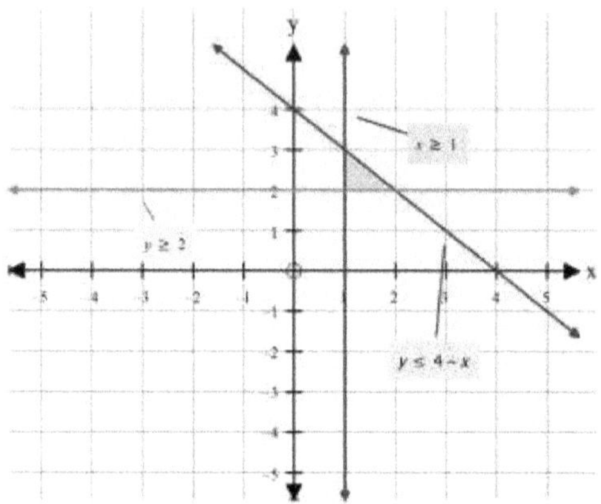

9. The following system of linear inequalities represents the situation described in the question:

$$2x + 3y \le 1000$$
$$x \ge 100$$
$$y \ge 50$$

10. To solve the system of linear inequalities $x + y \le 2$, $2x - y \ge -1$, $x \ge 0$, *and* $y \ge 0$, first graph the inequalities $y \le -x + 2$ *and* $y \le 2x + 1$. The solution to the system of inequalities is the region that is shaded by both of the lines.

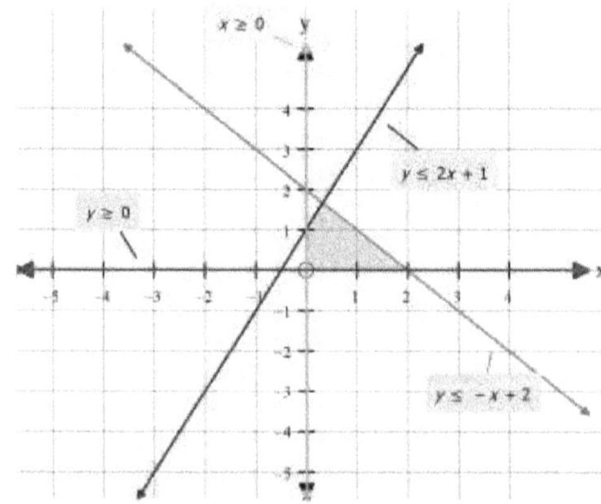

11. To graph the region, first graph the lines $x = 2, y = 3, and\ x + y = 5$. The solution to the system of inequalities is the region that is shaded by all three of the lines.

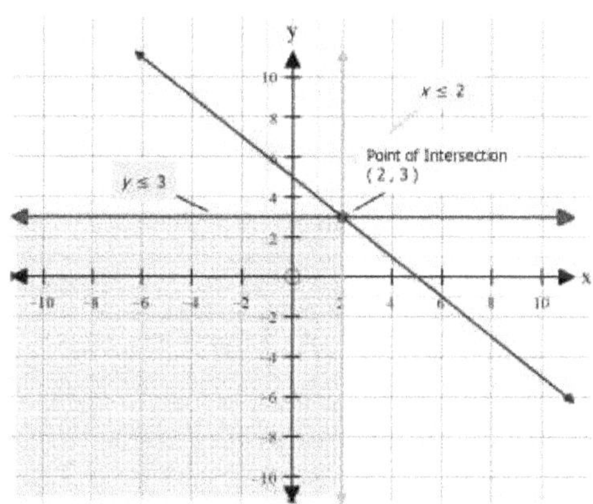

12. The line x = 1 is a vertical line that passes through the point (1, 0). The line y = 2 is a horizontal line that passes through the point (0, 2). The line x - y = 5 has a slope of 1 and a y-intercept of -5, so it can be graphed by plotting the points (0, -5) and (5, 0) and connecting them with a line.

Next, shade the region that satisfies all of the inequalities:

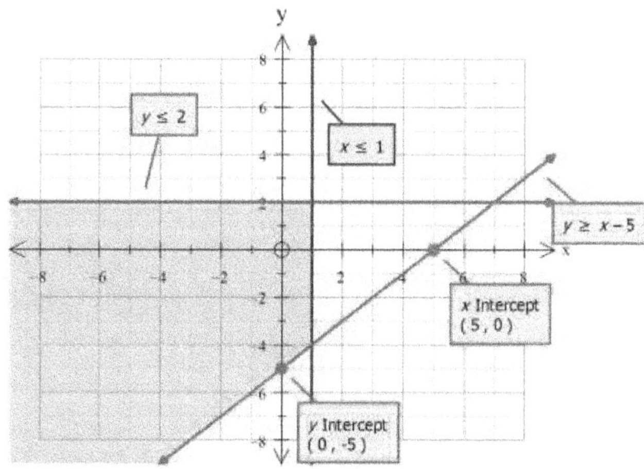

13.

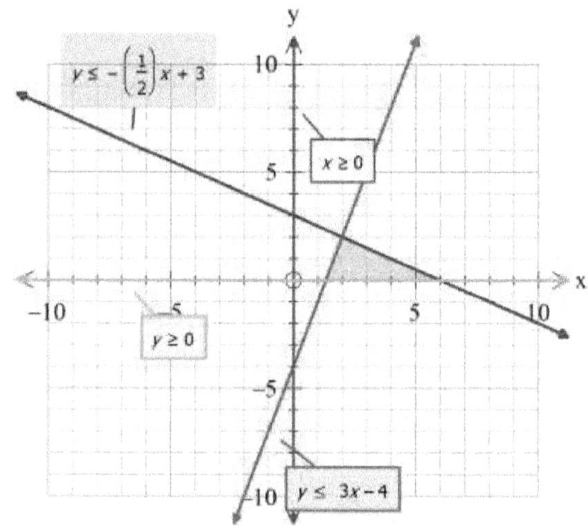

14. The shaded area above the line $2x + y = 4$ and above the line $x - 2y = 2$, restricted to the first quadrant.

15. The shaded area below the line $x + y = 3$ and below the line $2x - y = 1$, restricted to the first quadrant.

16. The shaded area below the line $4x + 2y = 8$ and below the line $2x - y = -1$, restricted to the first quadrant.

17. The shaded area above the line $2x + 3y = 6$ and above the line $x - 2y = 2$, restricted to the first quadrant.

18. A store sells two types of smartphones, A and B. Each type A smartphone costs $200, and each type B smartphone costs $250. The store wants to sell at least 30 smartphones and make a profit of at least $3000. If x represents the number of type A smartphones and y represents the number of type B smartphones sold,
The system of linear inequalities is:

$$200x + 250y \ge 3000 (Profit\ constraint)$$
$$x + y \ge 30 (Total\ smartphones\ constraint)$$
$$x \ge 0 (Non-negativity\ for\ type\ A)$$
$$y \ge 0 (Non-negativity\ for\ type\ B)$$

19. A company manufactures two models of laptops, X and Y. Each X model requires 4 hours of assembly time and 2 hours of testing time, while each Y model requires 3 hours of assembly time and 3 hours of testing time. The company has a total of 40 hours for assembly and 24 hours for testing each day. If the profit from each X model is $200 and from each Y model is $150,

The system of linear inequalities is:

$$4x + 3y \le 40 (Assembly\ time\ constraint)$$

$$2x + 3y \leq 24 (Testing\ time\ constraint)$$
$$200x + 150y \geq 0 (Profit\ constraint)$$
$$x \geq 0 (Non - negativity\ for\ model\ X)$$
$$y \geq 0 (Non - negativity\ for\ model\ Y)$$

20. **Graphical Representation:** The inequalities can be graphically represented as follows:

Financial Constraint: $30x + 20y \geq 150$

Time Constraint for Lawn Mowing: $x \leq 5$

Time Constraint for Hedge Trimming: $2y \leq 5$

Graphical Solution:

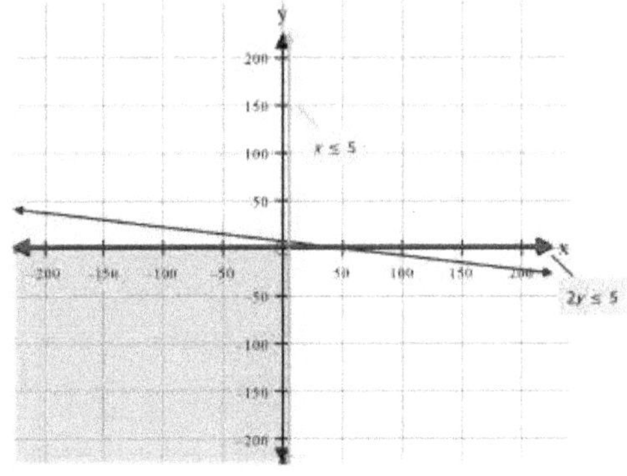

Part (II)
Advance Algebra

1. Absolute Value Equations, Inequalities and Graphs
2. Quadratic Equations, Polynomial Equations and Rational Equations
3. Exponential Equations, Radicals
4. Equivalent expressions, Isolating Quantities
5. Nonlinear equations and non-linear functions
6. Linear, Quadratic and Exponential Equations
7. Quadratic, Exponential, and Polynomial

Lesson 1 - Absolute Value Equations, Inequalities and Graphs

Introduction to Absolute Value:

Definition of Absolute Value: The absolute value of a real number, denoted by $|x|$, is the distance of that number from zero on the number line. Regardless of the sign of the number, the absolute value is always non-negative. Mathematically, it is defined as follows:

$$|x| = \begin{cases} x & if \ x \geq 0 \\ -x & if \ x < 0 \end{cases}$$

This definition highlights that if a number is positive or zero, its absolute value is the number itself. If the number is negative, its absolute value is the negation of the number, turning it into a positive value.

Notation and Basic Properties:

- **Notation:** The absolute value is represented using vertical bars.

  For example, $|5| = 5$ and $|-3| = 3$.

- **Basic Properties:**

  1. **Symmetry:** $|x| = |-x|$

  2. **Non-Negativity:** $|x| \geq 0$ for all values of x.

  3. **Identity:** $|x| = x \ if \ x \geq 0, and \ |x| = -x \ if \ x < 0$.

  4. **Triangle Inequality:** $|x + y| \leq |x| + |y|$

Understanding these properties is crucial for simplifying expressions involving absolute values and solving absolute value equations and inequalities.

Examples 1:

1. $|7| = 7$

2. $|-7| = 7$

3. $|0| = 0$

Practice Problems:

1. **Evaluate:** $|-8|$

- The absolute value of -8 is the distance of -8 from zero on the number line.

- $|-8| = 8$

2. **Simplify:** $|x - 3| \ for \ x = 4$

- Substitute $x = 4$ into the expression $|x - 3|$.

- $|4 - 3| = |1| = 1 \ |4 - 3| = |1| = 1$

3. **Solve for x:** $|2x - 1| = 5$

- Set up two cases based on the definition of absolute value:

    Case 1: $2x - 1 = 5$ (when $2x - 1$ is positive)

    Case 2: $-(2x - 1) = 5$ (when $2x - 1$ is negative)

- Solve each case separately:

    Case 1: $2x - 1 = 5$

    $\Rightarrow 2x = 6$

    $\Rightarrow x = 3$

    Case 2: $-(2x - 1) = 5$

    $\Rightarrow -2x + 1 = 5$

    $\Rightarrow -2x = 4$

    $\Rightarrow x = -2$

- The solution set is $x = 3 \ or \ x = -2.$

Solving Absolute Value Equations:

Isolating the Absolute Value Expression: When solving absolute value equations, it's crucial to isolate the absolute value expression to find the possible values of the variable.

Considering Positive and Negative Cases: When dealing with absolute value equations, it's essential to consider both positive and negative cases. This accounts for the fact that the absolute value of a number is its distance from zero, which can be either positive or negative.

Example 2: Solve for x: $| 2x - 3 | = 7$

1. **Isolate the Absolute Value Expression:** $| 2x - 3 | = 7$

    To isolate $| 2x - 3 |$, we set up two cases based on the definition of absolute value:

    - **Case 1:** $2x - 3 = 7$ (when $2x - 3$ is positive)
    - $2x - 3 = 7$
    - $2x = 10$
    - $x = 5$
    - Case 2: $-(2x - 3) = 7$ (when $2x - 3$ is negative)
    - $-(2x - 3) = 7$
    - $-2x + 3 = 7$
    - $-2x = 4$
    - $x = -2$

2. **Check Solutions:**

- Substitute $x = 5$ *and* $x = -2$ back into the original equation to ensure they satisfy the equation.

$$|\, 2(5) - 3 \,| = 7 \Rightarrow |\, 10 - 3 \,| = 7 \Rightarrow 7 = 7 \; (True)$$

$$|\, 2(-2) - 3 \,| = 7 \Rightarrow |\, -4 - 3 \,| = 7 \Rightarrow 7 = 7 \; (True)$$

Both solutions, $x = 5$ *and* $x = -2$, satisfy the original equation

Example 3: Solve for x: $|\, 3x + 2 \,| = 11$

1. **Isolate the Absolute Value Expression:** $|\, 3x + 2 \,| = 11$

Set up two cases:

- Case 1: $3x + 2 = 11$

$$3x + 2 = 11 \Rightarrow 3x = 9 \Rightarrow x = 3$$

- Case 2: $-(3x + 2) = 11$

$$-(3x + 2) = 11 \Rightarrow -3x - 2 = 11 \Rightarrow -3x = 13 \Rightarrow x = -\frac{13}{3}$$

2. **Check Solutions:**

- Substitute $x = 3$ and $x = -\frac{13}{3}$ back into the original equation:

$$|\, 3(3) + 2 \,| = 11 \Rightarrow |\, 9 + 2 \,| = 11 \Rightarrow 11 = 11 \; (True)$$

$$|\, 3(-\frac{13}{3}) + 2 \,| = 11 \Rightarrow |\, -13 + 2 \,| = 11 \Rightarrow 11 = 11 \; (True)$$

Both solutions, $x = 3$ and $x = -\frac{13}{3}$, satisfy the original equation.

Absolute Value Inequalities:

Solving Inequalities Involving Absolute Values: Absolute value inequalities represent situations where the distance between an expression and zero is less than, greater than, or equal to a certain value. To solve these inequalities, we follow a two-case approach:

Step 1: Split the inequality into two cases

Based on the absolute value sign, we split the inequality into two separate cases:

- Case 1: The expression inside the absolute value is positive or equal to zero.
- Case 2: The expression inside the absolute value is negative.

Step 2: Solve each case independently

For each case, we solve the inequality as a standard inequality. This involves isolating the expression inside the absolute value and then using the appropriate inequality sign ($>$, $<$, $\geq$, $\leq$).

Step 3: Combine solutions

Once we have solved each case, we combine the solutions, where possible, from both cases.

For < or <= absolute problems, we always join both solutions using AND, leading to 1 solution set

For > or >= absolute problems, we always join both solutions using OR, leading to 2 solution sets

Example 4: Solve the inequality $|x - 2| < 4$.

Step 1: Split the inequality into two cases

- Case 1: $x - 2 < 4$

- Case 2: $-(x - 2) < 4$

Step 2: Solve each case independently

- Case 1: $x < 6$

- Case 2: $x > -2$

Step 3: Combine solutions

Since it is absolute problem involving < sign , we combine using AND, leading to 1 solution set

$$x < 6 \; AND \; x > -2$$
$$-2 < x < 6$$

Example 5: Solve for x: $|2x - 1| < 5$

1. **Set Up Cases :** $|2x - 1| < 5$

   - **Case 1:** $2x - 1 < 5$

     $2x - 1 < 5$

     $2x < 6$

     $x < 3$

   - **Case 2:** $-(2x - 1) < 5$

     $-(2x - 1) < 5$

     $-2x + 1 < 5$

     $-2x < 4$

     $x > -2$

2. **Combine Cases:** Since it is absolute problem involving < sign , we combine using "AND" leading to 1 solution set $-2 < x < 3$

Example 6: Solve for x: $|x + 5| > 3$

1. **Set Up Cases :** $|x + 5| > 3$

- **Case 1:** $x + 5 > 3$

  $x > 3 - 5$

  $x > -2$

- **Case 2:** $-(x + 5) > 3$

  $-x - 5 > 3$

  $-x < 3 + 5$

  $-x < 8$

  $x < -8$

2. **Combine Cases:** Since it is absolute problem involving $<$ sign , we combine using "AND" leading to 1 solution set $x > -2 \; or \; x < -8$.

Graphical Representation:

Graphs of Basic Absolute Value Functions: The graph of the basic absolute value function, $y = |\, x \,|$, is a V-shaped graph with the vertex at the origin (0,0). Understanding the fundamental shape of this graph is essential for recognizing more complex absolute value functions.

Example 7: Graph $y = |\, x \,|$

- Plot points for $y = |\, x \,|$ by selecting various values of x, including positive and negative values.

- Connect the points to form a V-shaped graph.

- Emphasize symmetry around the y-axis.

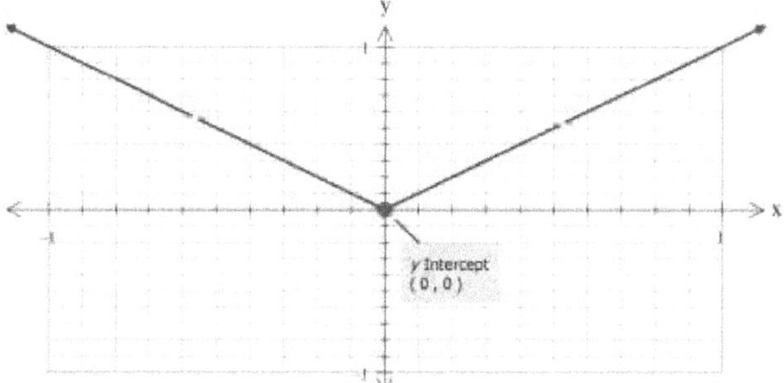

Key Features of Absolute Value Graphs: Absolute value graphs exhibit several key features that are important to recognize and understand:

- **Symmetry:** The graph is symmetrical about the y-axis. This means that if you reflect the graph across the y-axis, you will get the same graph back.

- **Vertex:** The highest or lowest point on the graph of an absolute value function is called the vertex. In this case, it is (0,0)

- **Zeroes:** This is where function $y = 0$, and in this case it is at $x=0$.

- **Direction of Opening:** The "arms" of the V-shaped graph open upwards. In general, the arms
  of the graph open in the direction determined by the sign in $y = |ax|$.

Recognizing Transformations: Understanding how different coefficients and constants affect the basic absolute value graph allows for the recognition of transformations.

Example 8: Graph $-2 \ | \ x - 3 \ | +4$: First plot the graph $y = |x|$

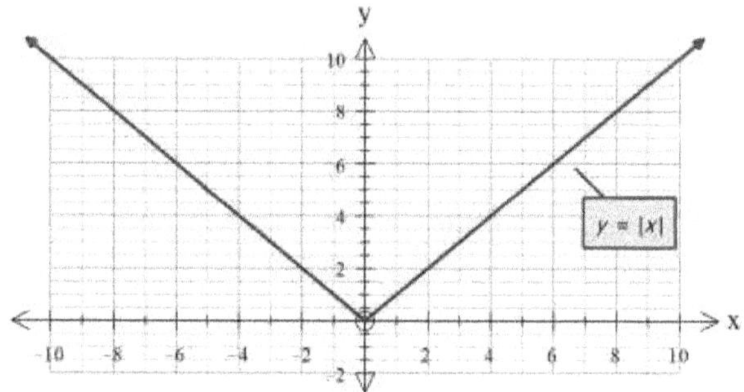

- **Horizontal Shift:** $x - 3$ shifts the graph right by three units.

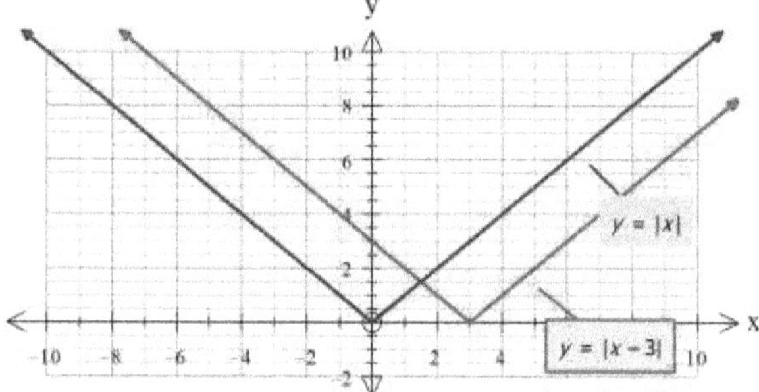

- **Vertical Shift:** $+4$ shifts the graph upward by four units.

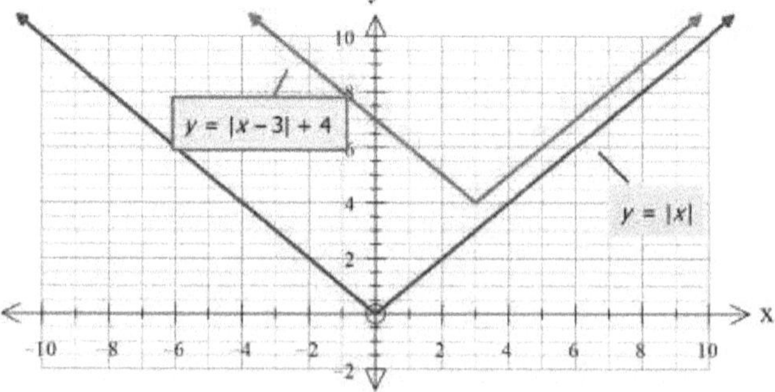

- **Vertical Stretch/Compression:** The coefficient 2 (which is greater than 1) shrinks it vertically by a factor of 2. The negative coefficient of same (-2) reflects the graph across the ~~~~

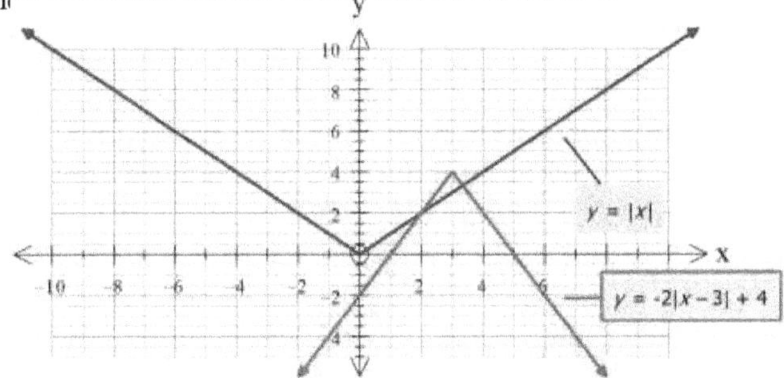

- **Final Transformation:** The combination of these transformations results in a downward-facing V-shaped graph shifted right by three units, stretched vertically by a factor of 2, and shifted upward by four units.

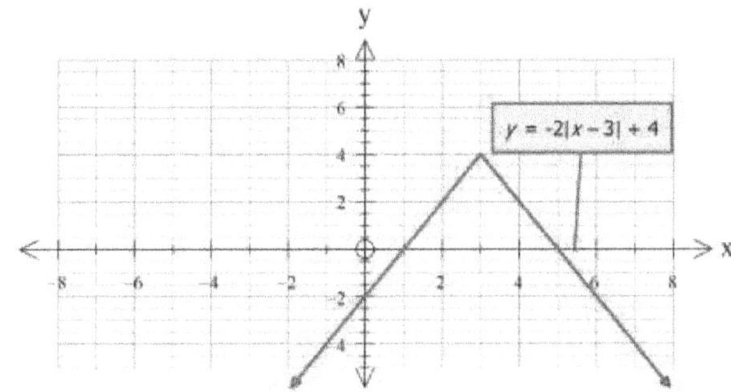

Transforming inequalities to absolute values

Transforming an inequality involving a range into an absolute value inequality involves a process of finding the midpoint and then determining the range around that midpoint. Let's break down the steps with an examples:

Example 9: $40 < x < 70$

3 step process

Step 1 : Calculate midpoint : $\frac{40+70}{2} = 55$

Step 2 : Subtract midpoint from all sides : $40 - 55 < x - 55 < 70 - 55$

Step 3 : Simplify : $-15 < x - 55 < 15$

Step 4 : Carry forward the "<" part of equation into absolute form : $|x - 55| < 15$

Final Absolute Value Inequality:

$|x - 55| < 15$

Example 10 $-8 < y < 4$

Step 1: Calculate Midpoint $= \frac{-8+4}{2} = -2$

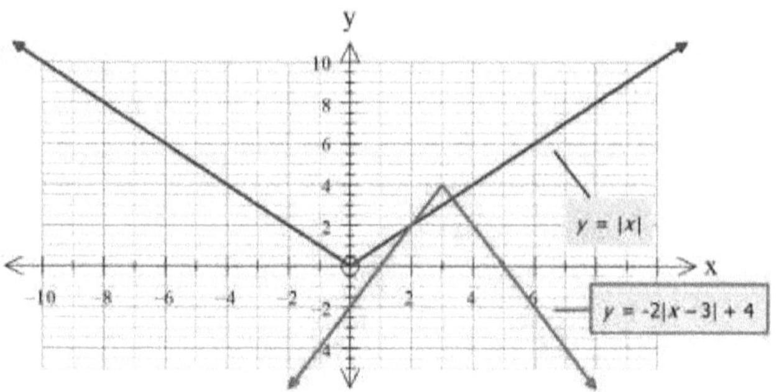

Step 2: Subtract Midpoint from All Sides –

$$=-8 - (-2) < y - (-2) < 4 - (-2)$$

$$-6 < y + 2 < 6$$

Step 3: Simplify $-6 < y + 2 < 6$

Step 4: Carry Forward the "<" Part of Equation into Absolute Form $|\, y + 2\, | < 6$

Final Absolute Value Inequality:

$$|\, y + 2\, | < 6$$

Practices Questions:

Transforming inequalities to absolute values

1. $4 < x < 14$
2. $9 < 2x < 15$
3. $50 < x < 120$
4. $250 < x < 1000$
5. $-3 < x < 21$
6. $-6 < 3y < 18$

Absolute Value Equations:

7. Solve for x: $|\,3x - 2\,| = 8$
8. Find the solution set for x: $|\,2x + 5\,| = 3$
9. Determine the value of k that satisfies the equation $|\,k - 4\,| = 6$
10. Solve the equation: $|2x - 3| = 4$
11. Solve the equation: $|x + 5| - 1 = 2$
12. A company's profit can be modeled by the absolute value function $P(x) = |x - 400|$, where x represents the number of units produced. What is the minimum profit the company can make?
13. Solve the equation: $|3x - 2| + 4 = 7$
14. A company's production cost can be modeled by the absolute value function $C(x) = |x - 100|$, where x represents the number of units produced. What is the production cost when 80 units are produced?
15. Solve the equation: $|2x - 1| - 3 = |x + 2|$

Absolute Value Inequalities:

16. Solve the inequality for x: $|\,2x - 1\,| < 4$
17. Determine the solution set for x in $|\,3x + 2\,| \geq 7$
18. Find the values of a that satisfy the inequality $|\,5a + 3\,| \leq 12$
19. Solve the inequality: $|3x + 4| \geq 7$
20. Solve the inequality: $|-4x + 6| < 1$

Graphical Representation:

21. Sketch the graph of the function $y = |-2x + 4|$.
22. Describe the transformation that occurs when the graph of $y = |x|$ is shifted 2 units to the right
23. Determine the transformation applied to $y = |\,x\,|$ to obtain the graph of $y = -|\,x - 3\,| + 5$.

Answer:

1. $|x - 9| < 5$
2. $|2x - 12| < 3$
3. $|x - 85| < 35$
4. $|x - 625| < 375$
5. $|x - 9| < 12$
6. $|3y - 6| < 12$
7. $x = 10/3, -2$
8. $x = -1, -4$
9. $k = 10, -2$
10. $x = \frac{7}{2}, -\frac{1}{2}$
11. $x = -2, -8.$
12. The minimum profit is $P(400) = |400 - 400| = 0$
13. $x = \frac{5}{3}$ and $x = -1/3.$
14. The production cost when 80 units are produced is 20.
15. $x = \frac{2}{3}, 6.$
16. $-\frac{3}{2} < x < \frac{5}{2}$
17. $x \leq -3$ or $x \geq 5/3$
18. $-3 \leq a \leq \frac{9}{5}$
19. $x \leq -\frac{11}{3}$ or $x \geq 1.$
20. $\frac{5}{4} < x < \frac{7}{4}.$
21.

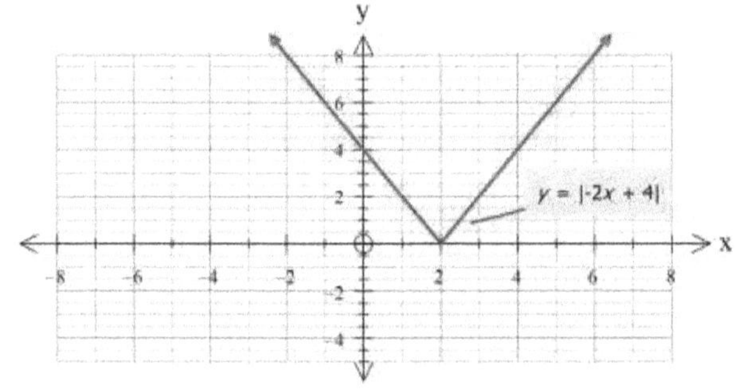

22. The new function $y = |x - 2|$. This transformation shifts the entire graph horizontally to the right, maintaining the V-shaped structure with the new vertex at (2, 0).
23. The transformation applied to $|y = |x|$ to obtain $y = -|x - 3| + 5$ includes a vertical reflection, a horizontal shift to the right by 3 units, and a vertical shift upward by 5 units.

Lesson 2 - Quadratic Equations, Polynomial Equations and Rational Equations

Introduction to Equations:

An equation is a statement that asserts the equality of two mathematical expressions. It involves an equal sign (=) that separates the two expressions. Equations are fundamental tools in mathematics, used to represent relationships between quantities and solve for unknowns.

Types of Equations: Equations can be classified into different categories based on the nature of the expressions involved and the degree of the polynomial. Here are the main types of equations:

Linear Equations: Linear equations represent a straight line when graphed. They are characterized by the presence of only one variable raised to the first power. The general form of a linear equation is $ax + b = c$, where a, b, and c are constants and $a \neq 0$.

Quadratic Equations: Quadratic equations represent a parabola when graphed. They involve the second power of a variable. The general form of a quadratic equation is

$ax^2 + bx + c = 0$, where a, b, and c are constants and $a \neq 0$.

Polynomial Equations: Polynomial equations involve any positive integer power of a variable. They can have multiple roots and represent a variety of curves when graphed. The general form of a polynomial equation is $a_n x^n + a_{n-1} x^{n-1} + ... + a_1 x + a_0 = 0$, where a_0, a_1, ..., a_{n-1}, and a_n are constants and $a_n \neq 0$.

Rational Equations: Rational equations involve expressions with fractions. They represent a quotient of two polynomials. The general form of a rational equation is $\frac{P(x)}{Q(x)} = 0$, where $P(x)$ and $Q(x)$ are polynomial expressions.

Quadratic Equations

Definition and General Form of Quadratic Equations: Basic Structure: A quadratic equation is an algebraic equation that can be written in the form $ax^2 + bx + c = 0$, where a, b, and c are real numbers and $a \neq 0$. The variable in the equation is typically denoted by x.

Coefficients and Variables: The coefficients a, b, and c are called the coefficients of the quadratic equation. The coefficient a is called the leading coefficient. The variable x represents the unknown quantity that we are trying to solve for.

Standard Form of Quadratic Equations:

- **Expressing Equations in Standard Form**
  Standard form is achieved by arranging terms in descending order of powers.
  Example: $2x^2 + 3x + 1 = 0$
- **Coefficient Notation:** Coefficient notation simplifies expression by denoting the coefficients $(a = 2, b = 3, c = 1)$ explicitly.

Recognizing Quadratic Equations:

- **Identifying Quadratic Forms**
  Quadratic equations can be identified by several key features:
    i. They involve the second power of the variable (x^2).
    ii. They can be rearranged into the form $ax^2 + bx + c = 0$
    iii. They represent a parabola when graphed.
- **Transformation to Standard Form**
  If a quadratic equation is not already in standard form, it can be manipulated to bring it into standard form by dividing both sides by the leading coefficient a (if necessary) and rearranging the terms.

Solving Quadratic Equations: There are three main methods for solving quadratic equations

Factoring the Quadratic Expression : This method involves factoring the quadratic expression $ax^2 + bx + c$ into two linear expressions ($p(x)$ and $q(x)$) and setting each factor equal to zero. The solutions to the quadratic equation are the values of x that make either $p(x)$ or $q(x)$ equal to zero. This includes the below common factoring formulas -

- $x^2 + ax + bx + ab = (x + a)(x + b)$
  $e.g. x^2 + 7x + 12 = (x + 3)(x + 4)$

- $x^2 + 2ax + a^2 = (x + a)^2$
  $e.g. x^2 + 10x + 25 = (x + 5)^2$

- $x^2 - 2ax + a^2 = (x - a)^2$
  $e.g. x^2 - 10x + 25 = (x - 5)^2$

- $x^2 - a^2 = (x + a)(x - a) (Difference\ of\ squares)$

  $e.g. x^2 - 25 = (x + 5)(x - 5)$

Completing the Square Method

This method involves manipulating the quadratic expression to create a perfect square trinomial. The perfect square can then be factored and solved, leading to the solutions of the quadratic equation.

Using the Quadratic Formula

The quadratic formula is a general formula that can be used to solve any quadratic equation of the form $ax^2 + bx + c = 0$. The formula is

$$x = \frac{-b \pm \sqrt{b^2 - 4ac}}{2a}$$

Each of these methods has its own advantages and may be more suitable for certain types of quadratic equations. Practice with different examples will help you develop an understanding of when to use each method effectively.

Example 1: Solving quadratic equation $x^2 - 3x - 4 = 0$

What are the solutions for the equation?

Factor the quadratic equation:

$$x^2 - 3x - 4 = 0$$

$$x^2 - 4x + x - 4 = 0$$

$$x(x - 4) + (x - 4) = 0$$

$$(x + 1)(x - 4)$$

Set each factor equal to zero and solve for x:

$$x + 1 = 0 \ or \ x - 4 = 0$$

$$x = -1 \ or \ x = 4$$

Example 2: Solving quadratic equation $x^2 + 10x - 25 = 0$

What are the solutions for the equation?

$$x^2 + 10x - 25 + 50 = 0 + 50$$

$$(x + 5)^2 = 50$$

$$x + 5 = \pm \sqrt{50}$$

$$x + 5 = \pm 5\sqrt{2}$$

$$x = -5 \pm 5\sqrt{2}$$

$$x = -5 + 5\sqrt{2} , x = -5 - 5\sqrt{2}$$

Example 3: Solving Quadratic Equation $2x^2 - 5x + 3 = 0$

What are the solutions for the equation?

Solution: To find the solutions, you can use the quadratic formula:

$$x = \frac{-b \pm \sqrt{b^2 - 4ac}}{2a}$$

For the given equation, $a = 2, b = -5, and \ c = 3$. Plug these values into the formula and calculate the solutions.

$$x = \frac{-(-5) \pm \sqrt{(-5)^2 - 4 * 2 * 3}}{2 * 2}$$

$$x = \frac{5 \pm \sqrt{25 - 24}}{4}$$

$$x = \frac{5 \pm 1}{4}$$

$$x = \frac{5 + 1}{4} , x = \frac{5 - 1}{4}$$

So, the solutions are $x = 1$ and $x = \frac{3}{2}$.

Example 4: Word Problem Involving Quadratic Equation

A rectangular garden with a length that is 5 meters more than its width. If the area of the garden is 24 square meters, find the dimensions of the garden.

Solution: Let w be the width of the garden. The length is $w + 5$. The area (A) is given by

$$A = length \times width.$$

$$A = w(w + 5)$$

Since the area is given as 7 square meters, set up the equation:

$$w(w + 5) = 24$$

This is a quadratic equation. Solve it to find the width (w) and then calculate the length

Expanding and rearranging: $w^2 + 5w - 24 = 0$

Now, you can factor or use the quadratic formula to solve for w. Factoring, you get:

$$(w + 8)(w - 3) = 0$$

So, we have two possible solutions for w:

1. $w - 3 = 0 \Rightarrow w = 3$

2. $w + 8 = 0 \Rightarrow w = -8$ (Discarded since the width cannot be negative)

Since the width of the garden cannot be negative, we have $w = 3$.

Now that we know the width is 3 meters, we can calculate the length:

Length = Width + 5 = 3 + 5 = 8 meters

Therefore, the dimensions of the garden are 3 meters wide by 8 meters long.

Discriminants and properties

The discriminant is a mathematical term associated with quadratic equations. For a quadratic a quadratic equation in the form $ax^2 + bx + c = 0$, the discriminant (Δ) is given by the expression $b^2 - 4ac$. The discriminant plays a crucial role in determining the nature of the solutions (roots) of the quadratic equation. Here are the three cases based on the discriminant: $i.e. \Delta = b^2 - 4ac$.

- If $\Delta > 0$: Two distinct real solutions.

  - Explanation: When the discriminant is positive, the quadratic equation has two real and distinct roots. Geometrically, this means the graph of the quadratic function intersects the x-axis at two distinct points.

- If $\Delta = 0$: One real solution (double root or repeated root).

- Explanation: When the discriminant is zero, the quadratic equation has one real solution. In this case, the graph of the quadratic function touches the x-axis at a single point, which means there is a repeated root.

- If $\Delta < 0$: No real solution; two imaginary solutions.

  - Explanation: When the discriminant is negative, the quadratic equation has no real solutions. Instead, it has two complex (imaginary) solutions. Geometrically, the graph of the quadratic function does not intersect the x-axis; it remains entirely above or below it.

Examples 5:

- $\Delta > 0$: Two distinct real solutions

  Equation: $x^2 + 6x + 5 = 0$

  The discriminant (Δ) for this equation is:

  $$\Delta = b^2 - 4ac = (6)^2 - 4(1)(5) = 16$$

  Since $\Delta > 0$, the quadratic equation has two distinct real solutions. To find the solutions, we can use the quadratic formula: $x = \dfrac{(-b \pm \sqrt{\Delta})}{2a}$

  $$x = \frac{(-6 \pm \sqrt{16})}{2}$$

  $$x = \frac{(-6 \pm 4)}{2}$$

  $$x = -1 \; or \; -5$$

  The root is x $= -1$ or -5

- $\Delta = 0$: One real solution (double root or repeated root)

  Equation: $x^2 + 4x + 4 = 0$

  The discriminant (Δ) for this equation is:

  $$\Delta = b^2 - 4ac = 4^2 - 4(1)(4) = 0$$

  Since $\Delta = 0$, the equation has one real solution (double root or repeated root):

  $$x = \frac{(-b \pm \sqrt{\Delta})}{2a}$$

  $$x = \frac{(-4 \pm \sqrt{0})}{(2)(1)}$$

  $$x = -2$$

  The root is x $= -2$ (a repeated root).

- $\Delta < 0$: No real solution; two imaginary solutions

Equation: $x^2 + 2x + 5 = 0$

The discriminant (Δ) for this equation is:

$$\Delta = b^2 - 4ac = 2^2 - 4(1)(5) = -16$$

Since $\Delta < 0$, the equation has no real solutions and two imaginary solutions:

$$x = \frac{\left(-b \pm \sqrt{\Delta}\right)}{2a}$$

$$x = \frac{\left(-2 \pm \sqrt{-16}\right)}{(2)(1)} = \frac{\left(-2 \pm \sqrt{i^2 16}\right)}{2} = \frac{\left(-2 \pm 4i\right)}{2} \qquad where \ i^2 = -1$$

$$x = -1 \pm 2i$$

The roots are complex (imaginary): $x = -1 + 2i \ and \ x = -1 - 2i$.

Sum and Product of solutions

For a quadratic equation in the form $ax^2 + bx + c = 0$, the sum and product of the roots (x_1 and x_2) can be expressed in terms of the coefficients a, b, and c.

Let the quadratic equation be $ax^2 + bx + c = 0$, and let x_1 and x_2 be the roots. The sum and product of the roots are given by the following formulas:

1. **Sum of the roots** $(x_1 + x_2) := -\frac{b}{a}$

2. **Product of the roots** $(x_1 * x_2) := \frac{c}{a}$

These formulas are derived from Vieta's formulas, which relate the coefficients of a polynomial to the sums and products of its roots.

Let's consider an example to illustrate these formulas:

Example 6 : Consider the quadratic equation $2x^2 - 5x + 2 = 0$

Sum of the roots $(x_1 + x_2): = -\frac{b}{a} \Rightarrow -\frac{(-5)}{2} = \frac{5}{2}$

Product of the roots $(x_1 * x_2): = \frac{c}{a} \Rightarrow \frac{2}{2} = 1$

So, for the given quadratic equation, the sum of the roots is 5/2 and the product of the roots is 1.

Polynomial Equations

Introduction to Polynomial Equations: Polynomial equations are algebraic equations that involve one or more non-negative integer powers of a variable. They are characterized by the presence of one or more polynomial terms, each consisting of a coefficient multiplied by a variable raised to a specific power.

- **Higher-Degree Polynomial Equations:** Higher-degree polynomial equations involve powers of the variable greater than or equal to 4 and represent more complex curves when graphed

    Example: $2x^4 + 5x^3 - 3x^2 + x - 1 = 0$

Definition and Classification of Polynomial Equations:

General Structure: $a_n x^n + a_{n-1} x^{n-1} + \ldots + a_1 x + a_0 = 0$, where $a_0, a_1, \ldots, a_{n-1}$, and an are constants and $a_n \neq 0$. The variable in the equation is typically denoted by x.

- Identifying Polynomial Forms
    - I.   Identify the presence of one or more polynomial terms.
    - II. Check for non-negative integer powers of the variable.
    - III. Ensure the presence of at least one term with a non-zero coefficient.

Solving Polynomial Equations:

Factoring Polynomial Expressions: Factoring polynomial expressions involves decomposing them into simpler polynomial terms. This method is often used for lower-degree polynomial equations. Let's explore factoring with an example.

Example 7 : Factor the Polynomial $3x^2 - 12x$.

Solution:

- **Common Factor:**

    Factor out the greatest common factor. In this case, both terms have a common factor of $3x$.

    $3x^2 - 12x = 3x(x - 4)$

    Now, we have factored out the common factor $3x$.

- **Factor the Remaining Expression:**

    The expression $x - 4$ is a binomial that can be factored no further.

    $3x^2 - 12x = 3x(x - 4)$

    The fully factored form is $3x(x - 4)$.

    This process involves identifying common factors and factoring the remaining expression. Factoring is an essential skill, and different techniques may be applied based on the structure of the polynomial. It plays a significant role in simplifying expressions and solving equations efficiently.

Example 8 : To find the value of b, if $(x^2 + bx - 2)(x + 3) = x^3 + 6x^2 + 7x - 6$

Let's expand the left side and simplify the expression:

$(x^2 + bx - 2)(x + 3) = x^3 + 6x^2 + 7x - 6$

Expand the left side:

$$x^3 + bx^2 - 2x + 3x^2 + 3bx - 6 = x^3 + 6x^2 + 7x - 6$$

Combine like terms:

$$x^3 + (bx^2 + 3x^2) + (3bx - 2x) - 6 = x^3 + 6x^2 + 7x - 6$$

$$x^3 + (b + 3)x^2 + (3b - 2)x - 6 = x^3 + 6x^2 + 7x - 6$$

Since the coefficients of corresponding terms on both sides of the equation are equal, we can set them equal to each other:

Coefficient of x^2

$$b + 3 = 6 \Rightarrow b = 3$$

Coefficient of x

$$3b - 2 = 7 \Rightarrow b = 3$$

So, the value of b is 3.

Polynomial Remainder Theorem: The Polynomial Remainder Theorem is a useful concept in algebra that relates polynomial division to remainders. It states that if a polynomial $P(x)$ is divided by $x-c$, then the remainder is $P(c)$. Let's explore this theorem with an example.

Example 9: Use the Polynomial Remainder Theorem to find the remainder when

$$f(x) = 2x^3 - 5x^2 + 3x - 9 \text{ is divided by } x - 3.$$

Solution:

Identify c:

In this case, $c = 3$, which is the root of the divisor $x - 3$.

Apply the Polynomial Remainder Theorem:

Substitute $x = 3$ into the polynomial $f(x)$ to find the remainder.

$$f(3) = 2(3)^3 - 5(3)^2 + 3(3) - 9$$

$$f(3) = 54 - 45 + 9 - 9$$

$$f(3) = 9$$

Interpret the Result:

The remainder when $f(x)$ is divided by $x - 3$ is 9.

Therefore, according to the Polynomial Remainder Theorem, when $f(x) = 2x^3 - 5x^2 + 3x - 9$ is divided by $x - 3$, the remainder is 9.

Rational Equations

Understanding Rational Equations:

Definition and Structure: Rational equations are mathematical expressions with variables in the numerator and denominator, often represented as $\frac{P(x)}{Q(x)} = 0$, where P(x) and Q(x) are polynomials.

- **Characteristics of Rational Equations:**
- Involves fractions with variables.
- May have restrictions on the values of variables (denominators cannot be zero).

Simplifying Rational Expressions: Several basic techniques can be used to simplify rational expressions:

- **Factoring out common factors:** This involves identifying the greatest common factor (GCD) of the numerator and denominator and dividing both by the GCD.
- **Canceling out common terms:** This involves finding terms that appear in both the numerator and denominator and canceling them out.
- **Combining like terms:** This involves combining terms with the same degree in the numerator and denominator separately.

Rational expressions can exist in various forms, including:

- **Proper rational expressions:** These expressions have a degree of the numerator that is less than the degree of the denominator.
- **Improper rational expressions:** These expressions have a degree of the numerator that is equal to or greater than the degree of the denominator.
- **Mixed rational expressions:** These expressions involve a combination of whole numbers, polynomials, and fractions.

Solving Rational Equations: Multiplying Both Sides by a Common Denominator: This technique involves multiplying both sides of the equation by the least common multiple (LCM) of the denominators of the rational expressions. This eliminates the fractions and allows for further manipulation of the equation.

Example 10 : Solve the rational equation $\frac{2}{x} + \frac{3}{2} = \frac{5}{4x}$

Identify the Common Denominator:

The common denominator for x and 2 is $2x$.

Multiply Both Sides by the Common Denominator:

Multiply both sides by $2x$ to clear the fractions.

$$2x \cdot \left(\frac{2}{x} + \frac{3}{2}\right) = 2x \cdot \frac{5}{4x}$$

Simplify each term:

Isolate the Variable:

$$4 + 3x = \frac{10}{4}$$

Subtract 4 from both sides to isolate x:

$$3x = \frac{10}{4} - 4$$

Simplify the right side:

$$3x = \frac{10 - 16}{4}$$

$$3x = \frac{-6}{4}$$

$$x = -\frac{1}{2}$$

So, the solution to the given rational equation is $x = -\frac{1}{2}$

Example 11 : Solve the equation $\frac{1}{x-2} - \frac{2}{x-1} = \frac{3}{2}$.

1. **Common Denominator:** Find a common bottom number for the fractions.

   It's $(x - 2)(x - 1)$.

2. **Multiply Both Sides:** Make the fractions simpler by multiplying both sides by $(x + 2)(x - 1)$.

   This gives you $(x - 1) - 2(x - 2) = \frac{3}{2} * (x - 2)(x - 1)$.

   Simplify the equation to $-x + 3 = \frac{3}{2} * (x^2 - 3x + 2)$.

   Solve the Equation: Solve the quadratic equation

   $$\frac{3}{2}x^2 - \frac{9}{2}x + x + 3 - 3 = 0$$

   $$\frac{3}{2} * x^2 - \frac{7}{2} * x + 3 - 3 = 0.$$

   $$3x^2 - 7x = 0.$$

   Factor it to $x(3x - 7) = 0$.

   Solutions: $x = \frac{7}{3}$ or $x = 0$.

Finding & Cancelling Out Common Factors: Finding common factors is a crucial step when simplifying expressions or solving equations, especially those involving rational expressions. Here's a simple explanation with an example:

Example 12 : Simplify the rational expression $\frac{6x^2 - 15x}{10x^2 - 25x}$.

Solution:

Factor the Numerator and Denominator:

Factor the numerator and denominator to find common factors.

$$\frac{6x^2 - 15x}{10x^2 - 25x.}$$

Factor the numerator: $3x(2x - 5)$

Factor the denominator: $5x(2x - 5)$

Write the Simplified Expression:

Write the expression with the common factors canceled out.

$$\frac{3x(2x - 5)}{5x(2x - 5)}$$

Cancel out the common factors: x & $(2x - 5)$

$$\frac{3(2x - 5)}{5(2x - 5)}$$

Final Simplified Expression:

Write the final simplified expression. $\frac{3}{5}$

Example 13 : Solve the equation:

$$\frac{x + 1}{x - 2} = \frac{3x - 2}{3x + 2}$$

Solution:

Step 1: Multiply both sides by the common denominator, which is the least common multiple of $(x - 2)$ and $(3x + 2)$. This is $(x - 2)(3x + 2)$.

$$(x + 1)(3x + 2) = (3x - 2)(x - 2)$$

Step 2: Expand both sides:

$$3x^2 + 5x + 2 = 3x^2 - 8x + 4$$

Step 3: Subtract $3x^2$ from both sides:

$$5x + 2 = -8x + 4$$

Step 4: Add $6x$ to both sides:

$$13x + 2 = 4$$

Step 5: Subtract 2 from both sides:

$$13x = 2$$

Step 6: Divide both sides by 13:

$$x = 2/13$$

Therefore, the solution to the rational equation is $x = 2/13$.

Practice questions

1. Solve the quadratic equation: $x^2 + 6x + 8 = 0$
2. Solve the quadratic equation $5x^2 + 9x = -4$
3. Solve the quadratic equation $k^2 - 31 - 2k = -6 - 3k^2 - 2k$
4. Solve the quadratic equation: $2x^2 - 5x + 2 = 0$
5. Solve the quadratic equation: $x^2 + 4x - 5 = 0$
6. Factor the expression $p^2 - 36$
7. *Factor the expression* $24x^3 - 54x$
8. *Factor the expression* $9x^2 - 16y^2$
9. *Factor the expression* $36a^4 - 25b^4$
10. Solve the quadratic equation: $3x^2 + 7x - 6 = 0$
11. Find the sum and product of the roots of each quadratic equation. $x^2 - 3x + 2 = 0$
12. Find the sum and product of the roots of each quadratic equation $x^2 + 6x + 5 = 0$
13. Find the sum and product of the roots of each quadratic equation $x^2 - 5x + 6 = 0$
14. Find the sum and product of the roots of each quadratic equation $x^2 = 4x + 3$
15. Find the sum and product of the roots of each quadratic equation $3x + 7x^2 - 1 = 0$
16. Solve the quadratic equation: $x^2 - 2x - 3 = 0$
17. Find the sum of the coefficients of the polynomial $4x^3 - 7x^2 + 2x - 1$
18. Solve the inequality $x^3 - 6x^2 + 9x \geq 0$
19. The sum of the roots of the polynomial $2x^2 - 5x + 3$ is:
20. Solve the equation $4x^3 - 12x^2 + 9x = 0$
21. Solve the equation: $\frac{2x-3}{x+1} = \frac{x-2}{2}$
22. Multiply the polynomials: $\frac{x^2-4}{(x-2)^2}$ *and* $\frac{x^2-4x+4}{x^2-5x+6}$
23. Solve for x: $\frac{1}{x+1} + \frac{1}{x} = \frac{2}{x-1}$
24. Solve the equation: $\frac{2x}{3} + 5 = \frac{4}{3}$.
25. Simplify: $\frac{5x-10}{x^2-4}$
26. Simplify: $\frac{2}{x^2-5x+6} - \frac{4}{x^2-2x-3} + \frac{2}{x^2+4x+3}$
27. Simplify: $\frac{5x}{1-2x} - \frac{2x}{2x+1} + \frac{3}{4x^2-1}$
28. Multiply the polynomials: $(3a^2 + 1) \times (4a^3 + 5)$
29. Without using long division, find each remainder:
    (a) $(2x^2 + 6x + 8) \div (x + 1)$
    (b) $(x^2 + 4x + 12) \div (x - 4)$
30. Find each remainder:
    (a) $(2x^2 + x - 6) + (x + 2)$
    (b) $(x^2 + 6x^2 - 4x + 2) + (x + 1)$

31. When $x^3 + kx^2 - 4x + 2$ is divided by $x + 2$ the remainder is 26, find k
32. When $2x^3 - 3x^2 + kx - 1$ is divided by $x - 1$ the remainder is 2, find k.

Answer:

1. $x = -2 \ and \ x = -4.$
2. $x = -\dfrac{4}{5} \ and \ x = -1.$
3. $k = 5/2 \ or \ k = -5/2$
4. $x = 2 \ and \ x = 1/2.$
5. $x = -5 \ or \ x = 1$
6. $(P - 6)(P + 6)$
7. $6x(2x + 3)(2x - 3).$
8. $(3x + 4y)(3x - 4y).$
9. $(6a^2 + 5b^2)(6a^2 - 5b^2).$
10. x = -3 and x = 2/3.
11. The sum of the roots is 3, and the product of the roots is 2.
12. The sum of the roots is -6, and the product of the roots is 5.
13. The sum of the roots is 5, and the product of the roots is 6.
14. The sum of the roots is 4, and the product of the roots is -3.
15. The sum of the roots is -3/7, and the product of the roots is -1/7.
16. $x = 3 \ or \ x = -1$
17. -2
18. All real numbers for x less than equal to 0 or greater than equal to 3
19. 5/2
20. $x = 0, x = \dfrac{3}{2}, \dfrac{3}{2}$
21. $x = 4 \ or \ x = 1$
22. $\dfrac{x+2}{x-3}$
23. $x = -1/3$
24. $x = -\dfrac{11}{2}$
25. $\dfrac{5}{x+2}$
26. $\dfrac{-6x+42}{(x-2)(x-3)(x+1)(x+3)}$
27. $-\dfrac{14x^2+3x-3}{(2x+1)(2x-1)}$
28. $12a^5 + 4a^3 + 15a^2 + 5$
29. (a) 4 (b) 44
30. (a) 0 (b) 13
31. $k = 6$
32. $k = 4$

Lesson 3 - Exponential Equations, Radicals

Exponential Equations: Exponential equations are equations in which the variable is found in the exponent. They typically take the form of $a^x = b$, where a is a fixed base, x is the variable exponent, and b is a constant.

Here are some examples of exponential equations:

- $2^x = 8$

- $3^x + 1 = 10$

- $e^{-2x} = \frac{1}{16}$

Solving exponential equations can be done using a variety of methods, including:

- **Isolating the exponent:** This involves moving all of the exponential terms to one side of the equation and then solving for the exponent.

- **Converting to logarithmic form:** This involves taking the logarithm of both sides of the equation and then solving for the variable.

- **Using properties of exponents:** This involves using the properties of exponents to simplify the equation and then solving for the variable.

Properties of Exponents:

- **Product rule:** The product rule states that the product of two powers of the same base is equal to the base raised to the sum of the exponents.

$$a^m \cdot a^n = a^{m+n}$$

For example, $2^3 \cdot 2^4 = 2^{3+4} = 2^7$.

- **Quotient rule:** The quotient rule states that the quotient of two powers of the same base is equal to the base raised to the difference of the exponents.

$$a^m \div a^n = a^{m-n}$$

For example, $3^5 \div 3^2 = 3^{5-2} = 3^3$.

- **Power of a power rule:** The power of a power rule states that the power of a power is equal to the base raised to the product of the exponents.

$$(a^m)^n = a^{mn}$$

For example, $(2^3)^2 = 2^{3 \cdot 2} = 2^6$.

- **Zero power rule:** The zero power rule states that any nonzero number raised to the power of zero is equal to one.

$$a^0 = 1$$

For example, $5^0 = 1, and\ 2^0 = 1$.

Negative exponent rule: The negative exponent rule states that any nonzero number raised to a negative exponent is equal to the reciprocal of the number raised to the positive exponent.

$$a^{-n} = \frac{1}{a^n}$$

For example, $2^{-3} = \frac{1}{2^3} = \frac{1}{8}$

- **Power of a Product Rule:** The power of a product rule states that the power of a product of two or more numbers is equal to the product of the powers of the individual numbers.
  In other words, for any numbers a and b, and any positive integer m,
  $$(ab)^m = a^m * b^m.$$

  For example $(2 * 3)^4 = 2^4 * 3^4$

- **Power of a Quotient Rule:** The power of a quotient rule states that the power of a quotient of two numbers is equal to the quotient of the powers of the individual numbers.
  In other words, for any numbers a and b, and any positive integer m,
  $$\left(\frac{a}{b}\right)^m = \frac{a^m}{b^m.} = a^m b^{-m}$$

  For example $\left(\frac{4}{2}\right)^3 = \frac{4^3}{2^3}$

- **Fractional Exponent Rule:** The fractional exponent rule states that the power of a number raised to a fractional exponent is equal to the nth root of the number raised to the power of the numerator of the exponent.
  In other words, for any number a, and any positive integers m and n,
  $$a^{\frac{m}{n}} = \sqrt[n]{(a^m)}$$

  For example $2^{\frac{3}{2}} = \sqrt[2]{(2^3)}$

Simplifying Exponential Expressions

Simplifying exponential expressions involves using the properties of exponents to rewrite expressions in their simplest form. Here's a breakdown of simplifying exponential terms with the same base, different bases, and negative exponents:

- **Simplifying exponential terms with the same base**

  The product rule and power of a power rule apply when simplifying exponential terms with the same base:

  Product rule: $a^m \times a^n = a^{m+n}$

  For example: $2^3 \times 2^4 = 2^{3+4} = 2^7$

  Power of a power rule: $(a^m)^n = a^{m \times n}$

  For example: $(3^2)^3 = 3^{2 \times 3} = 3^6$

- **Simplifying exponential terms with different bases**

  When simplifying exponential terms with different bases, you cannot directly apply the product or power of a power rule. However, you can use the following strategies:

- **Convert to a common base:** If possible, convert both terms to the same base and then apply the product or power of a power rule.

  For example: $4^2 \times 8^3 = (2^2)^2 \times (2^3)^3 = 2^4 \times 2^9 = 2^{13}$

- **Use factorization:** If the bases have common factors, factor them out and apply the product or power of a power rule.

  For example : $6^3 \times 2^4 = (2 \times 3)^3 \times 2^4 = 2^3 \times 3^3 \times 2^4 = 2^7 \times 3^3$

- **Simplifying exponential terms with negative exponents**

  The negative exponent rule states that $a^{-n} = \frac{1}{a^n}$. This rule allows you to simplify exponential terms with negative exponents.

  For example: $3^{-2} = \frac{1}{3^2} = \frac{1}{9}$

Solving Exponential Equations

The main method for solving exponential equations involve converting both sides of equation to same base and then solving

Example 1: Consider the equation $2^x = 16$, and we want to solve for x.

$$2^x = 16$$

Convert to the same base

$$2^x = 2^4$$

Since bases are the same, powers have to be equal. So $x = 4$

Radicals: Radicals are expressions that involve the roots of numbers. For example, $\sqrt{2}$ is a radical because it is the square root of 2. Radicals can be used to represent irrational numbers, which are numbers that cannot be expressed as a finite decimal or a fraction.

Properties of radicals:

- **Product rule:** The product of two radicals with the same index is equal to the product of their radicands.
  For example, $\sqrt{2} \times \sqrt{3} = \sqrt{2 \times 3} = \sqrt{6}$.
  This property is based on the fact that the square root of a product is equal to the product of the square roots.

$$\sqrt{a \times b} = \sqrt{a} \times \sqrt{b}$$

- **Quotient rule:** The quotient of two radicals with the same index is equal to the quotient of their radicands.

  For example, $\sqrt{8} \div \sqrt{2} = \sqrt{8 \div 2} = \sqrt{4} = 2$.

This property is also based on the fact that the square root of a quotient is equal to the quotient of the square roots.

$$\sqrt{a \div b} = \sqrt{a} \div \sqrt{b}$$

- **Power of a power rule:** The power of a radical is equal to the radical of the power of the radicand.

For example, $\left(\sqrt{2}\right)^3 = \sqrt{2^3} = \sqrt{8} = 2\sqrt{2}$.

- This property is based on the fact that the square root of a power is equal to the power of the square root.

$$\sqrt{a^n} = \sqrt{a^n} = a^{\frac{n}{2}}$$

- Zero power rule: Any nonzero number raised to the power of zero is equal to one.

For example, $\sqrt{2^0} = 1$.

This property is based on the fact that the square root of one is equal to one.

$$\sqrt{a^0} = a^{\frac{0}{2}} = 1$$

- Negative exponent rule: Any nonzero number raised to a negative exponent is equal to the reciprocal of the number raised to the positive exponent.

For example, $\sqrt{2^{-2}} = \frac{1}{\sqrt{2^2}} = \frac{1}{2}$.

This property is based on the fact that the square root of a reciprocal is equal to the reciprocal of the square root.

$$\sqrt{a^{-n}} = a^{-\frac{n}{2}} = \frac{1}{\sqrt{a^n}}$$

Simplifying radicals:

Simplifying a radical means expressing it in its most basic form. This involves removing any perfect squares from the radicand.

For example, $\sqrt{12}$ can be simplified to $2\sqrt{3}$ because 12 is equal to 4 × 3, and 4 is a perfect square.

$$\sqrt{12} = \sqrt{4 \times 3} = 2\sqrt{3}$$

Here are the steps on how to simplify a radical:

- Factor the radicand into its prime factorization.

- Identify any perfect squares in the radicand.

- Extract the perfect squares from the radicand and place them outside the radical symbol.

- Simplify the remaining radicand.

Combining radicals:

Combining radicals means adding or subtracting radicals with the same index. This can be done by using the distributive property and the fact that $\sqrt{a} + \sqrt{a} = 2\sqrt{a}$.

$$\sqrt{2} + 4\sqrt{2} = 5\sqrt{2}$$

Here are the steps on how to combine radicals:

- Identify the radicals with the same index.

- Factor out any common factors.

- Simplify the radicals using the properties of radicals.

- Add or subtract the simplified radicals.

Rationalizing radicals:

Rationalizing a radical means eliminating the radical from the denominator of an expression.

- In case of one term, this can be done by multiplying the numerator and denominator with the radical of the denominator.

    For example:

$$\frac{\sqrt{2}}{\sqrt{3}} = \frac{\left(\sqrt{2} \times (\sqrt{3})\right)}{\left(\sqrt{3} \times (\sqrt{3})\right)} = \frac{\sqrt{6}}{\sqrt{3} \times \sqrt{3}} = \frac{\sqrt{6}}{3}$$

- In the case of two terms, this can be done by multiplying the numerator and denominator by the conjugate of the denominator.
  The conjugate of a radical is the same expression with the opposite sign of the radical

- For Example

$$\frac{(\sqrt{2} + \sqrt{3})}{(\sqrt{6} + \sqrt{5})} = \frac{(\sqrt{2} + \sqrt{3}) \times (\sqrt{6} - \sqrt{5})}{(\sqrt{6} + \sqrt{5}) \times (\sqrt{6} - \sqrt{5})}$$

$$= \frac{\sqrt{12} - \sqrt{10} + \sqrt{18} - \sqrt{15}}{6 - 5}$$

$$= \frac{2\sqrt{3} - \sqrt{10} + 3\sqrt{2} - \sqrt{15}}{1}$$

Testing for extraneous solutions and eliminating

Testing for extraneous solutions and eliminating is a process of checking whether the solutions obtained by solving an equation are actually valid solutions to the original equation. This is particularly important when dealing with equations that involve radicals or other non-linear operations, as squaring both sides or taking other similar steps can sometimes introduce extraneous solutions.

- For example $\sqrt{x + 8} = x + 2$

  Following steps to solve and check for extraneous solutions are as follows:

1. **Solve the equation:**

   $$\sqrt{x + 8} = x + 2$$

   Square both sides of the equation:

   $$\left(\sqrt{x + 8}\right)^2 = (x + 2)^2$$

   Simplify:

   $$x + 8 = x^2 + 4x + 4$$

   Rearrange the terms to form a quadratic equation:

   $$x^2 + 3x - 4 = 0$$

2. **Solve the quadratic equation:**

   $$(x + 4)(x - 1) = 0$$

   $$x = -4 \; or \; x = 1$$

3. **Check for extraneous solutions:**

   Substitute x = -4 back into the original equation:

   $$\sqrt{-4 + 8} = -4 + 2$$

   $\sqrt{4} \neq -2$ (this is not true)

   Therefore, $x = -4$ is an extraneous solution.

   Substitute $x = 1$ back into the original equation:

   $$\sqrt{1 + 8} = 1 + 2$$

   $\sqrt{9} = 3$ (this is true)

   Therefore, $x = 1$ is a valid solution.

   Conclusion:

   The only valid solution to the equation $\sqrt{x + 8} = x + 2$ $is \; x = 1$

Practice Questions:

Exponential Equations:

1. Simplify: $(2x^3y^3)^{-2}$
2. Simplify: $5x^2y(2x^4y^{-3})$
3. Simplify: $\left(\frac{-7a^2b^3c^0}{3a^3b^4c^3}\right)^{-4}$
4. Simplify: $j^{-13}j^4j^6$
5. Simplify: $\frac{52x^6}{13x^{-7}}$
6. Solve for x in the equation $3^x = 81$.
7. If $2^x = 16$, what is the value of x?
8. The population of a city doubles every 5 years. If the current population is 100, what will the population be in 15 years?
9. Solve the exponential equation: $3^x = 81$
10. Solve the exponential equation: $3^x + 1 = 10$
11. Solve the exponential equation: $(2^3)^2 = 4^x$
12. Solve the exponential equation: $2^x = 2^{2x+2} * 4$
13. Solve the exponential equation: $3^{2x-1} = 27$
14. Solve the exponential equation: $e^{x-2} = e^4$
15. Solve the exponential equation: $\left(\frac{1}{36}\right)^x = (216)^{x+5}$
16. Solve the exponential equation: $\left(\frac{2}{3}\right)^{x-2} = \left(\frac{27}{8}\right)^x$
17. Solve the exponential equation: $(27)^{2x} = (81)^{\frac{x-1}{2}}$
18. Find all values of x, $\quad 5^x = \dfrac{1}{\sqrt[3]{5}}$
19. Find all values of x , $3^x = \left(\dfrac{1}{9}\right)^{4-x}$

Radicals:

20. Simplify: $\sqrt{25} + \sqrt{9}$
21. If $\sqrt{a} = 5$, what is the value of a?
22. Combine and simplify: $2\sqrt{3} - 3\sqrt{3}$
23. Solve the radical equation: $\sqrt{x} + 2 = 5$
24. Solve the radical equation: $\sqrt{x} - 1 = 4$
25. Factor the radical expression: $\sqrt{x^2 + 4x + 4}$
26. Solve the radical equation: $\sqrt{x} + \sqrt{x+1} = 3$
27. Solve the radical equation: $\sqrt{2x-1} = \sqrt{x+2}$
28. Rationalize the radical expression: $\dfrac{\sqrt{x}+1}{\sqrt{x}-1}$
29. Solve the radical equation: $\sqrt{x-1} + \sqrt{x+4} = 5$
30. $-n + \sqrt{(6n + 19)} = 2$

Answer:

1. $\dfrac{1}{4x^6y^6}$
2. $\dfrac{10x^6}{y^2}$
3. $\dfrac{81a^4b^4c^{12}}{2401}$
4. $\dfrac{1}{j^3}$
5. $4x^{13}$
6. $x = 4$
7. $x = 4$
8. 800 in 15 years.
9. $x = 3$
10. $x = 2$
11. $x = 3$
12. $x = -4$
13. $x = 2$
14. $x = 6$
15. $x = -3$
16. $x = 1/2$
17. $x = -1$
18. $x = -1/3$
19. $x = 8$
20. 8
21. $a = 25$
22. $-\sqrt{3}$
23. $x = 9$
24. $x = 17$
25. $x + 2$
26. $x = \dfrac{16}{9}$
27. $x = 3$
28. $\dfrac{x + 2\sqrt{x} + 1}{x - 1}$
29. $x = 5$
30. $n = 5$

Lesson 4 - Equivalent expressions, Isolating Quantities

Equivalent expressions

Equivalent expressions are algebraic expressions that have the same value for all values of the variables. In other words, if two expressions are equivalent, then they will always evaluate to the same number, no matter what value you substitute for the variables.

Here are some examples of equivalent expressions:

- $2x + 3 = 3 + 2x$

- $(x + 2)^2 = x^2 + 4x + 4$

- $\sin(x) = \cos(90 - x)$

Identify equivalent expressions: There are a few ways to identify equivalent expressions. One way is to simply evaluate both expressions for a few different values of the variables. If the expressions always evaluate to the same number, then they are equivalent.

Another way to identify equivalent expressions is to use the properties of equality. The properties of equality state that if two expressions are equal, then you can perform the following operations on them without changing the equality:

- Add or subtract the same number to both sides

- Multiply or divide both sides by the same number (except for zero)

- Swap the sides of the equation

Properties of equality that help you find equivalent expressions

The following properties of equality can be helpful for finding equivalent expressions:

- Reflexive property: For any expression A, A = A.

- Symmetric property: If A = B, then B = A.

- Transitive property: If A = B and B = C, then A = C.

- Additive property: For any expressions A and B, A + B = B + A.

- Multiplicative property: For any expressions A and B, A × B = B × A.

- Distributive property: For any expressions A, B, and C, A × (B + C) = A × B + A × C.

- Inverse operations property: For any expressions A and B, if A = B, then $B^{-1} = A^{-1}$ (where $^{-1}$ denotes the inverse operation).

Methods for finding equivalent expressions:

- **Factoring and Expanding:** Factoring and expanding are two techniques that can be used to transform expressions into equivalent forms. Factoring involves breaking down a complex expression into simpler expressions, while expanding involves combining simpler expressions into a more complex one.
  Factoring:

Factoring is the process of decomposing a mathematical expression into a product of simpler expressions. It's like breaking down a complex object into its smaller components.

For example, factoring the expression $2x^2 + 5x + 2$ gives:

$$2x^2 + 5x + 2 = (2x + 1)(x + 2)$$

Expanding:

Expanding is the opposite of factoring. It involves combining simpler expressions to form a more complex one. For instance, expanding the expression $(2x + 1)(x + 2)$ gives:

$$(2x + 1)(x + 2) = 2x^2 + 5x + 2$$

- **Combining Like Terms:** Combining like terms is a fundamental technique in algebra that involves grouping and adding terms that have the same variable and exponent. It's like collecting similar items together.

  For example, in the expression $3x^2 + 4x - 2x^2 + 5$, the terms $3x^2$ and $-2x^2$ are like terms since they both have the same variable (x) and the same exponent (2). Combining these terms gives:

$$3x^2 + 4x - 2x^2 + 5 = (3 - 2)x^2 + 4x + 5 = x^2 + 4x + 5$$

- **Using the Distributive Property:**

  The distributive property is a fundamental rule in algebra that describes how multiplication distributes over addition and subtraction. It's like distributing things equally among groups. For instance, consider the expression $2x(3y + 4)$. Using the distributive property, we can expand it as follows:

$$2x(3y + 4) = (2x * 3y) + (2x * 4) = 6xy + 8x$$

- **Using Inverse Operations:** Inverse operations are pairs of operations that undo each other. Examples include addition and subtraction, multiplication and division, and exponentiation and logarithms. Using inverse operations involves performing the inverse operation on one side of an equation to isolate a variable on the other side. For example, to solve for x in the equation $2x + 3 = 7$, we can use the inverse operation of subtraction (subtracting 3 from both sides) to isolate x:

$$2x + 3 = 7$$

$$2x = 7 - 3$$

$$2x = 4$$

$$x = 4/2$$

$$x = 2$$

Isolating a quantity: Isolating a quantity, also known as rearranging an equation, is the process of manipulating an equation or expression to isolate a specific variable or quantity on one side of the equation or expression. This technique is often used in algebra and mathematics to solve equations for unknown variables or to simplify complex expressions.

When do you Need to Isolate a Quantity?

You may need to isolate a quantity in various situations, such as:

- **Solving Equations:**

    - **Example:** In the equation $3x + 7 = 16$, isolating the variable x involves rearranging the equation to find the value of x.

- **Applications and Problem Solving:**

    - **Example:** In a physics problem, you might have an equation representing a physical relationship, and isolating a variable could help you find a specific measurement, like time, distance, or velocity.

- **Rearranging Formulas:**

    - **Example:** In scientific formulas, you might need to isolate a variable to express it explicitly in terms of other variables. For instance, in the formula for the area of a circle ($A = \pi r^2$), you can isolate $r = \sqrt{\dfrac{A}{\pi}}$

- **Comparing Quantities:**

    - **Example:** In financial calculations, you might need to isolate a variable to compare different scenarios. For instance, in compound interest formulas, isolating the principal or interest rate allows for easy comparison.

- **Graphical Representations:**

    - **Example:** When working with linear equations, isolating a variable allows you to express the equation in slope-intercept form ($y = mx + b$), making it easier to understand the graphical representation.

- **Manipulating Expressions:**

    - **Example:** Isolating a quantity might be necessary when simplifying expressions or proving algebraic identities. For example, in proving the quadratic formula, isolating x in the general form $ax^2 + bx + c = 0$ is a crucial step.

Methods for Isolating a Quantity:

Using Inverse Operations:

- **Example:**

    - **Equation:** $3x + 7 = 16$

    - **Isolating x:** $3x + 7 - 7 = 16 - 7 \Rightarrow 3x = 9 \Rightarrow\Rightarrow x = \dfrac{9}{3} \Rightarrow x = 3$

- **Explanation:** Subtracting 7 from both sides (inverse operation of addition) and then dividing by 3 (inverse operation of multiplication) isolates x.

Combining Like Terms:

- **Example:**

    - **Equation:** $2y + 3y - 5 = 10$

- **Isolating y:** $(2y + 3y) - 5 = 10 \Rightarrow\Rightarrow 5y - 5 = 10 \Rightarrow 5y = 15$

  $\Rightarrow y = \dfrac{15}{5} \Rightarrow y = 3$

- **Explanation:** Combining like terms (2y and 3y) simplifies the equation, making it easier to isolate y.

Factoring and Expanding:

- **Example:**

    - **Equation:** $4(x - 2) = 12$

    - **Isolating x:** $4x - 8 = 12 \Rightarrow 4x = 20 \Rightarrow x = \dfrac{20}{4} \Rightarrow x = 5$

- **Explanation:** Factoring out 4 from $4(x - 2)$ and then simplifying isolates x.

Using Distributive Property:

- **Example:**

    - **Equation:** $2(a + 3) = 14$

    - **Isolating a:** $2a + 6 = 14 \Rightarrow 2a = 8 \Rightarrow a = \dfrac{8}{2} \Rightarrow a = 4$

- **Explanation:** Distributing the 2 across $a + 3$ simplifies the equation, making it easier to isolate a.

Practice Problem:

1. Simplify the expression $2(3x - 5) + 4$ and write the result in standard form.
2. If $a - b = 8$, what is the equivalent expression for $3(a - b) + 2b$?
3. Expand and simplify the expression $(2x + 1)(x - 3)$.
4. If $4p - 2q = 10$, what is the equivalent expression for p in terms of q?
5. Combine like terms in the expression $5x - 3y + 2x + 2y$ and write the result in standard form.
6. Prepare yourself by making x the subject in each of the following cases:
   (a) $2w = 3x$
   (b) $y = 2x + 7$
   (c) $ax - y + z = b$
   (d) $y = x/5$
7. A recipe calls for 3 cups of flour for every 2 cups of sugar. Express the ratio of flour to sugar in two different equivalent forms.
8. The cost of a car rental is $50 per day plus a flat fee of $100. Express the total cost of renting a car for x days in two different equivalent forms.
9. In each case, make the letter at the end the subject of the formula.
   (a) $s = \dfrac{(u+v)t}{2}$, (u)
   (b) $S = ut + \dfrac{1}{2}at^2$, (u)
   (c) $\dfrac{y-x^2}{x} = 3z$, (y)
   (d) $S = \dfrac{(u+v)}{2}$, (u)
10. Rearrange the formula $V = \dfrac{4}{3}\pi r^3$ to solve for r in terms of V.
11. A rectangular garden has a length of x meters and a perimeter of 20 meters. Express the width of the garden in terms of x.
12. In each of the following cases make x the subject:
   (a) $\dfrac{x}{a} = \dfrac{x}{b} - 1$
   (b) $y(y + z) = 3z(x + y)$
   (c) $y = \dfrac{x+1}{x-1}$
   (d) $\sqrt{x} - 1 = y$
   (e) $x^3 - y^3 = 1$
   (f) $\sqrt{x^2 - y^2} = y$
13. In each case, make the letter at the end the subject of the formula:
   (a) $E = \dfrac{1}{2}mv^2 - \dfrac{1}{2}mu^2$, (u)
   (b) $\dfrac{x^2}{a^2} - \dfrac{y^2}{b^2} = 1$, (y)
   (c) $ay^2 = x^3$, (y)

Answer

1. $6x - 6$
2. $24 + 2b$
3. $2x^2 - 5x - 3$
4. $p = \frac{1}{2}q + \frac{5}{2}$
5. $7x - y$
6. $(a)\, x = \frac{2w}{3}$ $(b)\, x = \frac{y-7}{2}$ $(c)\, x = \frac{b+y-z}{a}$ $(d)\, x = 5y$
7. Flour: Sugar $= 3:2$; Flour: Sugar $= \left(\frac{3}{5}\right):\left(\frac{2}{5}\right)$
8. Total Cost $= 50(x + 2)$ or $50x + 100$
9. (a) $u = \frac{2s-vt}{t}$ (b) $u = \frac{2S-at^2}{2t}$ (c) $y = 3xz + x^2$ (d) $u = \frac{2S-vt}{t}$
10. $r = \sqrt[3]{\dfrac{3V}{4\pi}}$
11. Width $= 10 - x$
12.

    (a) $x = \dfrac{ab}{a-b}$

    (b) $x = \dfrac{y^2-2yz}{3z}$

    (c) $x = \dfrac{y+1}{y-1}$

    (d) $x = (y + 1)^2$

    (e) $x = \sqrt[3]{1 + y^3}$

    (f) $x = \sqrt{2}y$

13.

    (a) $u = \sqrt{\dfrac{mv^2-2E}{m}}$

    (b) $y = \dfrac{b}{a}\sqrt{x^2 - a^2}$

    (c) $y = \sqrt{\dfrac{x^3}{a}}$

Lesson 5 - Nonlinear equations and non-linear functions

Non-linear equations in one variable are mathematical expressions involving a single variable raised to a power other than one. In contrast to linear equations, which have a degree of 1, non-linear equations have a degree greater than 1. The term "non-linear" implies that the relationship between the variable and its coefficients is not a straight line when graphed. These equations can take various forms, including quadratic, cubic, exponential, and logarithmic expressions, but they all share the common characteristic that the relationship between the variable and its terms is not proportional.

Types of non-linear equations

There are many different types of non-linear equations, but some of the most common ones include:

- Quadratic equations: Quadratic equations are equations of the form $ax^2 + bx + c = 0$, where a, b, and c are constants and a is not equal to zero.

  Examples of quadratic equations include $x^2 + 5x + 6 = 0$ and $2x^2 - 3x - 5 = 0$.

- Cubic equations: Cubic equations are equations of the form $ax^3 + bx^2 + cx + d = 0$, where a, b, c, and d are constants and a is not equal to zero.

  Examples of cubic equations include $x^3 + 2x^2 - x - 2 = 0$ and $3x^3 - 5x^2 + 4x - 6 = 0$.

- Exponential equations: Exponential equations are equations of the form $a^x = b$, where a and b are constants and a is positive and different from 1.

  Examples of exponential equations include $2^x = 16$ and $e^x = 5$.

Properties of non-linear equations

Non-linear equations have several properties that distinguish them from linear equations. For instance:

- Non-linear equations do not always have a single solution. They may have multiple solutions, no solution, or an infinite number of solutions.

- Non-linear equations cannot be solved using simple algebraic methods like solving for x. They typically require more complex techniques such as graphing, factoring, or using numerical methods.

- Non-linear equations often represent more complex relationships between variables than linear equations. They are frequently used to model real-world phenomena that exhibit non-linear behavior.

Non-linear Functions:

A **non-linear function** is a mathematical function that does not have a constant rate of change. Unlike linear functions, where the graph is a straight line, non-linear functions exhibit a curved or more complex pattern. The degree of non-linearity can vary, and non-linear functions can take different forms, including quadratic, cubic, exponential, logarithmic, and more.

Examples of non-linear functions:

- Quadratic function: $f(x) = x^2$

- Cubic function: $f(x) = x^3$

- Exponential function: $f(x) = a^x$ (where a is a positive constant and $a \neq 1$)

Properties of Non-linear Functions:

Domain and Range:

- **Domain:** The set of all possible input values (x-values) for which the function is defined.

- **Range:** The set of all possible output values (y-values) corresponding to the input values in the domain.

Example 1 : The quadratic function $f(x) = x^2$ is defined for all real numbers. However, radical function root x is defined only for $x \geq 0$.

Example 2 : Consider the quadratic function $f(x) = x^2 + 3x + 2$.

Domain: All real numbers, as the function is defined for any x.

Range: The minimum value of the function occurs at the vertex. Using the vertex form, the minimum value is $\left[-\frac{b}{2a}, f\left(\frac{b}{-2a}\right)\right]$, which is $\left(-\frac{3}{2}, -\frac{1}{4}\right)$ Therefore, the range is $\left(-\frac{1}{4}, \infty\right)$.

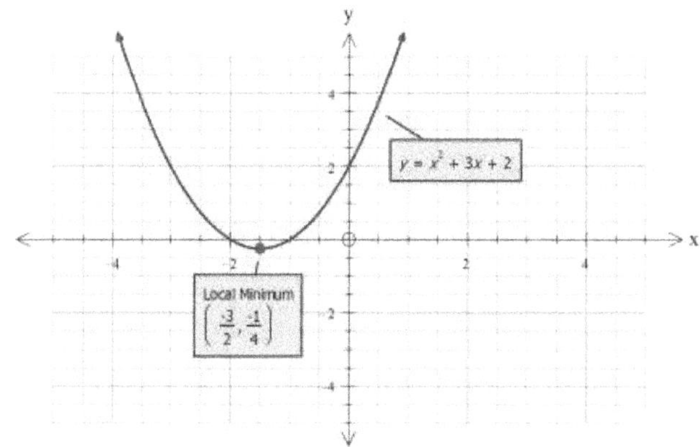

Increasing and Decreasing Intervals:

- **Increasing Interval:** The set of x-values over which the function is strictly increasing.

- **Decreasing Interval:** The set of x-values over which the function is strictly decreasing.

- **Example 1, Quadratic function** $f(x) = x^2$

  Increasing intervals: The function $f(x) = x^2$ is increasing over the interval $(0, \infty)$ and decreasing over the interval $(-\infty, 0)$ and

  Example 2: Cubic function

  Consider the cubic function $f(x) = x^3 - 3x^2 + 2$. The graph of this function has three turning points, indicating that the function changes its direction (increases or decreases) at these points.

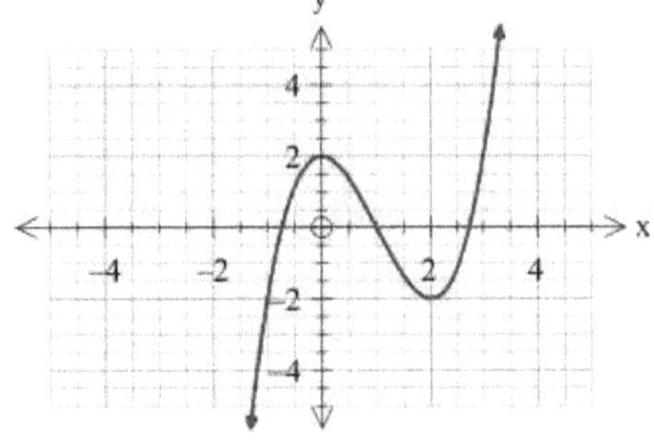

End Behavior:

- **End Behavior:** Describes the behavior of the function as x approaches positive or negative infinity.

- For example, a quadratic function may have an upward or downward end behavior.

- For example, the exponential function $f(x) = 2^x$ increases indefinitely as x approaches positive infinity and decreases indefinitely as x approaches negative infinity.

Symmetry:

- **Symmetry:** Describes whether a function has symmetry and, if so, the type of symmetry (e.g., symmetry about the y-axis or origin).

  - For example, a quadratic function $f(x) = ax^2 + bx + c$ may exhibit symmetry about the axis of symmetry $x = -\dfrac{b}{2a}$.

  - For instance, the function $f(x) = x^3$ is odd symmetric, while the function $f(x) = x^2$ is even symmetric.

Periodicity:

- **Periodicity:** Describes whether a function repeats its pattern over a specific interval.

  - For example, trigonometric functions like sine and cosine exhibit periodic behavior.

- For example, the sine function $f(x) = sin(x)$ is periodic with a period of 2π.

Types of non-linear functions

- **Quadratic functions:** Quadratic functions are a type of non-linear function that is represented by the general formula $f(x) = ax^2 + bx + c$, where a, b, and c are constants and a $\neq$ 0.

  These functions are characterized by their parabolic-shaped graphs, which can open upwards or downwards depending on the sign of the coefficient a.

  Examples of Quadratic Functions:

  $$f(x) = x^2 + 2x + 1$$
  $$f(x) = -2x^2 + 3x - 4$$
  $$f(x) = 0.5x^2 - x + 2$$

- **Cubic functions:** Cubic functions are another type of non-linear function represented by the general formula f(x) = ax^3 + bx^2 + cx + d, where a, b, c, and d are constants and a $\neq$ 0. Their graphs exhibit a more complex shape than quadratic functions, with a single point of inflection (where the curve changes concavity).

  Examples of Cubic Functions:

  $$f(x) = x^3 + 3x^2 + 2x - 1$$
  $$f(x) = -2x^3 + 5x^2 - 4x + 3$$
  $$f(x) = 0.25x^3 - 1.5x^2 + 0.75x + 1$$

- **Exponential functions:** Exponential functions are non-linear functions represented by the general formula $f(x) = a^x$, where a is a positive constant and a $\neq$ 1. Their graphs exhibit rapid growth or decay as the input value increases, depending on whether the constant a is greater or less than 1.

  Examples of Exponential Functions:

  $$f(x) = 2^x$$
  $$f(x) = \left(\frac{1}{2}\right)^x$$
  $$f(x) = 3.14^x$$

- **Trigonometric functions:** Trigonometric functions are a fundamental class of non-linear functions that describe the relationship between the sides and angles of triangles

  Examples of Trigonometric Functions:

  $$f(x) = sin(x)$$
  $$f(x) = cos(x)$$
  $$f(x) = tan(x)$$

- **Piecewise functions:** Piecewise functions are a versatile type of non-linear function defined by different rules for different parts of their domain

  Examples of Piecewise Functions:

  Absolute Value Function: $f(x) = |x| = \begin{cases} x, & if\ x \geq 0; \\ -x, & if\ x < 0 \end{cases}$

  Step Function: $f(x) = \begin{cases} 0, & if\ x < 0; \\ 1, & if\ 0 \leq x < 2; \\ 2, & if\ x \geq 2 \end{cases}$

  Piecewise Linear Function: $f(x) = \begin{cases} 3x, & if\ x \leq 1 \\ 2x + 1, & if\ x > 1 \end{cases}$

- **Composite Function :** A composite function can be represented using the composition operator ($\circ$), where $f \circ g(x)$ denotes the composition of functions f and g. This means that $f \circ g(x)$ is equivalent to $f(g(x))$. In other words, $f \circ g(x)$ is the result of applying function f to the output of function g, evaluated at input x.

  For example, consider the functions $f(x) = x^2 and\ g(x) = 2x + 1$. The composite function $f \circ g(x)$ is:

  $$f \circ g(x) = f(g(x)) = f(2x + 1) = (2x + 1)^2 = 4x^2 + 1 + 4x$$

  Evaluating $f \circ g(x)\ at\ x = 3$, we get:

  $$f \circ g(3) = f(g(3)) = f(2(3) + 1) = f(7) = 7^2 = 49$$

  Therefore, the value of the composite function $f \circ g(x)\ at\ x = 3\ is$ 49.

Properties of composite functions:

- **Associativity:** $(f \circ g) \circ h = f \circ (g \circ h)$

  This means that the order in which the composition is performed does not matter as long as the functions are composed in the same order.

- **Identity property:** $f \circ I = f$

  where I is the identity function, $I(x) = x$. This means that composing a function with the identity function leaves the function unchanged.

- **Composition of inverses:** If f and g are invertible functions, then $(f \circ g)^{-1} = g^{-1} \circ f^{-1}$

  This means that the inverse of a composite function is the composition of the inverses of the individual functions, in reverse order.

Practices Question

1. Evaluate the function $f(x) = 2x^2 + 3x - 1$ for $x = 2$.
2. Evaluate the function $f(x) = \sqrt{x}$ for $x = 4$.
3. Evaluate the function $f(x) = (x + 1)^2$ for $x = -2$.
4. Evaluate the function $f(x) = e^x$ for $x = 0$.
5. Evaluate the expression $f(g(x))$ if $f(x) = 2x + 1$ and $g(x) = x^2$.
6. Evaluate the expression $h(f(x))$ if $h(x) = x^3$ and $f(x) = sqrt(x)$.
7. Evaluate the expression $g(f(x))$ if $g(x) = |x|$ and $f(x) = 3x - 2$.
8. Compose the functions $f(x) = x^2$ and $g(x) = x + 1$ to obtain the composite function $h(x)$.
9. Compose the functions $g(x) = 2x - 1$ and $f(x) = \sqrt{x}$ to obtain the composite function $h(x)$.
10. If $f(x) = 2x - 5$, then what is the value of $f(2) + f(5)$?
11. If $h(x) = 3x + 5$ and $h(a) = 27$, then what is the value of a ?
12. If $z(q) = 4q + \dfrac{1}{2}$ The zoomster function z used in space flight engineering is defined above. If, for some number u, $z\left(u + \dfrac{1}{2}\right) = \dfrac{1}{2}$, then what is the value of u ?
13. For the function f graphed in the xy-plane above, if $f(-2.5) = k$, then what is $f(2k)$?

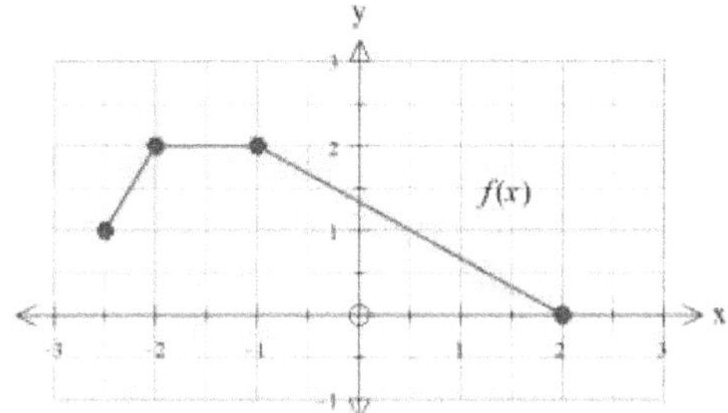

14. If $f(x) = \sqrt{x} + 4$, find
    (a) $f(-1)$
    (b) $f(a)$
    (c) $f(x + h)$
    (d) $f(☺)$
15. Determine which of the curves are graphs of functions. For the graphs that are functions, find the domain and range.
    (a

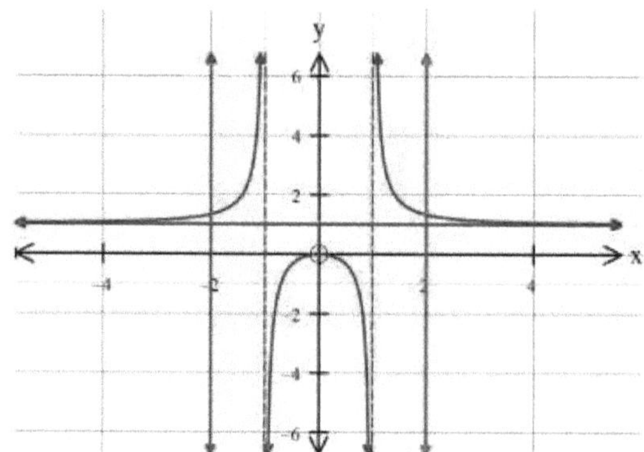

(b)

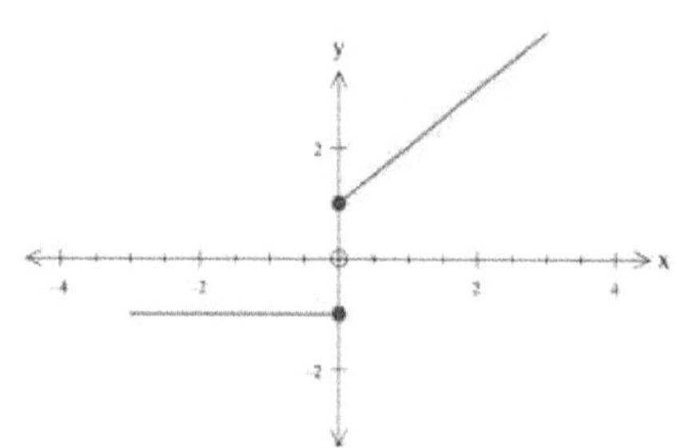

16. Find the domain and range of each function.

    (a) $f(x) = \sqrt{x^2 - 9}$

    (b) $f(x) = \sqrt{\dfrac{x-2}{x-1}}$

    (c) $f(x) = \sqrt{x^2 - x - 2}$

    (d) $f(x) = f(x) = \begin{cases} x^3, & \text{if } x \geq 0 \\ -2x, & \text{if } x < 0 \end{cases}$

17. Find $f + g, f - g, f \cdot g, \text{and } f / g$.

    (a) $f(x) = \dfrac{1}{x}$; $g(x) = \dfrac{x}{x-2}$

Answer:

1. 13
2. 2
3. 1
4. 1
5. $f(g(x)) = f(x^2) = (2x^2) + 1$
6. $h(f(x)) = x^{\frac{3}{2}}$
7. $g(f(x)) = g(3x - 2) = |3x - 2|$
8. $h(x) = f(g(x)) = x^2 + 2x + 1$
9. $h(x) = f(g(x)) = \sqrt{(2x - 1)}$
10. 4
11. $\frac{22}{3} = 7.33$
12. $-\frac{1}{2}$
13. 0
14. . $(a)\sqrt{3}$ $(b)\sqrt{a + 4}$ $(c)\sqrt{x + h + 4}$ $(d)\sqrt{\smiley + 4}$

15. (a) Is a function. Domain: $(-\infty, -2) \cup (-2, 2) \cup (2, \infty)$, Range: $(-\infty, 0) \cup (1, \infty)$.
    (b) Is a function. Domain: $(-\infty, \infty)$, Range: $\{-1\} \cup (1, \infty)$
16. (a) Domain: $(-\infty, -3] \cup [3, \infty)$, Range: $[0, \infty)$
    (b) Domain: $(-\infty, 1) \cup (2, \infty)$, Range: $[0, 1) \cup (1, \infty)$
    (c) Domain: $(-\infty, -1] \cup [2, \infty)$, Range: $[0, \infty)$
    (d) Domain: $(-\infty, \infty)$, Range: $[0, \infty)$
17. $(f + g)(x) = \frac{1}{x} + \frac{x}{x-2}$; $(f - g)(x) = \frac{1}{x} - \frac{x}{x-2}$; $(f \cdot g)(x) = \frac{1}{x-2}$; $\left(\frac{f}{g}\right)(x) = \frac{x-2}{x^2}$

Lesson 6 - Linear, Quadratic and Exponential Equations

Relationship between Linear and Quadratic Equations

Linear and quadratic equations, despite their distinct properties, share a fundamental connection. Both types of equations represent relationships between variables and can be expressed algebraically. Quadratic equations can be considered an extension of linear equations, incorporating an additional term that introduces curvature.

- **Transition from Linear to Quadratic Equations**: The transition from linear to quadratic equations involves the introduction of a quadratic term (x^2) to a linear equation, thereby transforming it into a quadratic form. Let's break down the transition process:

  Linear Equation: A linear equation is an equation of the first degree, meaning the highest power of the variable (x) is 1. The general form of a linear equation is $y = mx + c$, where m is the slope (rate of change) and c is the y-intercept (the y-value when $x = 0$).

  Example: $y = 2x + 3$

- **Transition to Quadratic Equation:** To transition from a linear to a quadratic equation, we introduce a quadratic term (x^2) to the equation. The general form of a quadratic equation is $y = ax^2 + bx + c$, where a, b, and c are constants.

  Example: $y = 2x^2 + 3$

- In this example, linear equation $y = 2x + 3$ is transitioned to the quadratic equation $y = 2x^2 + 3$ by introducing the quadratic term $2x^2$.

x	y
0	3
1	5
2	11

- So we can see that the x^2 term in the equation causes the rate of change to increase as x increases

- Here is a table that summarizes the key differences between linear and quadratic equations:

Feature	Linear Equation	Quadratic Equation
Rate of change	Constant	Not constant
Graphical representation	Straight line	Parabola
Example equation	$y = 2x + 3$	$y = 2x^2 + 3$

- **Graphical interpretation of combined linear and quadratic equations**

Example 1: Two Intersections (Two Solutions)

    Linear Equation: $y = 2x + 3$

    Quadratic Equation: $y = 2x^2 + 3$

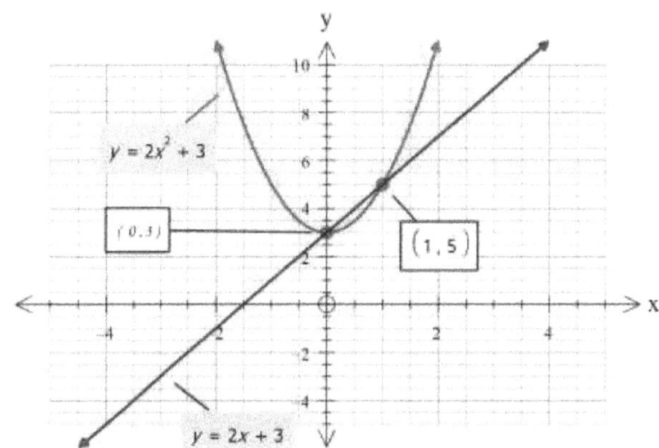

If the lines intersect at two points, then the system has two solutions. This occurs when the linear equation and the quadratic equation have different slopes.

Example 2: Solving the system of equations to find the point of intersection

Linear Equation: $y = 2x + 3$
Quadratic Equation: $y = (x + 1)^2 + 4$

Setting y equal in both equations:

$$2x + 3 = (x + 1)^2 + 4$$

Now, let's solve for x:

$$2x + 3 = x^2 + 2x + 1 + 4$$

Combine like terms:

$$2x + 3 = x^2 + 2x + 5$$

Subtract $2x + 3$ from both sides:

$$x^2 + 2$$

Now, set this quadratic equation to zero and solve for x:

$$x^2 + 2 = 0$$

$$x = \sqrt{-2}$$

This quadratic equation has no real solutions because the term x^2 is always non-negative, and adding 2 to it results in a positive value. Therefore, the system of equations does not have a real point of intersection

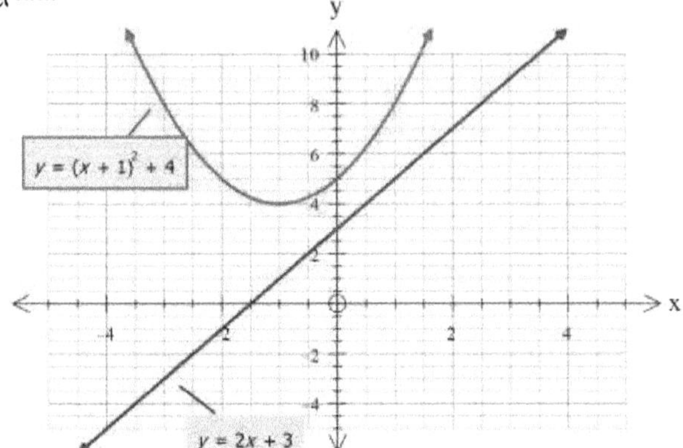

Graphically, this implies that the line $y = 2x + 3$ and the parabola $y = (x + 1)^2 + 4$ do not intersect on the real number plane. The parabola is situated above the line, and they do not cross each other.

Hence no real solutions are available. Hence no point of intersection

Example 3: One Intersection (One Solution)

- **Linear Equation:** $4y - 8x = -21$
  Quadratic Equation: $y - x^2 = 7 - 5x$

Let's first substitute the expression for y from the quadratic equation into the linear equation
$$4(x^2 - 5x + 7) - 8x = -21$$

Simplify and Rearrange:
$$4x^2 - 28x + 49 = 0 \Rightarrow (2x - 7)^2 = 0$$
$$(2x - 7) = 0$$

Solve for x:

$$2x = 7$$

$$x = \frac{7}{2} = 3.5$$

Substitute $x = \dfrac{7}{2}$ *into the linear equation* $4y - 8x = 21 \Rightarrow y = 2x - \dfrac{21}{4}$:

$$y = 2\left(\frac{7}{2}\right) - \frac{21}{4} \Rightarrow \frac{7}{4} = 1.75$$

So, the point of intersection is $(3.5, 1.75)$

So we can see that $(3.5, 1.75)$ is the one point of intersection, since this resolves to a perfect square. And hence only 1 solution

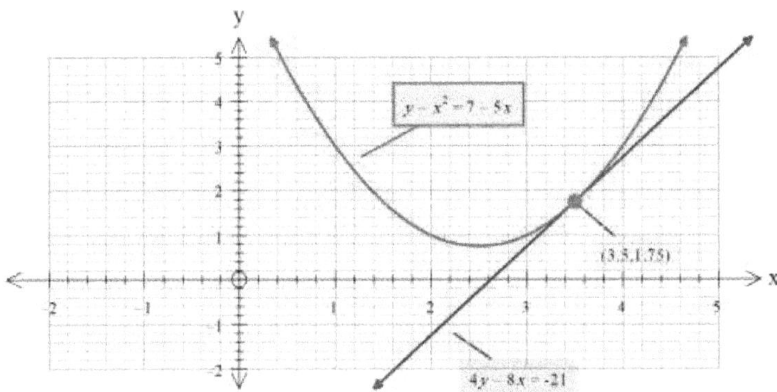

Graphically, in this example, the purple dot on the graph marks the point of intersection, representing the unique solution to the system of equations.

Solving Linear and Quadratic Equations

- Techniques for solving equations that combine linear and quadratic terms Equations that combine linear and quadratic terms can be solved using a variety of techniques, including:
- **Substitution:** This method involves solving one of the equations for one variable and substituting that value into the other equation.

Example 4: Solving a system of linear and quadratic equations

Consider the system of equations:

$$2x + y = 4$$

$$x^2 - y = -1$$

To solve this system using substitution, we can solve the first equation for y:

$$y = 4 - 2x$$

Then, substitute this expression for y into the second equation:

$$x^2 - y = -1$$

$$x^2 - (4 - 2x) = -1$$

$$x^2 + 2x - 3 = 0$$

$$(x - 1)(x + 3) = 0$$

Solve for x:

$$x = 1 \ or \ x = -3$$

Substitute the values of x back into the first equation to solve for y:

For $x = 1$:

$$2(1) + y = 4$$

$$2 + y = 4$$

$$y = 2$$

For $x = -3$:

$$2(-3) + y = 4$$

$$-6 + y = 4$$

$$y = 10$$

Solutions:

$$(x, y) = (1, 2) \ or \ (x, y) = (-3, 10)$$

- **Graphing:** Graphing both the linear and quadratic terms on the same coordinate plane and identifying the point(s) of intersection can provide visual solutions.

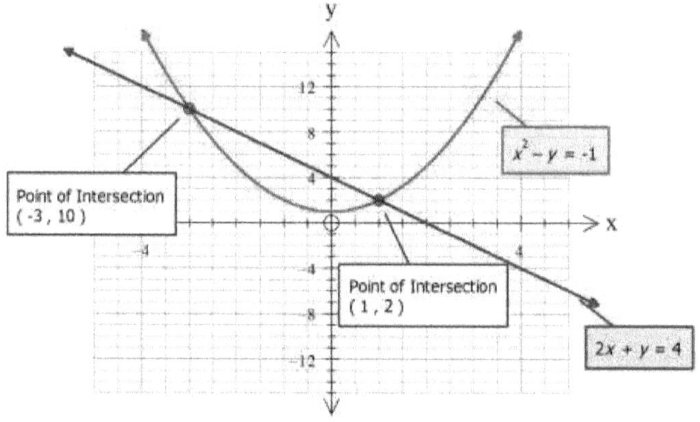

Transition from Linear to Exponential Functions

Linear and exponential functions are two fundamental types of functions with distinct characteristics and growth patterns.

Characteristics of linear functions:

- Constant rate of change: The value of the function increases or decreases by a constant amount for each unit increase in the independent variable.

- Represented by the equation $y = mx + c$, where m is the slope and c is the y-intercept.

- Graphical representation: A straight line with a constant slope.

Characteristics of exponential functions:

- Rate of change proportional to the current value: The change in the function's value is proportional to its current value at a particular point.

- Represented by the equation $y = a\,b^x$, where a is the initial value and b is the growth factor (b is also called the base).

  If $b > 1$ for exponential growth, $0 < b < 1$ for exponential decay.

- Graphical representation: A curve that increases or decreases rapidly, depending on the value of b.

Transition between linear and exponential functions:

- As the independent variable increases, the rate of change of an exponential function becomes increasingly different from that of a linear function.

- In the initial stages, an exponential function may closely resemble a linear function, but the difference becomes more pronounced as the independent variable increases in magnitude. For exponential function, the key difference is that the base (b) represents a multiplier, which is driving the exponential increase/decrease.

Example 5: Linear to Exponential Transition:

Consider the linear function $y = 2x + 1$. As we transition to an exponential function, let's transform it to $y = 2.(3)^x$.

- **Base (b):**

  - In the given exponential equation $y = 2 \cdot 3^x$, the base (b) is 3.

- **Table of Values:**

  - We've chosen values of x and calculated the corresponding y values based on the exponential equation.

x	y
0	2
1	6
2	18

  - As x increases by 1, y is multiplied by the base 3.

- **Deriving the Multiplier (b):**

  - By comparing the values in the table, you can observe that each y value is obtained by multiplying the previous y value by 3. This implies that 3 is the multiplier or base (b).

- **Deriving the Y-Intercept (a):**

    - When $x = 0$, we have $y = 2$. This corresponds to the initial value or the y-intercept (

    a) in the exponential function.

- **Final Exponential Equation:**

    - Combining these observations, we can express the exponential equation as
    $y = 2 \cdot 3^x$

    - 2 is the initial value (a), and 3 is the base (b).

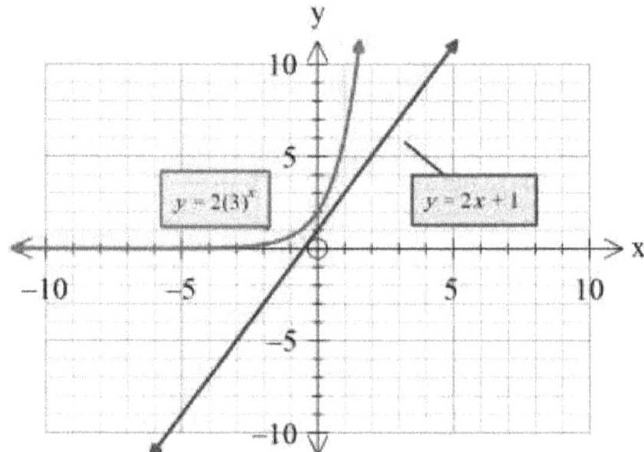

In this example, observe the graphical transition from a linear function (left) to an exponential function (right) with a base of 3 (or also known as multiplier). The curve in the exponential function showcases the accelerating growth characteristic.

Common quadratic functions used in word problems include:

- Perfect square trinomials: These are of the form $ax^2 + bx + c$, where a, b, and c are constants and $a \neq 0$. They represent situations where the variable being measured is squared, such as the area of a square or the distance traveled by a falling object.

- Factored quadratic expressions: These are of the form $a(x + h)(x + k)$, where $a, h, and\ k$ are constants and $a \neq 0$. They represent situations where there are two distinct values of the variable that make the expression equal to zero, such as the height of a projectile or the time it takes to travel a certain distance.

Steps to solve word problems:

- Read the problem carefully and identify the variables. What is the quantity being measured, and what symbols will you use to represent it?
- Translate the problem into a mathematical equation. This may involve defining variables, writing down equations that represent the relationships between the variables, and using algebraic manipulations to simplify the equations.
- Solve the equation(s) using appropriate methods. This may involve converting between exponential and logarithmic forms, using properties of logarithms, or using graphical methods.
- Interpret the solution(s) in the context of the problem. This may involve checking for extraneous solutions, considering the units of measurement, and drawing conclusions about the relationship between the variables.

Example 6 : The path of a projectile launched from the ground is modeled by the quadratic function $h(t) = -5t^2 + 20t + 10$, where $h(t)$ represents the height of the projectile (in meters) above the ground at time t (in seconds).

1. Find the initial height of the projectile.

2. Find the time it takes for the projectile to hit the ground.

Solution:

1. **Initial height:** The initial height of the projectile is the height at time $t = 0$. So, we can find the initial height by evaluating $h(0)$:
   $h(0) = -5(0)^2 + 20(0) + 10 = 10$ meters
   Therefore, the initial height of the projectile is 10 meters

2. **Find the time to hit the ground:** The time to hit the ground is determined by setting $h(t)$ equal to 0 and solving for t: $-5t^2 + 20t + 10 = 0$
   Solve using the quadratic formula to find t.
   $$t = \frac{-b \pm \sqrt{b^2 - 4ac}}{2a}$$
   $$t = \frac{-20 \pm \sqrt{20^2 - 4(-5)10}}{2(-5)}$$
   $$t = \frac{-20 \pm \sqrt{600}}{-10}$$
   $$t = \frac{-10-5\sqrt{6}}{-5} \quad \text{(Discard the negative root)}$$
   So, the time it takes for the projectile to hit the ground is approximately $t \approx 4.45$ seconds

Common exponential functions used in word problems include:

- **Exponential functions:** These are of the form $f(x) = ab^x$, where a and b are constants and $a, b > 0$. They represent situations where the quantity is growing exponentially, such as the population of a city or the amount of money in a bank account with compound interest.
(rounded to two decimal places).

Exponential Growth Equation:

The general formula for exponential growth is:

$$P = P_0 \times (1 + r)^t$$

where:

- P is the final quantity

- P_0 is the initial quantity

- r is the growth rate

- t is the time

Example 7: The population of a city is 50,000, and it grows at a rate of 3% per year. Write an equation for the population P after t years and find the population after 10 years. Solution: Identify P and t as unknowns, write the equation, solve for P after 10 years, and interpret the solution.

Solution:

Identifying P and t as unknowns:

- Let P be the population of the city after t years

- Let t be the number of years that have passed since the initial population of 50,000.

Writing the equation:

Since the population grows at a rate of 3% per year, we can model the population growth using an exponential function of the form:

$$P = P_0 \times (1 + r)^t$$

where:

- P_0 is the initial population (50,000)

- r is the annual growth rate (3%)

Substituting the given values, we get:

$$P = 50,000 \times (1 + 0.03)^t$$

Solving for P after 10 years:

After 10 years ($t = 10$), the population will be:

$$P = 50,000 \times (1 + 0.03)^{10} \approx 67,195.82$$

Therefore, the population of the city after 10 years is approximately 67,196.

Interpretation:

The population of the city is expected to grow from 50,000 to 67,196 in 10 years, representing an increase of about 34%. This growth is due to the annual growth rate of 3%.

Exponential Decay

Exponential Decay (1-r): Exponential decay is a process in which a quantity decreases at a constant rate over time. This means that the rate of decay is proportional to the current value of the quantity. The formula for exponential decay is:

$$y = a \, (1 - r)^t$$

where:

- y is the quantity at time t
- a is the initial quantity
- r is the decay rate $(0 < r < 1)$
- t is the time

The decay rate (r) is a fraction between 0 and 1. It represents the proportion of the quantity that is lost in each unit of time. For example, if the decay rate is 0.5, then half of the quantity is lost in each unit of time.

Example 8 : Radioactive Decay: Suppose a radioactive substance has an initial quantity of 200 grams, and it decays at a rate of 10% per year.

The exponential decay equation is $y = 200 \times (1 - 0.10)^x$.

where:

- y is the quantity of the radioactive substance remaining after x years
- 200 is the initial quantity of the radioactive substance
- 0.1 is the decay rate (10% = 1/10 = 0.1)
- x is the number of years that have passed

This equation can be used to calculate the amount of the radioactive substance remaining after any number of years.

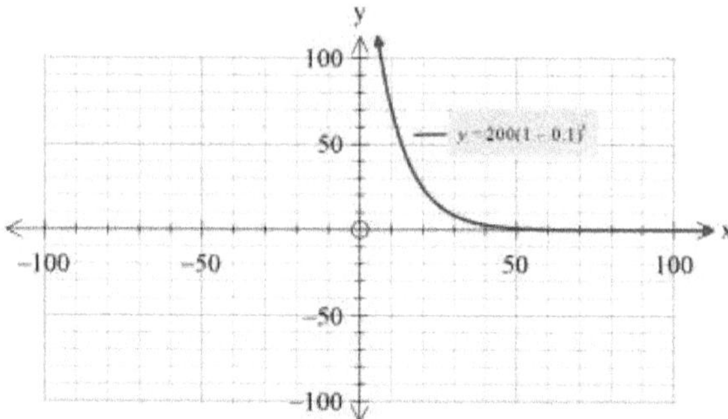

The graph shows the rapid decrease in quantity over time, characteristic of exponential decay.

For example, to calculate the amount of the radioactive substance remaining after 5 years, we would plug in x = 5 into the equation:

$$y = 200 * (1 - 0.1)^5$$

$$y = 200 \times 0.59049$$

$$y \approx 118.098$$

$$y \approx 118.098 \; grams$$

Therefore, after 5 years, there would be approximately 118.098 grams of the radioactive substance remaining.

Changing Time/Exponential Units

When time/exponential units change, then we need to consider growth in terms of interval units.

Example 9 : Changing Time Units from Years to Months

Suppose we have an exponential function $y = 50 \times 1.05^x$ representing yearly growth. To change it to monthly growth, we can use the formula (1 $years = 12 \; months$) $y = 50 \times 1.05^{\frac{x}{12}}$

Explanation:

- Original Function:$y = 50 \times 1.05^x$ (YearlyGrowth)

- Modified Function: $y = 50 \times 1.05^{\frac{x}{12}}$ (Monthly Growth)

Fraction of Time

The concept of fraction of time can be applied to various situations where exponential growth or decay occurs. Here's an example to help you understand it better:

Example 10: A population that starts with 1000 people and increases by 5% every 2 years. We want to know the population after 5 years.

Fractional Time: Instead of directly applying the 5% annual growth for 5 years, we need to consider the fraction of time involved. We know the population increases every 2 years, and we want to calculate the population after 5 years. So, the fraction of time is:

- Fraction of time $= \dfrac{\text{Total time}}{\text{Growth interval}}$
- Fraction of time $= \dfrac{5\ \text{years}}{2\ \text{years}}$
- Fraction of time $= \dfrac{5}{2}$

Exponential Growth Equation:

The general formula for exponential growth is:

$$P = P_0 \times (1 + r)^t$$

where:

- P is the final quantity

- P_0 is the initial quantity (1000 in this case)

- r is the growth rate (5% = 0.05)

- t is the time

Applying Fraction of Time:

In this case, we need to consider the fraction of time instead of the total time directly. Therefore, the equation becomes:

$$y = P \times (1 + r)^{\text{fraction of time}}$$

Calculating Population:

Now, we can plug in the values:

$$y = 1000 \times (1 + 0.05)^{\frac{5}{2}}$$

$$y \approx 1127.46$$

Interpretation:

After 5 years, the population will be approximately 1127.46 people, which is an increase of about 12.75% from the initial population.

Practice Questions:

Decide whether the word problem represents a linear or exponential function and write the function formula.

1. "A library has 8000 books, and is adding 500 more books each year."
   Linear or exponential? $y =$ _______________

2. "A gym's customers must pay \$50 for a membership, plus \$3 for each time they use the gym."
   Linear or exponential? $y =$ _______________

3. "A bank account starts with \$10. Every month, the amount of money in the account is tripled."
   Linear or exponential? $y =$ _______________

4. "There are 20,000 owls in the wild. Every decade, the number of owls is halved."
   Linear or exponential? $y =$ _______________

Decide whether the table represents a linear or exponential function & write the function formula.

5.

x	0	1	2	3	4	5	6	7
y	2	5	8	11	14	17	20	23

Linear or exponential? $y =$ _______________

6.

x	0	1	2	3	4	5	6	7
y	3	6	12	24	48	96	192	384

Linear or exponential? $y =$ _______________

7.

x	0	1	2	3	4	5	6	7
y	10	5	2.5	1.25	.625	.3125	.15625	.078125

Linear or exponential? $y =$ _______________

8.

x	0	1	2	3	4	5	6	7
y	40	35	30	25	20	15	10	5

Linear or exponential? $y =$ _______________

9.

x	0	1	2	3	4	5	6	7
y	.4	.6	.9	1.35	2.025	3.0375	4.55625	6.834375

Linear or exponential? $y =$ _______________

10. Make a table for $f(x) = 8\left(\frac{1}{2}\right)^x$ Express answers as fractions.

x	$f(x) = 8\left(\frac{1}{2}\right)^x$ in fractions
0	
1	
2	
3	
4	
5	
6	

11. Julie gets a pre-paid cell phone. Initially she has a \$40.00 balance on the phone. Each minute of talking costs \$0.15.

Let x stand for the amount of time in minutes that Julie has talked on the phone, and let $f(x)$ stand for the remaining dollar value of the phone.

    (a) Is $f(x)$ a linear function or an exponential function? Explain how you know.

    (b) Find a function formula equation $f(x) =$ _______________

    (c) Find the value of $f(0)$ and explain its meaning in terms of the cell phone

    (d) Find the value of $f(100)$ and explain its meaning in terms of the cell phone.

    (e) Find the value of x that makes $f(x) = 10$, and explain its meaning in terms of the cell phone.

    (f) Find the value of x that makes $f(x) = 0$, and explain its meaning in terms of the cell phone

Linear and Quadratic Systems:

12. Solve the system of equations:
$$2x + y = 10$$
$$x^2 + y = 13$$

13. Solve the system of equations:
$$y = -3x$$
$$x^2 + y^2 = 3$$

14. Solve the system of equations:
$$x^2 + x + 5 = y$$
$$2x + 7 = y$$

15. Solve the system of equations:
$$x^2 - 5x + 7 = y$$
$$2x + 1 = y$$

16. Solve the system of equations:
$$x^2 + y^2 = 25$$

$$3y - 2x = 6$$

Exponential Growth and Decay

17. $y = 1200(1 + 0.3)^t$
    (a) Does this function represent exponential growth or exponential decay?
    (b) What is your initial value?
    (c) What is the rate of growth or rate of decay?
18. $y = 14000(0.92)^t$
    (a) Does this function represent exponential growth or exponential decay?
    (b) What is your initial value?
    (c) What is the rate of growth or rate of decay?
19. The population of a small town was 3600 in 2005. The population increases by 4% annually.
    (a) Write an exponential growth function to represent this situation.
    (b) What will the population be in 2025? Round your answer to the nearest person
20. Your car cost $42,500 when you purchased it in 2015. The value of the car decreases by 15% annually.
    (a) Write an exponential decay function to represent this situation.
    (b) How much will your car be worth in 2022? Round your answer to the nearest dollar.
21. A piece of land was purchased for $65,000. The value of the land has slowly been decreasing by 1% annually.
    (a) Write an exponential decay function to represent this situation.
    (b) How much will the land be worth in 20 years? Round your answer to the nearest dollar.
22. The number of bacteria present in a colony is 180 at 12 noon and the bacteria grows at a rate of 22% per hour. How many will be present at 8 p.m.?
23. A house purchased for $226,000 has lost 4% of its value each year for the past five years. What is it worth now?
24. A 1970 comic book has appreciated 10% per year and originally sold for $0.35. What will it be worth in 2010?
25. A concert has been sold out for weeks, and as the date of the concert draws closer, the price of the ticket increases. The cost of a pair of tickets was $150 yesterday and is $162 today. Assuming that the cost continues to increase at this rate:
    (a) What is the daily rate of increase? What is the multiplier?
    (b) What will be the cost one week from now, the day before the concert?
    (c) What was the cost two weeks ago?

Answer

1. Linear, $y = 8000 + 500x$
2. Linear, $y = 50 + 3x$
3. Exponential $y = 10(3)^x$
4. Exponential $y = 20{,}000 \left(\frac{1}{2}\right)^x$
5. Linear, $y = 2 + 3x$
6. Exponential $y = 3(2)^x$
7. Exponential $y = 10 \left(\frac{1}{2}\right)^x$
8. Linear, $y = 40 + 5x$
9. Exponential $y = 0.4(1.5)^x$
10.

x	$f(x) = 8 \left(\frac{1}{2}\right)^x$ in fractions
0	8
1	4
2	2
3	1
4	1/2
5	1/4
6	1/8

11.

    (a) The function $f(x)$ is linear. In a linear function, the rate of change is constant. In this case, the cost per minute is constant at $0.15.

    (b) f(x) = 40.00 − 0.15x

    (c) f(0) is $40.00

    (d) f(100) is $25.00

    (e) $f(x) = 10$. This means that Julie can talk for 200 minutes before her balance reaches $10.00.

    (f) when x ≈ 266.67, f(x) = 0. This means that Julie can talk for approximately 267 minutes before her balance reaches $0.00, and she needs to recharge or add more funds to her cell phone.

12. $x = 3, y = 4$

13. $\left(-\sqrt{\frac{3}{10}}, \frac{3\sqrt{3}}{\sqrt{10}}\right), \left(\sqrt{\frac{3}{10}}, -\frac{3\sqrt{3}}{\sqrt{10}}\right)$

14. $(2,11)$ & $(-1,5)$

15. $(1,3)$ & $(6,13)$

16. $(3,4)$ & $(-63/13, -16/13)$

17.

    (a) Exponential Growth

    (b) 1200

(c) 0.3 or 30%

18.

    (a) Exponential Decay

    (b) B. 14000

    (c) C. 0.08 or 8%

19.

    (a) $y = 3600(1.04)^t$

    (b) 7888 people

20.

    (a) $y = 42500(0.85)^t$

    (b) $13625

21.

    (a) $y = 65000(0.99)^t$

    (b) $53,164

22. ≈ 883

23. $184,274

24. $15.84

25.

    (a) 8%, 1.08

    (b) $277.64

    (c) $55.15

Lesson 7 - Quadratic, Exponential, and Polynomial Graphs

Graphing quadratic functions

Quadratic equations are second-degree polynomial equations, and their graphs are represented by parabolas. The general form of a quadratic equation is:

$$ax^2 + bx + c = 0$$

Here, a, b, and c are constants, and a must not be equal to zero for the equation to be quadratic. The graph of a quadratic equation is a parabola, which can open upwards or downwards.

Forms of Quadratic Equations

Quadratic equations can be expressed in different forms, each providing insights into the characteristics of the parabola:

- **Standard Form:**

$$f(x) = ax^2 + bx + c$$

where a, b, and c are real numbers and a $\neq$ 0. The coefficient of the x^2 term, 'a', determines the direction of the parabola. If a > 0, the parabola opens upwards; if a < 0, it opens downwards.

- **Vertex Form:**

$$f(x) = a(x - h)^2 + k$$

where a, h, and k are real numbers and a $\neq$ 0. This form explicitly reveals the vertex coordinates: (h, k). The coefficient 'a' still determines the direction of the parabola.

To convert from standard form to vertex form, we use the following formulas:

$$h = -\frac{b}{2a},$$

$$k = f(h)$$

where $f(h)$ is the value of the quadratic function at $x = h$.

- **Intercept Form:**

$$f(x) = a(x - r)(x - s)$$

where a, r, and s are real numbers and a $\neq$ 0. This form directly provides the x-intercepts: r and s. The coefficient $'a'$ indicates the direction of the parabola.

Graphical Characteristics of Quadratic Functions

- **Vertex:** The vertex is the minimum or maximum point of the parabola, depending on the direction it opens.

- **Axis of Symmetry:** The axis of symmetry is a vertical line passing through the vertex, dividing the parabola into two symmetrical halves.

- **Direction:** The sign of a determines whether the parabola opens upwards or downwards.

- **Intercepts:**

    - **x-intercepts (roots):** The points where the parabola intersects the x-axis. Solve $ax^2 + bx + c = 0$ to find these.

    - **y-intercept:** The point where the parabola intersects the y-axis. Set $x = 0$ to find this point.

- **Determining Maximum or Minimum:**
    - If $a > 0$, the parabola opens upwards, and the vertex represents the minimum point.
    - If $a < 0$, the parabola opens downwards, and the vertex represents the maximum point.

Transformations of the Parabola:

- **Horizontal Translations (Left/Right):**

    - In the form $y = a(x - h)^2 + k$, changing h shifts the parabola horizontally.

    If $h > 0$, the parabola shifts right; if $h < 0$, it shifts left.

- **Vertical Translations (Up/Down):**

    - In the form $y = a(x - h)^2 + k$, changing k shifts the parabola vertically.

    If $k > 0$, the parabola shifts up; if $k < 0$, it shifts down.

- **Vertical Stretch/Compression:**

    - In the form $y = a(x - h)^2 + k$, changing the absolute value of a alters the steepness of the parabola.

    $|a| > 1$ stretches the parabola vertically; $0 < |a| < 1$ compresses it vertically.

- **Reflections:**

    - Replacing $f(x)$ with $-f(x)$ or $y = -y$, reflects the parabola across the x-axis.
    Replacing $f(x)$ with $f(-x)$ reflects the parabola across the y-axis.

Example 1: Quadratic Equation: $y = -2x^2 + 4x + 6$

Vertex Form: $y = -2(x - 1)^2 + 8$

Analysis:

- The vertex is $(1,8)$.

- The parabola opens downwards because the coefficient of x^2 is negative.

- Axis of symmetry: $x = 1$.

Graphical Representation:

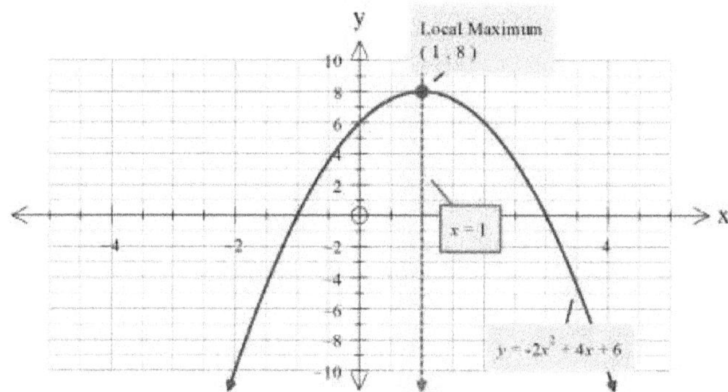

Example 2:

Consider the quadratic equation $y = (x - 2)^2 - 3$.

- **Vertex Form:**

    - Vertex: $(2, -3)$

    - Translations: Shifted right by 2 units and down by 3 units.

- **Standard Form:**

    - Expand the vertex form to standard form: $y = x^2 - 4x + 1$

    - Coefficients: $a = 1, b = -4, c = 1$

Now, let's explore transformations:

- **Horizontal Translation (Right):**

    - If we replace x with $x - 3$, the parabola shifts right by 3 units: $y = (x - 3)^2 - 3$

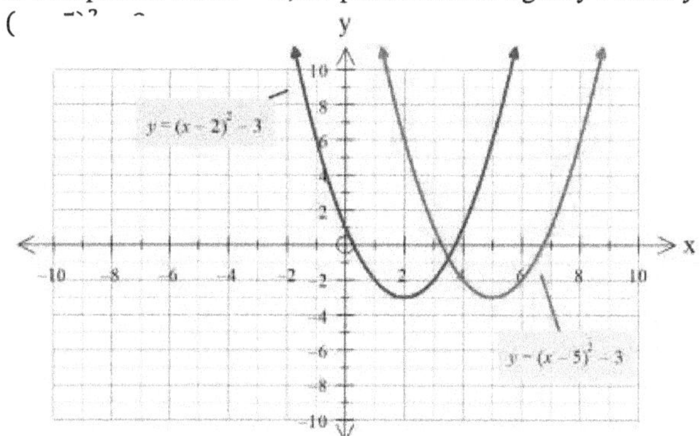

- **Vertical Stretch:**
  - If we replace y with $2y$, the parabola is stretched vertically: $2y = (x - 2)^2 - 3$.

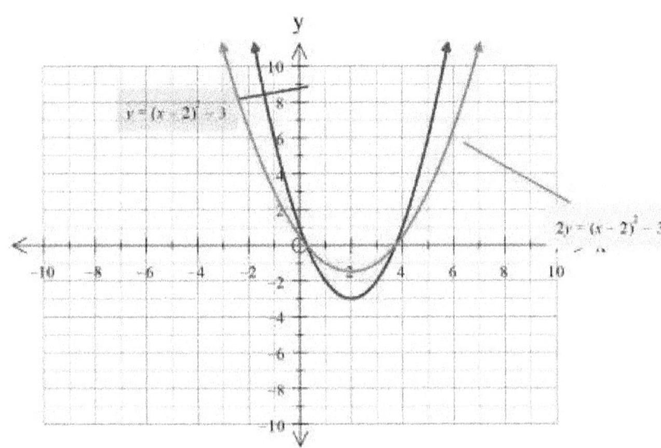

- **Reflection across x-axis:**
  - If we replace y with $-y$, the parabola reflects across the x-axis: $-y = (x - 2)^2 - 3$.

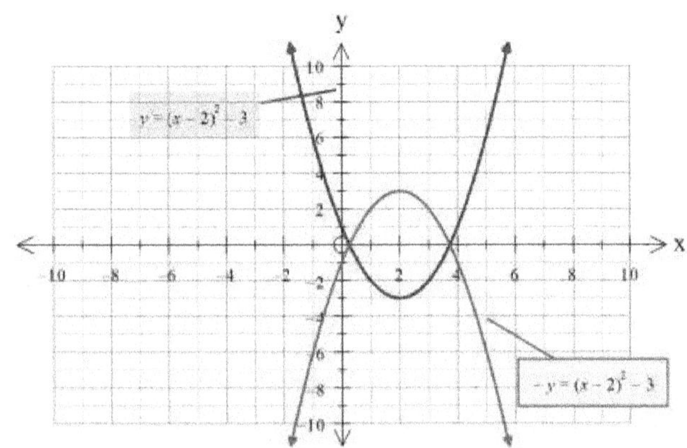

These transformations showcase how changes in coefficients and terms impact the position, shape, and orientation of the quadratic graph.

Example 3: Consider the quadratic function $y = x^2 - 4x + 3$.

- **Standard Form:**

  - $a = 1, b = -4, c = 3$.

- **Vertex Form:**

  - Complete the square to find (h, k): $y = (x - 2)^2 - 1$.

- **Factored Form:**

  - Roots are $r = 1$ and $s = 3$: $y = (x - 1)(x - 3)$.

Now, let's apply transformations:

- **Right Shift by 2 Units:** $y = (x - 2)^2 - 1 \rightarrow y = (x - 4)^2 - 1$

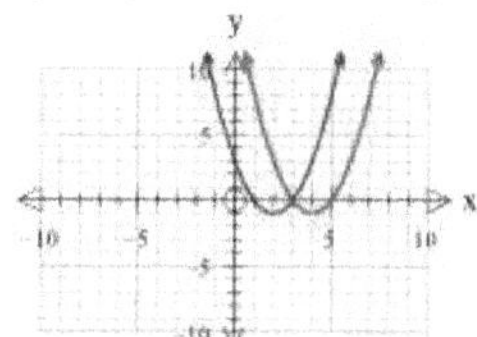

- **Left Shift by 2 Units:** $y = (x - 2)^2 - 1 \rightarrow y = (x)^2 - 1$

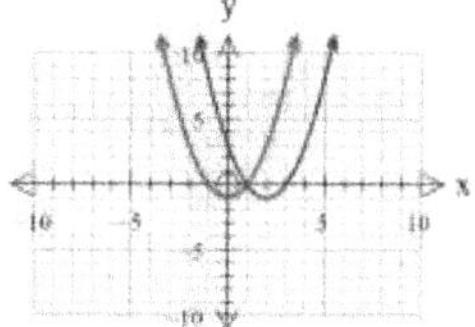

- **Upward Shift by 2 Units:** $y = (x - 2)^2 - 1 \rightarrow y = (x - 2)^2 + 1$

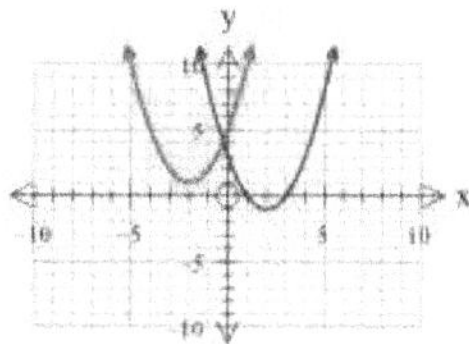

- **Downward Shift by 2 Units:** $y = (x - 2)^2 - 1 \rightarrow y = (x - 2)^2 - 3$

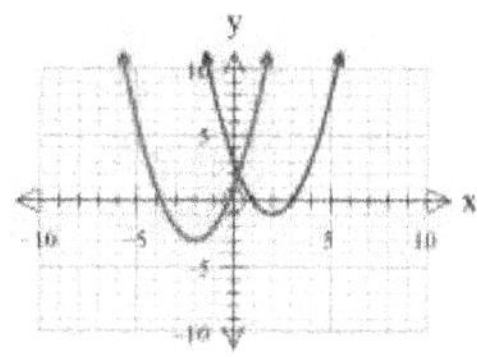

- **Reflection across x-axis:** $y = -(x^2 - 4x + 3) \rightarrow y = -x^2 + 4x - 3$

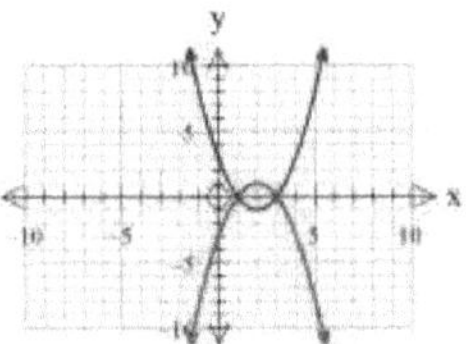

- **Reflection across y-axis:** $y = y = f(-x) = (-x)^2 - 4(-x) + 3 = x^2 + 4x + 3$

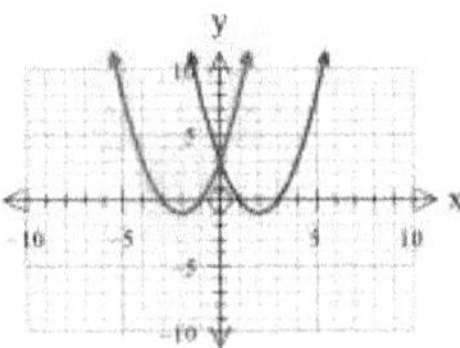

- **Vertical Stretch by 2:** $y = 2(x - 2)^2 - 1$

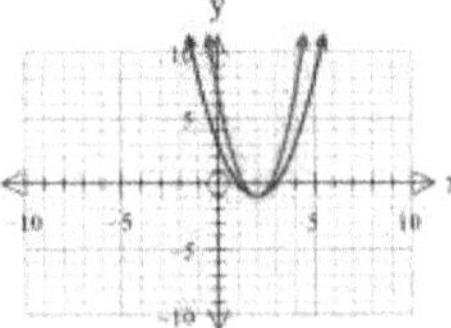

These transformations help visualize how changes in the function affect the position, shape, and orientation of the parabola.

Example 4:

Given the quadratic equation $y = -2x^2 + 8x + 6$ let's convert it to vertex form and find the vertex:

- **Identify a, b, and c:**

  - $a = -2, b = 8, c = 6.$

- **Find h using h=−b/2a:**

  - $h = -\dfrac{8}{-2.2} = 2$

- **Find k using $k = f(h)$:**

  - Substitute $h = 2$ back into the original equation: $k = f(2) = -2.2^2 + 8 \cdot 2 + 6 = 14.$

- **Write Vertex Form $y = a(x - h)^2 + k$:**

  - $y = -2(x - 2)^2 + 14.$

- **Determine Minimum:**

- Since $a = -2 < 0$, the parabola opens downwards, and the vertex represents the maximum point.

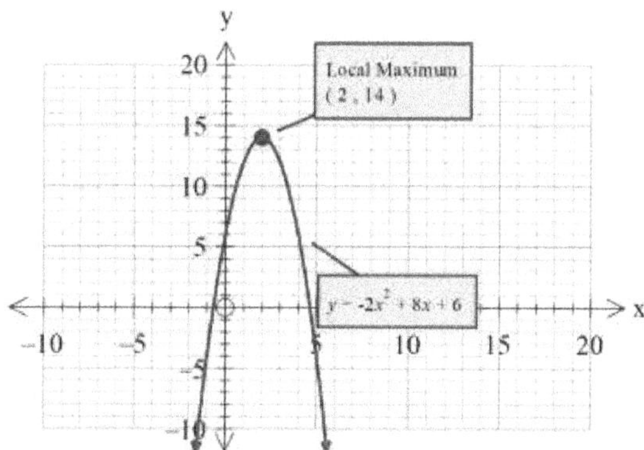

In this example, we converted the quadratic equation to vertex form, identified the vertex, and determined that the parabola has a maximum point. The graphical representation shows the downward-opening parabola with its vertex at (2, 14).

Graphing Exponential functions

Exponential functions are mathematical functions that have the form $y = ab^x$, where a and b are constants, and b is a positive constant not equal to 1. The exponent x can take on any real number, making exponential functions a broad class of functions. These functions are used to model various phenomena, such as population growth, radioactive decay, compound interest, and more.

Features of Exponential Functions:

- **Initial Value (a):**

    - Represents the value of the function when $x = 0$.
    This is the same as y-intercept For any/all values of b, the y-intercept is always a

- **Base (b):**

    - Determines whether the function represents exponential growth ($b > 1$) or decay ($0 < b < 1$).

    - The larger the b, the steeper the growth; the smaller the b, the steeper the decay.

- **Shifting the Horizontal Asymptote:**

- **For $f(x) = b^x$:**

- The function approaches infinity on one end and zero on the other.
  - This is the standard behavior for exponential growth and decay with a base b.
- For $f(x) = b^x + d$:
  - The function still approaches infinity on one end, but it approaches d on the other end.
  - Adding d shifts the horizontal asymptote upwards by d.

Shifting the Y-Intercept:

- For $f(x) = b^x + d$
  - The y-intercept is $1 + d$.
  - The base b still determines the growth or decay rate, and d shifts the y-intercept vertically.
- For $f(x) = a \cdot b^x$
  - The y-intercept is $a \cdot 1 = a$.
  - a is the initial value or the y-intercept when $x=0$.
- For $f(x) = a \cdot b^x + d$
  - The y-intercept is $a + d$.
  - a represents the initial value, and d shifts the y-intercept vertically.

Example 5: Consider the exponential function $f(x) = 2^x$. Now, let's create variations of this function by adding constants to shift the asymptote and adjusting the y-intercept.

1. **Original Function:** $f(x) = 2^x$
2. **Shifting the Horizontal Asymptote:**
   - To shift the asymptote upwards by 3 units, we add $d = 3$: $g(x) = 2^x + 3$
3. **Shifting the Y-Intercept:**
   - To shift the y-intercept upwards by 5 units, we add $d = 5$:
   $$h(x) = 2^x + 5$$
   - To adjust the initial value to 2, we multiply the function by 2:
   $$k(x) = 2 \cdot 2^x$$
- **Graphical Characteristics:**
  - **Exponential Growth ($b > 1$):**
    - The graph increases as x increases.
    - The initial value (a) is the y-intercept.

- As x increases, the function grows rapidly.
  - The graph approaches, but never reaches, the x-axis.
- **Exponential Decay ($0 < b < 1$):**
  - The graph decreases as x increases.
  - The initial value (a) is the y-intercept.
  - As x increases, the function decays gradually.
  - The graph approaches, but never reaches, the x-axis.

Example 6 : Consider the exponential function $y = 2^x$.

- **Initial Value (a):**
  - $a = 1$ (initial value is 1).
- **Base (b):**
  - $b = 2$ (positive base, representing exponential growth).
- **Select Points:**
- Choose $x = 0, 1, 2, -1, -2$ and calculate corresponding y values.

x	y
0	1
1	2
2	4
-1	0.5
-2	0.25

- **Graphical Characteristics:**
  - As x increases, the function grows rapidly.
  - The graph approaches, but never reaches, the x-axis.
  - The initial value is 1, so the function starts at the point (0, 1).
- **Graph:**

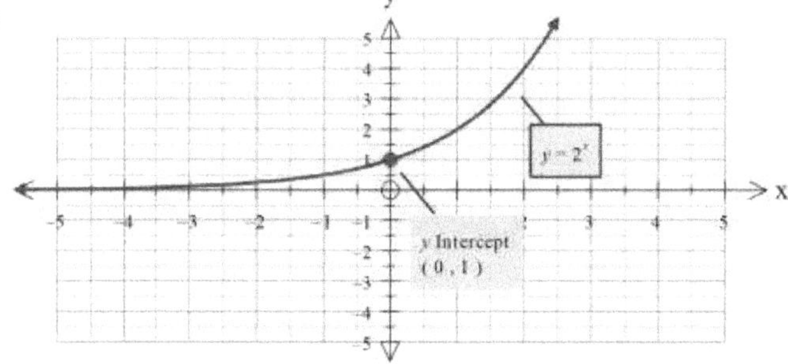

Polynomial Graphs:

Polynomial graphs are a type of mathematical graph that represents the behavior of a polynomial function. Polynomial functions are functions that can be expressed as a sum of terms, each of which is a product of a constant and a power of the variable x. The degree of a polynomial is the highest power of x that appears in the function.

There are several key features that can be used to identify polynomial graphs:

- **Zeros of Polynomials:**

    - **Definition:** The zeros (roots) of a polynomial are the values of x for which the polynomial equals zero.

    - **Graphically:** Zeros are the x-intercepts of the polynomial graph.

    - **Example:** If $f(x) = (x - 2)(x + 1)(x - 3)$, the zeros are $x = 2, x = -1, and\ x = 3$.

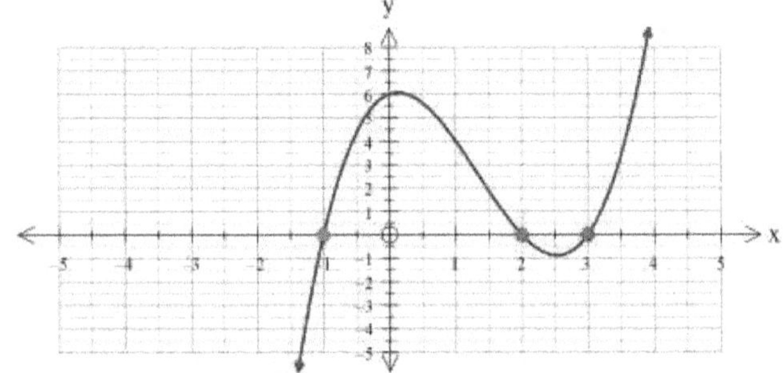

- **Features of Polynomial Graphs:**

    - **Degree:** The highest power of the variable in the polynomial determines its degree.

    - **End Behavior:** It describes the behavior of the graph as x approaches positive and negative infinity.

    - **Leading Coefficient:** The coefficient of the term with the highest power influences the direction of the end behavior.

- **Factored Form and Zeros:**

    - **Factored Form:** Expressing a polynomial as a product of linear factors.

    - **Zeros:** The roots of the polynomial are the values that make each factor equal to zero.

- **Standard Form, *y*-Intercept, and End Behavior:**

    - **Standard Form:** $f(x) = a_n x^n + a_{n-1} x^{n-1} + \cdots + a_1 x + a_0$.

    - **y-Intercept:** The point where the graph intersects the y-axis, found by setting $x=0$.

    - **End Behavior:** Determined by the degree and leading coefficient.

Example 7: A polynomial function as x approaches positive or negative infinity, based on the leading term ax^n, where a is the leading coefficient, and n is the degree of the polynomial.

- **If $a > 0$, then y ultimately approaches positive infinity as x increases:**
  - This is true for a polynomial with a positive leading coefficient. As x becomes very large, the positive leading term dominates, and the function approaches positive infinity.

- **If $a < 0$, then y ultimately approaches negative infinity as x increases:**
  - This is true for a polynomial with a negative leading coefficient. As x becomes very large, the negative leading term dominates, and the function approaches negative infinity.

- **If n is even, then the ends of the graph point in the same direction:**
  - For even-degree polynomials, both ends of the graph behave similarly. As x approaches positive or negative infinity, the graph rises or falls in the same direction.

- **If n is odd, then the ends of the graph point in different directions:**
  - For odd-degree polynomials, the ends of the graph behave differently. As x approaches positive infinity, the graph may rise, while as x approaches negative infinity, it may fall (or vice versa).

- **Turning Points (Local Extrema):**
  - **Definition:** Points where the graph changes direction, either reaching a maximum

    (local maximum) or minimum (local minimum).
  - **Influence:** Related to the degree of the polynomial.

- **Symmetry:**
  - **Definition:** Polynomials can be symmetric with respect to the y-axis, x axis, or the origin.
  - **Example:** Even-degree polynomials are symmetric with respect to the y-axis; odd-degree polynomials are symmetric with respect to the origin.

Example 8 : Consider the polynomial $f(x) = x^3 + x^2 - 10x + 8$

Zeros of the Polynomial:

- **Procedure:** Set $f(x) = 0$ and solve for x.
- **Equation:** $x^3 + x^2 - 10x + 8 = 0$.
- **Solutions:** Zeros or roots of the function can be found using factoring techniques or a graphing calculator.
  $x^3 + x^2 - 10x + 8$ is the same as $(x - 1)(x - 2)(x + 4)$; so we can find that the

zeros of $f(x)$ are $x = 1, x = 2,$ and $x = -4$. This means that the graph of $f(x)$ intersects the x-axis at these three points.

2. Degree of the Polynomial:

- **Definition:** The degree is the highest power of the variable in the polynomial.

- **Example:** The degree of $f(x) = x^3 + x^2 - 10x + 8$ is 3.

3. End Behavior:

- **Example:** The leading term is x^3, and the degree is odd. As x approaches positive and negative infinity, the graph goes in opposite directions.

4. Leading Coefficient:

- **Example:** The leading coefficient is 1.

6. y-Intercept:

- **Procedure:** Set $x = 0$ and find $f(0)$.

- **Example:** For $f(x) = x^3 + x^2 - 10x + 8$, the y-intercept is $y = f(x) = 8$.

7. Turning Points (Local Extrema):

- **Procedure:** Locate points where the graph changes direction.

- **Example:** The number of turning points is related to the degree; in this case, there may be two turning points.

Graphical Representation:

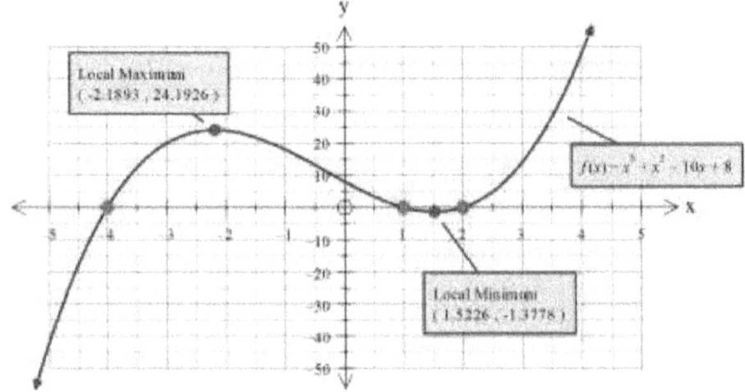

Practice question:

1. Find the Vertex Form of Parabolas
   (a) $y = x^2 - 6x + 5$
   (b) $\frac{1}{2}(y + 4) = (x - 7)^2$
   (c) $y = x^2 - 12x + 46$
   (d) $y = x^2 + 4x$
   (e) $y + 6 = (x + 3)^2$
2. Identify the vertex and axis of symmetry of each. Then sketch the graph.
   (a) $f(x) = -3(x - 2)^2 - 4$

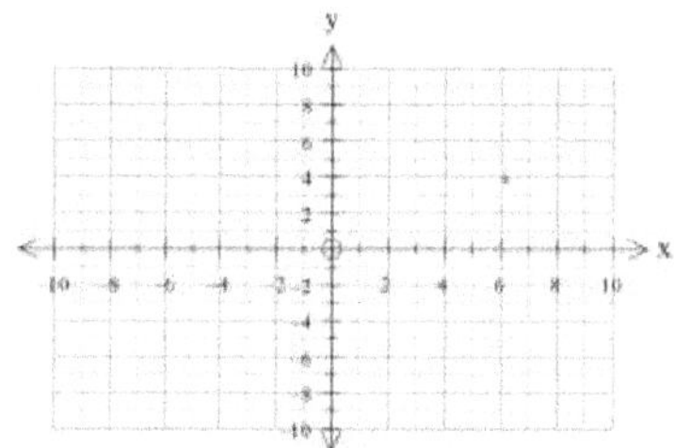

   (b) $f(x) = -\frac{1}{4}(x - 1)^2 + 4$

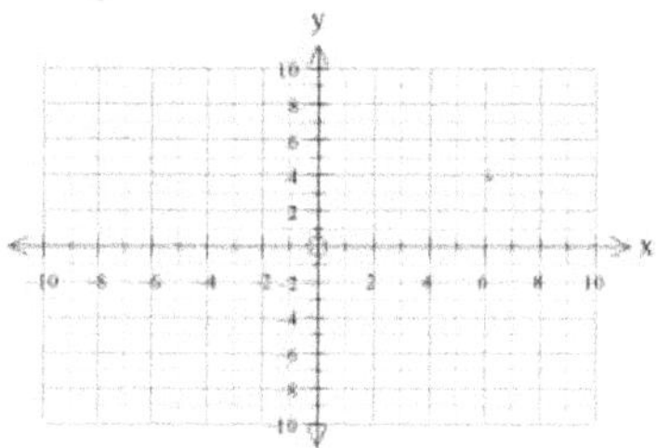

   (c) $f(x) = \frac{1}{4}(x + 4)^2 + 3$

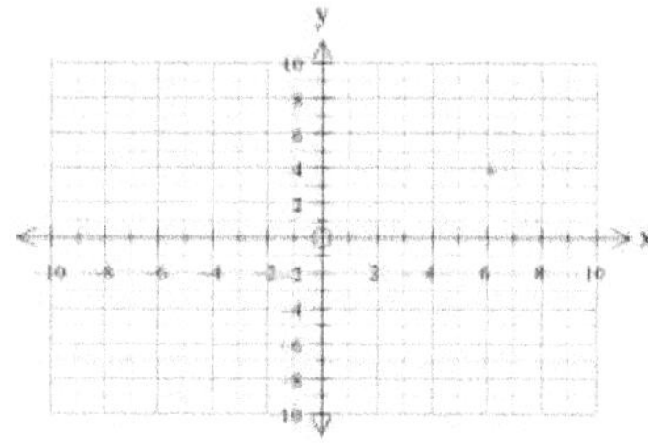

   (d) $f(x) = -2(x + 5)^2 - 3$

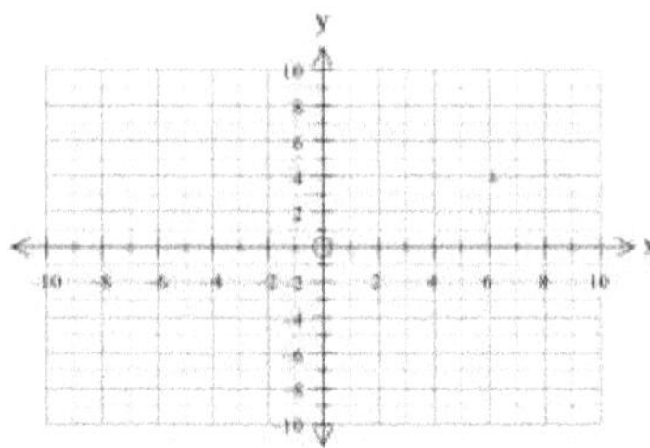

3. Identify the vertex, axis of symmetry, and min/max value of each.

   (a) $f(x) = 3x^2 - 54x + 241$

   (b) $f(x) = -\frac{4}{5}x^2 + \frac{48}{5}x - \frac{114}{5}$

   (c) $f(x) = -\frac{1}{4}x^2 + 7$

   (d) $f(x) = \frac{1}{4}x^2 - x + 9$

   (e) $f(x) = x^{\wedge}2 + 4x + 5$

4. Identify the min/max value of each. Then sketch the graph.

   (a) $f(x) = -x^2 + 8x - 20$

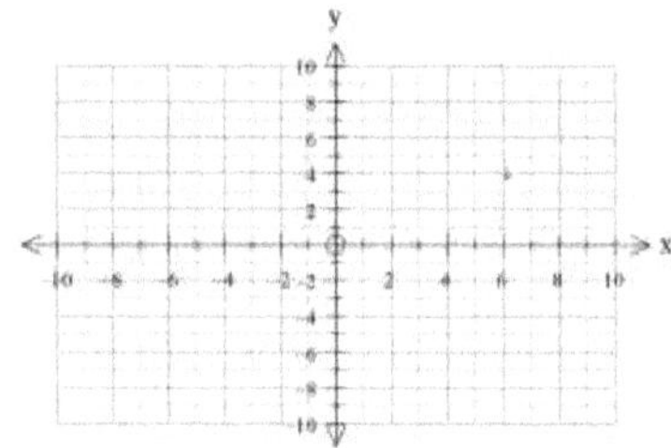

   (b) $f(x) = -x^2 - 10x - 30$

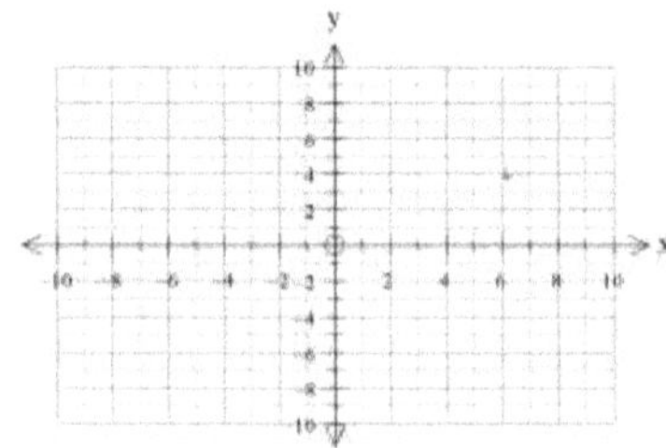

5. Consider the quadratic function $f(x) = -2x^2 + 4x - 3$.

   (a) Find the vertex of the parabola.

   (b) Determine the axis of symmetry.

   (c) Identify the direction in which the parabola opens.

   (d) Calculate the y-intercept of the graph.

6. A company's profit, in thousands of dollars, is modeled by the quadratic function $P(t) = -t^2 + 100t - 200$, where t is the time in months.

   (a) Determine the time when the company reaches its maximum profit.

   (b) Find the maximum profit the company can achieve.

7. Given Quadratic Function: $h(x) = -x^2 + 6x - 9$

   (a) Determine the vertex of the parabola.

   (b) Find the axis of symmetry.

   (c) Identify the direction in which the parabola opens.

   (d) Calculate the x-intercepts of the graph.

8. Given Cost Function: $C(x) = 4x^2 - 80x + 400$

   (a) Find the number of unit's x that minimizes the cost.

   (b) Determine the minimum cost.

9. A farmer has a rectangular field that he wants to fence in. He has 1000 feet of fencing material. What are the dimensions of the field that will maximize the area of the field?

10. A projectile is launched from a height of 100 feet at an initial velocity of 200 feet per second. What is the maximum height that the projectile will reach?

11. A radioactive substance has a half-life of 10 years. If you start with 100 grams of the substance, how much will be left after 50 years?

12. Find the degree of the polynomial function $f(x) = 3x^4 - 2x^2 + 5x - 1$.

13. Factor the polynomial function $f(x) = x^3 - 4x^2 - 4x + 16$.

14. Find the end behavior asymptotes of the polynomial function $f(x) = -2x^3 + 5x^2 - 1$.

15. Sketch the graph of the polynomial function $f(x) = x^2 - 4x + 3$.

16. Find the x-intercepts of the polynomial function $f(x) = 2x^3 - 5x^2 + 3x - 1$.

17. A projectile is launched from a height of 100 feet at an initial velocity of 200 feet per second. What is the maximum height that the projectile will reach?

The height of the projectile as a function of time can be modeled by the following cubic function: $h(t) = -5t^3 + 100t^2 + 200t + 100$

18. A box has a volume of 125 cubic inches. The dimensions of the box are x inches, y inches, and z inches. If x = 2y, find the dimensions of the box that will minimize the surface area of the box.

19. A population of bacteria is growing exponentially. The initial population is 100 bacteria, and the population triples every hour. How long will it take for the population to reach 1 billion bacteria?

20. A company produces widgets at a cost of $10 per widget. The company sells the widgets for $15 per widget. If the company produces and sells x widgets, find the polynomial function that represents the company's profit.

Answer

1.

(a) $y = (x - 3)^2 - 4$
(b) $y = 2(x - 7)^2 - 4$
(c) $y = (x - 6)^2 + 10$
(d) $y = (x + 2)^2 - 4$
(e) $y = (x + 3)^2 - 6$

2.

(a)

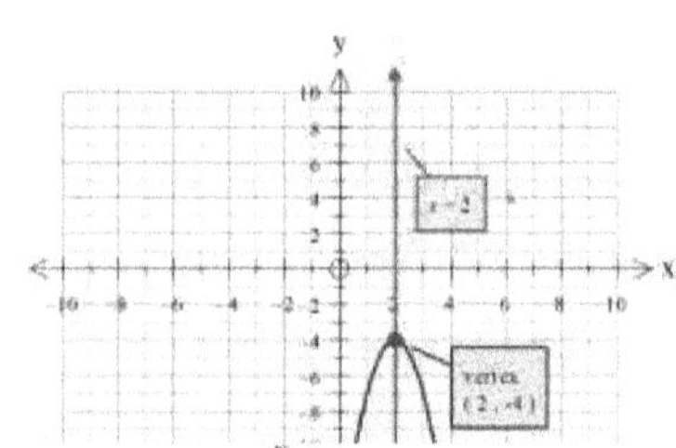

(b)

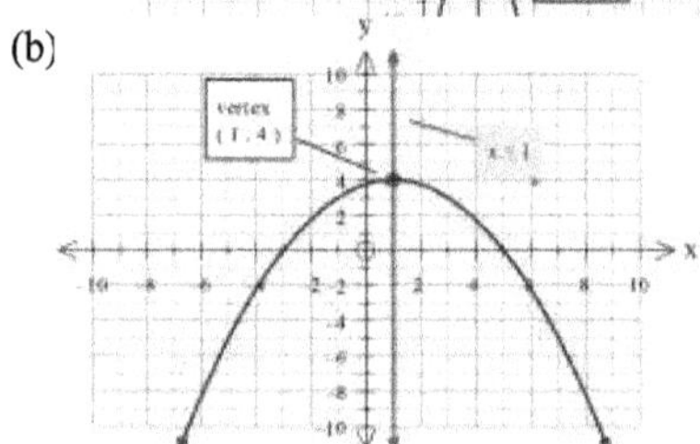

(c)

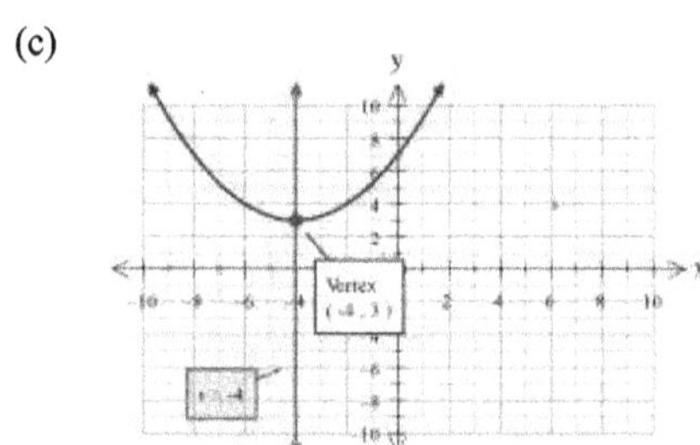

(d)

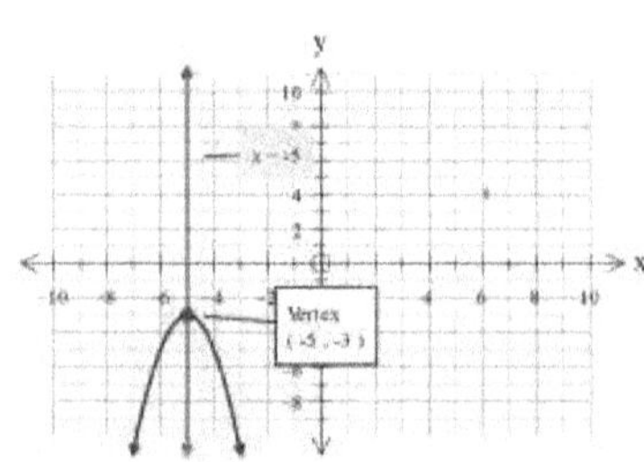

3.

(a) Vertex: (9, −2)
Axis of Sym.: x = 9
Min value = −2

(b) Vertex: (6, 6)
Axis of Sym.: x = 6
Max value = 6

(c) Vertex: (0, 7)
Axis of Sym.: x = 0
Max value = 7

(d) Vertex: (2, 8)
Axis of Sym.: x = 2
Min value = 8

(e) Vertex: (−2, 1)
Axis of Sym.: x = −2
Min value = 1

4.

(a)

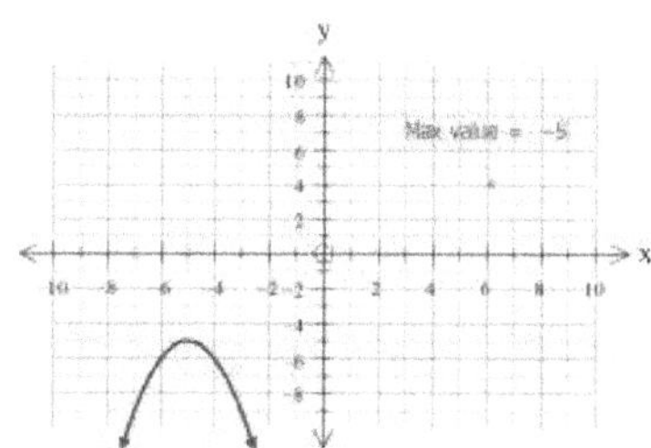

(b)

5.

(a) vertex of the parabola is (1,1).
(b) The axis of symmetry is $x = 1$.
(c) $-2 < 0$, the parabola opens downward
(d) y-intercept of the graph is (0, −3)

6.
    (a) The company reaches its maximum profit after 50 months.
    (b) The maximum profit the company can achieve is $2,300,

7.
    (a) The vertex of the parabola is (3,0)
    (b) The axis of symmetry for this parabola is $x = 3$.
    (c) $-1 < 0$, the parabola opens downward.
    (d) (3,0)

8.
    (a) The number of unit's x that minimizes the cost is 10.
    (b) The minimum cost is $0.

9. The dimensions of the field that will maximize the area are 250 feet by 250 feet.

10. The maximum height that the projectile will reach is 725 feet.

11. After 50 years, 3.125 grams of the radioactive substance will remain.

12. 4

13. The polynomial can be factored as $(x - 2)(x - 2)(x + 4)$.

14. The end behavior asymptotes are $y = -\infty$ and $y = \infty$.

15. The vertex is (2, -3).

16. x-intercepts are x = 1, x = 1/2, and x = -1.

17. 900 feet

18. The minimum surface area of the box is 128 square inches.

19. It will take about 15.41 hours for the population of bacteria to reach 1 billion bacteria.

20. The polynomial function that represents the company's profit is P(x) = 5x.

Part (III)
Problem Solving and Data Analysis

1. Ratios, Rates, Proportional Relationships, and Units/Conversions
2. Percentages
3. Two-Variable Data - Models and Scatterplots
4. Probability and Conditional Probability
5. Distributions and Measures of Center and Spread
6. Data Inferences - Inference from Sample Statistics and Margin of Error, Evaluating Statistical Claims - Observational Studies and Experiments

Lesson 1: Ratios, Rates, Proportional Relationships, and Units/Conversions

Ratios: A ratio is a way of comparing two quantities of the same kind. It expresses how many times one quantity is contained in another. There are three common ways to write a ratio:

- **a:b**: This is the most common notation. It means a is to b. For example, a ratio of 3:2 means that there are 3 of the first quantity for every 2 of the second quantity.

- **a to b**: This is a more informal way of writing a ratio. It means the same thing as a:b.

- $\frac{a}{b}$: This is the fraction form of a ratio. It is equivalent to a:b, but it is not as common in formal writing.

Identifying Part-to-Part and Part-to-Whole Ratios: There are two main types of ratios:

- **Part-to-part ratios:** These compare two parts of a whole.

  For example, a ratio of 3 boys to 2 girls in a classroom is a part-to-part ratio.

- **Part-to-whole ratios:** These compare a part of a whole to the whole itself.

  For example, a ratio of 3 red marbles to 5 total marbles is a part-to-whole ratio.

Simplifying and Expanding Ratios: A ratio can be simplified by dividing both the numerator and denominator by the greatest common factor (GCD). For example, the ratio 6:9 can be simplified to 2:3 by dividing both numbers by 3.

- A ratio can be expanded by multiplying both the numerator and denominator by the same number.
  For example, the ratio 3:4 can be expanded to 6:8 by multiplying both numbers by 2.

Equivalent Ratios: Equivalent ratios are ratios that represent the same relationship between two quantities. They can be obtained by simplifying or expanding a ratio, or by multiplying both the numerator and denominator by the same number.

  For example, the ratios 3:4, 6:8, and 9:12 are all equivalent ratios.

Converting Between Ratios and Fractions

- A ratio can be converted to a fraction by dividing the numerator by the denominator.
  For example, the ratio 3:4 is equivalent to the fraction 3/4.
- A fraction can be converted to a ratio by multiplying both the numerator and denominator by the same number.
  For example, the fraction 3/4 is equivalent to the ratio 6:8.

> Here are some additional notes on the types of ratios:
>
> - **Complementary ratios:** These are two ratios whose sum is 1.
>
>   For example, the ratios 2:3 and 1:3 are complementary ratios.
>
> - **Supplementary ratios:** These are two ratios whose difference is 1.
>
>   For example, the ratios 3:4 and 2:4 are supplementary ratios.
>
> - **Multiplicative relationships:** These are relationships where the ratio of two quantities is constant.
>
> - For example, the ratio of the circumference to the diameter of a circle is always π.

Example 1:

A bag is filled with red marbles and blue marbles. There are 54 total marbles in the bag, and $\frac{1}{3}$ of the marbles are blue.

   (a) The ratio of blue marbles to total marbles is
   (b) The ratio of red marbles to total marbles is
   (c) The ratio of red marbles to blue marbles is
   (d) How many red marbles are in the bag?

Solution: Ratios:

(a) **Blue Marbles to Total Marbles:**

- Blue marbles: $\frac{1}{3} \times (54) = 18$

- Ratio of blue marbles to total marbles: $\frac{18}{54}$

(b) **Red Marbles to Total Marbles:**

- Red marbles: $54 - 18 = 36$

- Ratio of red marbles to total marbles: $\frac{36}{54}$

(c) **Red Marbles to Blue Marbles:**

- Ratio of red marbles to blue marbles: $\frac{36}{18}$

Simplify Ratios:

(a) **Simplify Ratio of Blue Marbles to Total Marbles:**

- $\frac{18}{54} = \frac{1}{3}$ (Simplify by dividing both numerator and denominator by 18)

(b) **Simplify Ratio of Red Marbles to Total Marbles:**

- $\frac{36}{54} = \frac{2}{3}$ (Simplify by dividing both numerator and denominator by 18)

(c) **Simplify Ratio of Red Marbles to Blue Marbles:**

- $\frac{36}{18} = 2$

(d) Number of Red Marbles in the Bag: There are 36 red marbles in the bag.

Example 2: A high school randomly selected 50 students to take a survey about extending their lunch period. Of students selected for the survey, 14 were freshmen and 13 were sophomores.

(a) Ratio of freshmen to sophomores is

(b) Ratio of sophomores to total students surveyed is

(c) Ratio of freshmen to total students surveyed is

Solution:

(a) **Freshmen to Sophomores:**

- Ratio of freshmen to sophomores: 14:13

(b) **Sophomores to Total Students Surveyed:**

- Ratio of sophomores to total students surveyed: 13:50

(c) **Freshmen to Total Students Surveyed:**

- Ratio of freshmen to total students surveyed: 14:50

- Simplify the Freshmen to Total Students Surveyed Ratio:
- The ratio 14:50 can be reduced by dividing both parts by the greatest common factor, which is 2.

$$\frac{14}{2} : \frac{50}{2} = 7:25$$

Proportional Relationships: A proportional relationship is a relationship between two variables where their ratios are always equal. This means that as one variable increases or decreases, the other variable changes proportionally.

Here are some key characteristics of proportional relationships:

- **Constant of proportionality:** There is a constant value (k) that relates the two variables. This means that the product of one variable and k is always equal to the other variable.

- **Linear relationship:** When graphed, a proportional relationship forms a straight line that passes through the origin (0,0).

- **Rate of change:** The slope of the line represents the rate of change of one variable with respect to the other.

Direct vs. Inverse Proportion:

There are two types of proportional relationships:

- **Direct proportion:** In this type of relationship, both variables increase or decrease together. For example, the distance traveled is directly proportional to the time spent traveling at a constant speed.

- **Inverse proportion:** In this type of relationship, as one variable increases, the other variable decreases proportionally. For example, the time it takes to complete a task is inversely proportional to the number of people working on it.

Writing Proportions:

Proportions can be written in several ways:

- Fraction form: $\frac{a}{b} = \frac{c}{d}$

- Colon form: $a : b = c : d$

- Equation form: $a = kc$, where k is the constant of proportionality

Solving Proportions for Unknowns:

To solve a proportion for an unknown variable, we can use the following steps:

1. Cross-multiply the terms. $\frac{a}{b} = \frac{c}{d}$ implies $ad = bc$.

2. Simplify the equation.

3. Solve for the unknown variable.

Example 3: We're making cookies, and the recipe calls for 1 cup of sugar for every 3 cups of flour. What if we want to use 9 cups of flour: how much sugar do we need?

- The ratio of sugar to flour must be $1 : 3$ to match the recipe.

- The ratio of sugar to flour in our batch can be written as $x : 9$.

To determine how much sugar we need, we can set up the proportion $\frac{1}{3} = \frac{x}{9}$ and solve for x:

$$\frac{1}{3} * 9 = \frac{x}{9} * 9 \Rightarrow x = 3$$

We need 3 cups of sugar.

Example 4: There are 340 students at Du Bois Academy. If the student-to-teacher ratio is 17:2 how many teachers are there?

Student-to-teacher ratio$= 17 : 2$

This ratio implies that for every 17 students, there are 2 teachers. To find the number of teachers, we need to set up a proportion and solve for the unknown quantity (the number of teachers).

Let x be the number of teachers.

The proportion can be set up as:

$$\frac{17}{2} = \frac{340}{x}$$

Now, cross-multiply to solve for x:

$$17 \times x = 2 \times 340$$

$$17x = 680$$

Now, solve for x:

$$x = \frac{680}{17}$$

$$x = 40$$

So, there are 40teachers at Du Bois Academy.

Inverse proportion: Inverse proportion refers to a relationship between two variables in which an increase in one variable leads to a decrease in the other, and vice versa. Mathematically, if x is inversely proportional to y, it can be expressed as:

$$x \cdot y = k$$

where k is a constant.

Example 5: If it takes 8 hours for 5 workers to complete a task, what would be the time required for 10 workers to complete the same task?

Solution: Let's denote:

- t: time required to complete the task
- w: number of workers

The relationship can be expressed as:

$$t \cdot w = k$$

where k is a constant.

For the initial scenario with 5 workers:

$$8 \cdot 5 = k \Rightarrow k = 40$$

Let's use the inverse proportion formula:

$$t \cdot w = k$$

Now, for the scenario with 10 workers:

$$t \cdot 10 = 40 \Rightarrow t = \frac{40}{10} \Rightarrow t = 4$$

So, with 10 workers, it would take 4 hours to complete the task.

Example 6: If it takes 3 hours to travel a certain distance at a speed of 40 miles per hour, what would be the time required to travel the same distance at a speed of 60 miles per hour?

Solution:

Let's use the inverse proportion formula: $t \cdot s = k$

For the initial scenario with a speed of 40 miles per hour:

$3 \cdot 40 = k \Rightarrow k = 120$

Now, for the scenario with a speed of 60 miles per hour:

$$t \cdot 60 = 120 \Rightarrow t = \frac{120}{60} \Rightarrow t = 2$$

So, at a speed of 60 miles per hour, it would take 2 hours to travel the same distance.

Rates

Definition and Units (Unit Rate): A rate is a measure of how quickly something changes. It expresses the amount of one quantity per unit of another quantity.

Rates are often expressed in units of:

- **Per unit time:** Miles per hour (mph), kilometers per hour (km/h), meters per second (m/s)

- **Per unit area:** Dollars per square meter ($/m^2$), pounds per square inch (psi)

- **Per unit volume:** Liters per gallon (L/gal), milligrams per cubic centimeter (mg/cm^3)

The unit rate is a special type of rate that expresses the amount of one quantity per unit of another quantity, where the second quantity is 1.

For example, a rate of 50 miles per hour (50 mph) can also be expressed as a unit rate of 50 miles per 1 hour (50 miles/1 hour).

Converting Units with Rates: Rates can be converted from one unit to another by using dimensional analysis. This involves multiplying and dividing by factors that are equal to 1, but expressed in different units.

For example, to convert 50 miles per hour to kilometers per hour, we can use the following conversion factor:

1 mile = 1.6 kilometers

Therefore:

50 miles/hour $*$ 1.6 kilometers/mile $=$ 80.46 kilometers/hour

Rates Expressed as "Per" or "For Each"

Rates can also be expressed using words like "per" or "for each". These expressions are equivalent to the fraction form of the rate.

For example, "50 miles per hour" can also be expressed as "50 miles for each hour".

Calculating Average Speed

Average speed is a measure of the total distance traveled divided by the total time taken. It is calculated using the following formula:

$$\text{Average speed} = \frac{\text{Total Distance}}{\text{Total Time}}$$

For example, if you traveled 100 miles in 2 hours, your average speed would be:

$$\text{Average speed} = \frac{100 \text{ miles}}{2 \text{ hours}} = 50 \text{ miles/hour}$$

Example 7: Tony is on a road trip and records details for two segments of his journey:

Segment 1:

- Speed: 5 miles per hour
- Distance: 10 miles

Segment 2:

- Speed: 10 miles per hour
- Distance: 30 miles

Calculate the average speed for the entire road trip, considering both Segment 1 and Segment 2 combined.

Solution:

1. **Calculate Time for Each Segment:**

   - Time (t_1) for Segment 1 = Distance / Speed =
   - Time (t_1) for Segment $= \dfrac{10 \text{ miles}}{5 \text{ miles per hour}} = 2 \text{ hours}$
   - Time (t_2) for Segment 2 = Distance / Speed =
   - Time (t_2) for Segment $= \dfrac{30 \text{ miles}}{10 \text{ miles per hour}} = 3 \text{ hours}$

2. **Calculate Total Distance and Total Time:**

   - Total Distance = Distance of Segment 1 + Distance of Segment 2 =

     Total Distance $= 10 \text{ miles} + 30 \text{ miles} = 40 \text{ miles} 10 \text{ miles} + 30 \text{ miles} = 40 \text{ miles}$

   - Total Time = Time for Segment 1 + Time for Segment 2 =

$$\text{Total Time} = 2\,\text{hours} + 3\,\text{hours} = 5\,\text{hours}$$

3. **Calculate Average Speed:**

- $\text{Average Speed} = \dfrac{\text{Total Distance}}{\text{Total Time}} = \dfrac{40\,\text{miles}}{5\,\text{hours}} = 8\,\text{miles per hour}$

Example 8: Sarah is buying jellybeans for her best friend's birthday party. She buys a bag of 10 lb of jellybeans that costs \$45. Sarah is wondering how much 1 lb of jellybeans cost.

$$\$45 = 4500\,cents$$

$$\frac{4500\,cents}{10\,lb} = \frac{4500\,cents \div 10}{10\,lb \div 10} = \frac{450\,cents}{1\,lb}$$

$$1\,lb = 450\,cents = \$4.50$$

Example 9: Tony buys 6 large pizzas for \$ 77.94 before tax.

(a) The price for a single large pizza is --------------\$.
(b) The price of 10 large pizzas before tax would be

$$\text{Price per pizza} = \frac{\text{Number of pizzas}}{\text{Total cost}}$$

For Tony's purchase:

$$Price\ per\ pizza = \frac{\$77.94}{6}$$

Now, calculate the price per pizza:

$$Price\ per\ pizza = \frac{\$77.94}{6} \approx \$12.99$$

(a) So, the price of a single large pizza is approximately \$12.99.

Now, to find the cost of 10 large pizzas, you can multiply the price per pizza by the number of pizzas:

Total cost = Price per pizza $\times$ Number of pizzas

Total cost = \$12.99 $\times$ 10

Total cost = \$129.90

Therefore, the price of 10 large pizzas before tax would be \$129.90.

Units and Conversions

- **Units:** Standardized measures used to quantify physical quantities like length, mass, time, temperature, and many more.

- **Types of units:** Several unit systems exist, each with its own set of units.

  - **Metric system:** The most widely used system, based on the meter, kilogram, second, and ampere (SI units).

- **US customary system:** Used primarily in the United States, with units like inches, feet, miles, pounds, and gallons.

- Other systems: Less widely used systems like the Imperial system and nautical units.

Unit Conversion:

- **Conversion factors:** Ratios that relate different units of the same quantity (conversion factor will be generally provided in test paper).

  - Example: 1 inch = 2.54 centimetres.

  - 1 yard = 12 feet

  - 12inch =1 foot

  - 1 yard =36 inch

- **Conversion methods:**

  - Direct conversion: Using a single conversion factor to convert from one unit to another.

  - Dimensional analysis: A systematic approach that utilizes conversion factors and multiplication/division to ensure the desired unit is obtained.

Example 10: Examples of Unit Conversion:

- Converting 5 feet to meters:

  - Identify the conversion factor: 1 foot = 0.30 meters.

  - Set up the conversion expression: 5 feet * (0.30 meters/foot).

  - Simplify: 5 feet * 0.30 meters/foot = 1.52 meters.

- Converting a speed from mph to km/h:

  - Identify the conversion factors: 1 mile = 1.6 kilometers and 1 hour = 1 hour.

  - Set up the conversion expression: Speed (mph) * (1.6 kilometers/mile) * (1 hour/1 hour).

  - Simplify: Speed (mph) * 1.6 kilometers/mile = Speed (km/h).

Example 11: How much of 25% Saline solution needs to be mixed with 3g of 10% saline solution to make a 15% Saline solution?

Solution: **Given Information:**

	Percent	Amount	Total
Mixture 1	0.25	x	0.25x
Mixture 2	0.10	3	0.1 times 3
Net Mixture (Result):	0.15	(x+3)	0.15(x+3)

Equation from the Mixtures:

The equation to solve is based on the principle that the amount of saline in the mixtures should be the same before and after mixing:

$$0.25x + 0.1 \times 3 = 0.15 \times (x + 3)$$

Solve the Equation:

1. **Distribute the 0.15 on the right side:** $0.25x + 0.3 = 0.15x + 0.45$

2. **Subtract 0.15x from both sides:** $0.1x + 0.3 = 0.45$

3. **Subtract 0.3 from both sides:** $0.1x = 0.15$

4. **Divide by 0.1 to solve for** $x = 1.5$

To make a 15% saline solution, 1.5 grams of the 25% saline solution needs to be mixed with 3 grams of the 10% saline solution.

Therefore, the answer is 1.5 grams.

Example 12: An object initially has a kinetic energy (K_1) given by $K_1 = \frac{1}{2}mv^2$, where m is the mass, and v is the velocity. If the mass of the object is halved, and its velocity is doubled, what is the impact on the kinetic energy (K_2)?

Solution:

Given that the mass (m) is halved and the speed (v) is doubled, let's explore the impact on the kinetic energy (K).

Original Kinetic Energy (K₁):

$$K_1 = \frac{1}{2}mv^2$$

Changes in Mass and Speed:

1. **Halving the Mass (*m/2*):**

   - New mass $(m') = \frac{1}{2}m$

2. **Doubling the Speed (*2v*):**

   - New speed $(v') = 2v$

New Kinetic Energy (K₂):

$$K_2 = \frac{1}{2}m'v'^2$$

Substitute the new mass and new speed:

$$K_2 = \frac{1}{2}\left(\frac{1}{2}m\right)(2v)^2$$

Simplify:

$$K_2 = mv^2$$

Impact on Kinetic Energy (K_2 vs. K_1):

To determine the impact, let's compare K_2 to K_1:

$$\text{Impact on Kinetic Energy} = \frac{K_2}{K_1} = \frac{mv^2}{\frac{1}{2}mv^2}$$

Simplify the expression:

Impact on Kinetic Energy= 2

The Kinetic energy (K) doubles when mass is halved and speed is doubled.

Practice Question:

1. A recipe calls for 2 cups of flour to 3 cups of sugar. If you only want to make half the recipe, how many cups of flour do you need?
2. A cafeteria with 40 tables can sit 600 people. Some tables can sit 10 people and some can sit 20 people. What is the ratio of the number of 10-person tables to the number of 20-person tables?
3. The first term in a sequence is m. If every term thereafter is 5 greater than 1/10 of the preceding term, and m≠0, what is the ratio of the second term to the first term?
4. Two cars were traveling 630 miles. Car A traveled an average speed of 70 miles per hour. If car B traveled 90 miles an hour, how many miles had car A traveled when car B arrived at the destination?
5. A particular ball always bounces back to 2/5 of the height of its previous bounce after being dropped. After the first bounce it reaches a height of 175 inches. Approximately how high (in inches) will it reach after its fifth bounce?
6. The flow of water through a certain pipe is 20 cubic meters per minute. How many minutes would it take for 4 of such pipes to fill 2 tanks, if each tank is a cube with a side length of 20 m?
7. Two numbers have a ratio of 5: 2. If they are positive and differ by 21, what is the value of the larger number?
8. The ratio of coins to notes in a bag is 3 to 8. If there are total of 24 coins, then how many notes are there?
9. The volume of water in two containers is in the ratio of 6 to 7. If the volume of first container is 36 liters, find the volume of second container?
10. A bag contains 240 marbles that are either red, blue, or green. The ratio of red to blue to green marbles is 5 : 2 : 1. If one-third of the red marbles and two-thirds of the green marbles are removed, what fraction of the remaining marbles in the bag will be blue?
11. If x varies directly as y, and x = 27 when y =6, find x when y = 2.
12. If y varies inversely as x, and y = 23 when x = 8, find y when x = 4.
13. If z varies directly as x, and z = 30 when x = 8, find z when x = 4.
14. If y varies inversely as x, and y = 14 when x= 8, find y when x = 7.
15. Laura has a mass of 60 kg and is sitting 265 cm from the fulcrum of a seesaw. Bill has a mass of 50 kg. How far from the fulcrum must he be to balance the seesaw? (Hint: The distance from the fulcrum varies inversely as the mass).
16. Tina's mass is 40 kg, and she is sitting 2 m from the fulcrum of a seesaw. Jasmine's mass is 20 kg. How far from the fulcrum must she sit to balance the seesaw?
17. A small company's workforce consists of store employees, store managers, and corporate managers in the ratio 10:3:1. How many employees are either corporate managers or store managers if the company has a total of 126 employees?
18. The volume (V) of a cylinder is given by $V = \frac{4}{3}\pi r^2 h$, where r is the radius and h is the height. If the radius is tripled and the height is doubled, how does this impact the volume?
19. The gravitational force (F) between two masses (m_1 and m_2) separated by a distance (r) is given by $F = \frac{Gm_1 m_2}{r^2}$, where G is the gravitational constant. If both masses are doubled and the distance is halved, how does this impact the gravitational force?

20. The potential energy (U) of an object in a gravitational field is given by $U=mgh$, where m is the mass, g is the acceleration due to gravity, and h is the height. If the mass is halved and the height is doubled, how does this impact the potential energy?
21. The ratio of x to y is 2 to 5, while the ratio of y to z is 2 to 3. What is the ratio of x to z?
22. A solution of pure antifreeze is mixed with water to make a 65% antifreeze solution. How much of each should be used to make 70 L?

	Amount	Part	Final
Antifreeze	a	1	
Water	w	0	
Final	70	0.65	

We use a and w for our variables. Antifreeze is pure, 100% or 1 in our table, written as a decimal. Water has no antifreeze; its percentage is 0. We also fill in the final percent.

23. In a candy shop, chocolate which sells for S4 a pound is mixed with nuts which are sold for S2.50 a pound is mixed to form a chocolate-nut candy which sells for S3.50 a pound. How much of each are used to make 30 pounds of the mixture?

	Amount	Part	Total
Chocolate	c	4	
Nut	n	2.5	
Final	30	3.5	

Using our mixture table, use c and n for variables We do know the final amount (30) and price, include this in the table. (Hint: replace n with (30-c), so you only have 1 variable to resolve)

24. How many grams of pure water must be added to 50 g of pure acid to make a solution that is 40% acid?
25. A lumber company combined oak wood chips that cost S3.10 per pound with pine wood chips that cost S2.50 per pound. How many pounds of each were used to make an 80 lb mixture costing S2.65 per pound?
26. How many ounces of pure water must be added to 50 oz of a 15% saline solution to make a saline solution that is 10% salt?
27. If a pail collects x ounces of dripping water every 15 minutes, how many ounces will it collect in h hours?
28. Convert 3500 meters to kilometers.
29. A rectangular field has dimensions of 40 meters by 60 meters. What is the area of the field in square kilometers?

30. A thermometer reads 30 degrees Celsius. What is the equivalent temperature in Fahrenheit? $\left(F = \frac{9}{5}C + 32\right)$.

31. Convert 3.5 gallons to liters. (1 gallon $\approx$ 3.78541 liters)

32. If the speed of a car is 60 miles per hour, what is its speed in feet per second? (1 mile = 5280 feet)

Answer

1. 1 cups
2. 1:1
3. (11m+50)/10m
4. 490
5. 4.5
6. 200
7. 35
8. 64
9. 42
10. 6/17
11. 9
12. 46
13. 15
14. 16
15. 318 cm
16. 4 m
17. 36
18. 18
19. 16
20. The potential energy is that it remains the same.
21. 4:15
22. 24.5L of water
23. 20 lbs of chocolate and 10 lbs of nuts
24. 75
25. 20, 60
26. 25
27. 4xh
28. 3.5 km
29. 0.0024 square kilometers
30. 86°F
31. 10.57 L
32. 80 ft/s

Lesson 2: Percentages

Understanding Percentages:

- **Definition:** A percentage is a ratio out of 100 that represents a part-to-whole relationship.

- **Notation:** Percent means "parts per hundred" and is denoted by the symbol "%".

- **Converting percentages:**

  - **Percentage to decimal:** Divide the percentage by 100. For example, 50% is equal to $50/100 = 0.5$.

  - **Decimal to percentage:** Multiply the decimal by 100 and add the percent sign. For example, 0.75 is equal to $0.75 * 100 = 75\%$.

- **Calculating percentages:**

  - Finding a percentage: Use the formula: Percentage = (Part / Whole) * 100.

  - Finding a part: Use the formula: Part = (Percentage * Whole) / 100.

  - Finding a whole: Use the formula: Whole = (Part / Percentage) * 100.

Converting Between Percentages, Decimals, and Fractions

Conversion Formulas:

- To convert a percentage to a decimal, divide by 100.

  - Example: Convert 25 % to a decimal.

$$25\% = \frac{25}{100} = 0.25$$

  - Example: Convert 75% to a decimal.

$$75\% = \frac{75}{100} = 0.75$$

  - Remove the percent sign.

- To convert a decimal to a percentage, multiply by 100 and add the "%" symbol.

  - Example: Convert 0.4 to a percentage.
    $0.4 = 0.4 \times 100 = 40\%$
  - Example: Convert 0.6 to a percentage.
  - $0.6 = 0.6 \times 100\% = 60\%$

- To convert a percentage to a fraction, write it over 100 and simplify if possible.

  - Example: Convert 40% to a fraction.
    $$40\% = \frac{40}{100} = \frac{2}{5}$$
  - Example: Convert 33.33% to a fraction.

$$33.33\% \; = \frac{33.33}{100} = \frac{10}{30} = \frac{1}{3}$$

- Fractions to percentages:

- Multiply the numerator and denominator of the fraction by the same number to get a denominator of 100.

  Convert the resulting fraction to a percentage.

- Example: Convert 3/4 to a percentage.

$$\frac{3}{4} \times \frac{100}{100} = \frac{300}{400} = 75\%$$

Percentages are used in many everyday situations, including:

- Calculating discounts and sales tax: You can use percentages to find the amount of a discount or sales tax that needs to be added or subtracted from a price.

- Determining grades in school: Your grades are often calculated as a percentage of the total points possible in a class.

- Measuring interest rates on loans: Interest rates are expressed as a percentage of the principal amount of a loan.

- Analyzing statistics and data: Percentages are used to represent and compare data in many different contexts.

- Comparing prices and quantities: You can use percentages to compare prices of different items or quantities of the same item.

Steps to Calculate Percent Changes:

1. **Find the Difference:**

   - Subtract the initial value from the final value. The result represents the absolute change in quantity.

$$\text{Difference} = \text{Final Value} - \text{Initial Value}$$

2. **Divide by the Initial Value:**

   - Divide the difference obtained in Step 1 by the initial value. This step normalizes the change relative to the initial quantity.

$$\text{Relative Change} = \frac{\text{Difference}}{\text{Initial Value}}$$

3. **Convert to a Percentage:**

   - Multiply the relative change (obtained in Step 2) by 100 to express the result as a percentage.

$$\text{Percent Change} = \text{Relative Change} \times 100$$

Example 1:

Let's say the initial price of a product is $50, and it increases to $65.

1. **Find the Difference:** Difference = $65 − $50 = $15

2. **Divide by the Initial Value:** Relative Change $= \frac{\$15}{\$50} = 0.3$

3. **Convert to a Percentage:** *Percent Change* $= 0.3 \times 100 = 30\%$

    In this example, the percent change is 30%, indicating a 30% increase from the initial value to the final value.

Calculating Net Price with Tax and Discount

Understanding how to calculate tax, discount, and net price is crucial for making informed purchasing decisions. Let's break down the steps involved

Steps to Calculate Net Price:

1. **Find the Discount Amount:**

    - Subtract the discounted price from the original price to determine the absolute discount.

    $$\text{Discount Amount} = \text{Original Price} - \text{Discounted Price}$$

2. **Apply Tax:**

    - Add the tax amount to the discounted price. This step represents the tax as a percentage of the discounted price.

    $$\text{Tax Amount} = \text{Discounted Price} \times \left(\frac{\text{Tax Rate}}{100}\right)$$

3. **Calculate Net Price:**

    - Add the tax amount to the discounted price to obtain the final cost after both discount and tax.

    $$\text{Net Price} = \text{Discounted Price} + \text{Tax Amount}$$

Example 2: Suppose a laptop originally costs $1200, and there's a 10% discount. Additionally, a 7% sales tax is applied to the discounted price.

1. **Find the Discount Amount:** Discount Amount $= \$1200 - (\$1200 \times 0.10) = \$1080$

2. **Apply Tax:** Tax Amount $= \left(\$1080 \times \frac{7}{100}\right) = (\$1080 \times 0.07) = \$75.60$

3. **Calculate Net Price:** Net Price $= \$1080 + \$75.60 = \$1155.60$

In this example, the net price, considering both the 10% discount and 7% tax, is $1155.60.

Example: You're purchasing a product with a listed price of $150. The sales tax rate in your region is 12%. Calculate the following:

1. **Tax Amount:**

   - What is the amount of sales tax you would pay on this purchase?

2. **Net Price:**

   - After accounting for the sales tax, what is the final cost, or net price, you would pay for the product?

1. **Tax Amount:**

   - To calculate the tax amount, use the formula:

   $$\text{Tax Amount} = \text{Price} \times \left(\frac{\text{Tax Rate}}{100}\right)$$

   $$\text{Tax Amount} = \$150 \times \left(\frac{12}{100}\right)$$

   $$\text{Tax Amount} = \$150 \times 0.12$$

   $$\text{Tax Amount} = \$18$$

2. **Net Price:**

   - The net price is obtained by adding the tax amount to the original price:

   $$\text{Net Price} = \text{Price} + \text{Tax Amount}$$

   $$\text{Net Price} = \$150 + \text{Tax Amount}$$

   $$\text{Net Price} = \$150 + \$18$$

   $$\text{Net Price} = \$168$$

Net Price Calculation:

The formula for calculating the net price, considering a discount applied before tax, is:

$$\text{Net Price} = \text{Price} \times \left(1 - \frac{\text{Discount Rate}}{100}\right) \times \left(1 + \frac{\text{Tax Rate}}{100}\right)$$

$$\text{Net Price} = P \times \left(1 - \frac{D}{100}\right) \times \left(1 + \frac{T}{100}\right)$$

Example 3: You are considering purchasing an item with a listed price of $150. The store is offering a discount of 7%, and there is a sales tax of 7%. Calculate the Net price.

Solution:

- Price(P): $150

- Discount Rate(D): 7

- Tax Rate(T): 7

$$\text{Net Price} = P \times \left(1 - \frac{D}{100}\right) \times \left(1 + \frac{T}{100}\right)$$

$$\text{Net Price} = \$150 \times \left(1 - \frac{7}{100}\right) \times \left(1 + \frac{7}{100}\right)$$

$$\text{Net Price} = \$150 \times 0.93 \times 1.07$$

$$\text{Net Price} = \$150 \times 0.9951$$

$$\text{Net Price} \approx \$149.27$$

Practice question:

1. James had 24 pages to write. By the evening, he had completed 25% of his work. How many pages were left?
2. In an orchard, 16 2/3 % of the trees are apple trees. If the number of trees in the orchard is 240, find the number of other type of trees in the orchard.
3. A number is decreased by 10% and then increased by 10%. The number so obtained is 10 less than the original number. What was the original number?
4. If 20% of x = y, what is the value of y% of 20 in terms of x?
5. A person multiplied a number by 3/5 instead of 5/3, What is the percentage error in the calculation?
6. In a cricket tournament, team Red has won 7 games out of 8 games played, while team Blue has won 19 out of 20 games played. Which cricket team has a higher percentage of wins?
7. What is 5/8 as a percentage?
8. A company sells a product for $80, and there is a 20% discount on the original price. In addition, a sales tax of 8% is applied to the discounted price. What is the final cost, including the discount and sales tax?
9. An item originally priced at $120 is on sale with a 15% discount. If a customer also has a coupon for an additional 10% off the sale price, what is the final cost of the item?
10. A store marks up the cost of a product by 25% and then offers a 20% discount. If the original cost of the product is $60, what is the final selling price?
11. A compact disk player costs $269.00. It is on sale for 20% off and there is a 6% sales tax. Find the final price of the CD player.
12. A television costs $375.00. It is on sale for 25% off and there is a 6.5% sales tax. Find the final price of the TV.
13. What number increased by 30% equals 260?
14. Eighteen is 25% less than what number?
15. The Sweater Shack is offering a 20% discount on sweaters. If the regular price of a sweater is $15.00, what is the discount? What is the sale price?
16. There are 30 students in Mrs. Jones' class. Twenty percent of the students received an A on the last math test. How many students received an A?
17. There are 435 representatives in the U.S. House of Representatives. Approximately 12.2% of the representatives are from California. How many representatives from California are there in the U.S. House of Representatives? Round your answer to the nearest whole number.
18. Your family went out to eat. The total bill was $68.50. How much tip should you leave using 15%?
19. The value of a stock increased from $50 to $65 over the past month. Calculate the percentage increase in the stock's value.
20. The Consumer Price Index (CPI) increased from 150 to 165. Calculate the percentage increase in the CPI, indicating the level of inflation.

Answer

1. 18 pages
2. 200 trees
3. 1000
4. 4% *of x*
5. 64 %
6. Blue has a higher percentage of wins with **95 %.**
7. 62.5%
8. $69.12
9. $92.40.
10. $60
11. $228.11.
12. $299.63.
13. 200
14. 24
15. $12.00.
16. 6 students received an A
17. 53
18. $10.28.
19. 30%.
20. CPI increased by 10%

Lesson 3: Two-Variable Data - Models and Scatterplots

Bivariate data involves the analysis of two variables to understand their relationship or correlation. These variables can be either quantitative or categorical.

Quantitative variables:

- Numerical variables that represent a measurable quantity

- Examples: height, weight, time, temperature

Categorical variables:

- Represent groupings/categories rather than numbers

- Examples: gender, blood type, country, job type

Here's an overview of bivariate data and some common data representations used for analysis:

Scatterplots: A scatterplot is a graphical representation of bivariate data, displaying individual data points on a two-dimensional coordinate system. It is a visual tool used to investigate the relationship between two variables, often denoted as X and Y. Each data point on the scatterplot represents a unique observation or pair of values for the two variables.

Key characteristics of scatterplots include:

- **Axis Representation:**

    - The horizontal axis (x-axis) typically represents one variable (independent variable).

    - The vertical axis (y-axis) represents the other variable (dependent variable).

- **Data Points:**

    - Each point on the scatterplot corresponds to a specific combination of values for the two variables.

- **Patterns and Trends:**

    - Scatterplots are used to visually identify patterns, trends, and relationships between the variables. This includes looking for correlations, associations, or clusters of data points.

- **Correlation:**

    - The arrangement of points on the scatterplot can suggest the strength and direction of the relationship between the two variables.

    - **Positive correlation:** As one variable increases, the other tends to increase as well. Points generally move upward from left to right.

    - **Negative correlation:** As one variable increases, the other tends to decrease. Points generally move downward from left to right.

- **No correlation:** There is no discernible pattern between the two variables. Points are scattered with no clear pattern.

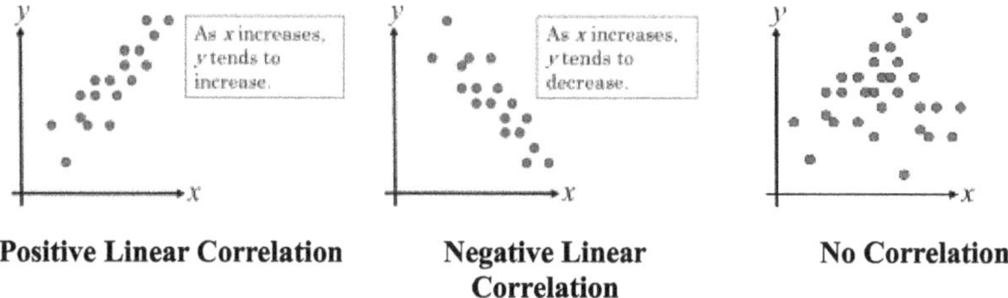

Positive Linear Correlation **Negative Linear Correlation** **No Correlation**

- **Outliers:**

  - Outliers, or data points that significantly deviate from the general pattern, can be easily identified on a scatterplot.

Determine the Line of Best Fit:

- Use statistical methods, such as the method of least squares, to calculate the slope (m) and y-intercept (b) for the line of best fit. The equation of the line is $y = mx + b$, where y is the dependent variable, x is the independent variable, m is the slope, and b is the y-intercept.

Plot the Line on the Scatterplot:

- Once you have the equation of the line, plot it on the scatterplot along with the data points. The line should visually represent the overall trend observed in the data.

Example 1: Linear Fit

Suppose you have a scatterplot of the distance traveled by a car over time. A linear fit might be appropriate for this scenario:

$$Y = mX + b$$

where Y is the distance traveled, X is time, m is the speed of the car, and b is the initial distance. The linear fit helps estimate the speed and initial position of the car.

Example 2: The scatterplot below illustrates the distance traveled by a car over time. A linear fit has been applied with the equation $Y=10X+30$, where Y is the distance traveled, X is time, and the coefficients represent the speed and initial distance. Based on the linear fit, what is the estimated initial distance, in miles, of the car?

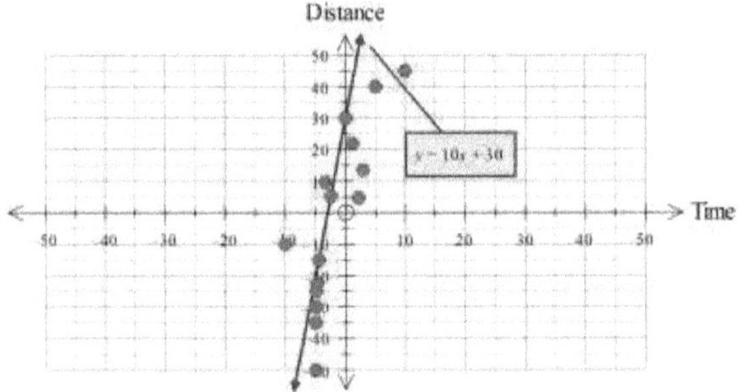

Based on the linear fit equation $Y = 10X + 30$. This indicates that the estimated initial distance of the car is 30 miles.

Example 3: Suppose you have a scatterplot of students' study hours (X) and their exam scores (Y), and you have determined the line of best fit with the equation:

$$Y = 2X + 70$$

Now, you want to make predictions for the exam scores based on specific study hours.

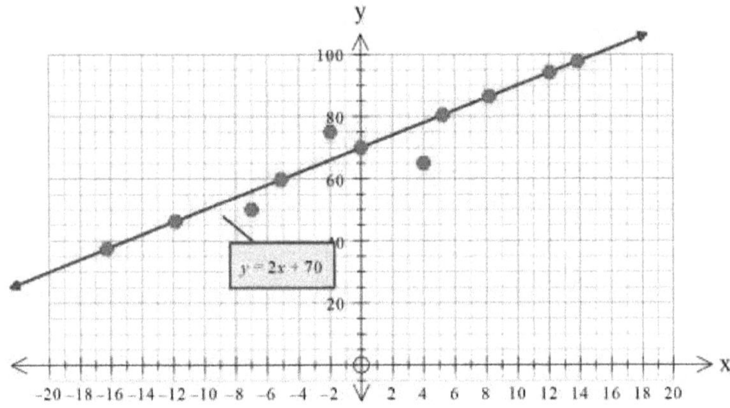

Solution:

Prediction 1: Let's predict the exam score when a student studies for 5 hours (X=5).

$$Y = 2 \times 5 + 70 = 10 + 70 = 80$$

So, the predicted exam score for a student who studies for 5 hours is 80.

Prediction 2: Now, predict the exam score when a student studies for 8 hours (X=8).

$$Y = 2 \times 8 + 70 = 16 + 70 = 86$$

The predicted exam score for a student who studies for 8 hours is 86.

Prediction 3: Let's make a prediction for a value outside the observed range, say when a student studies for 12 hours ($X=12$).

$$Y = 2 \times 12 + 70 = 24 + 70 = 94$$

The predicted exam score for a student who studies for 12 hours is 94.

- **How many scores lie above and below the predicted scores ?**
  Solution:
  Above - 1
  Below - 2

Data Representations:

Line Graph:

A line graph is a type of chart that displays data points connected by straight line segments. It is particularly useful for illustrating trends and changes in data over a continuous interval or time. Line graphs are effective for showing the relationship between two variables and highlighting patterns, fluctuations, or trends in the data.

Example 4: The following table gives information on the favourite colours by the group of people.

Colours	Yellow	Pink	Blue	Green	Orange
No.of people	16	20	30	26	35

Draw the line graph for the information provided.

Solution:

To draw the line graph for the information provided, plot the colours on the x-axis and the number of people on the y-axis.

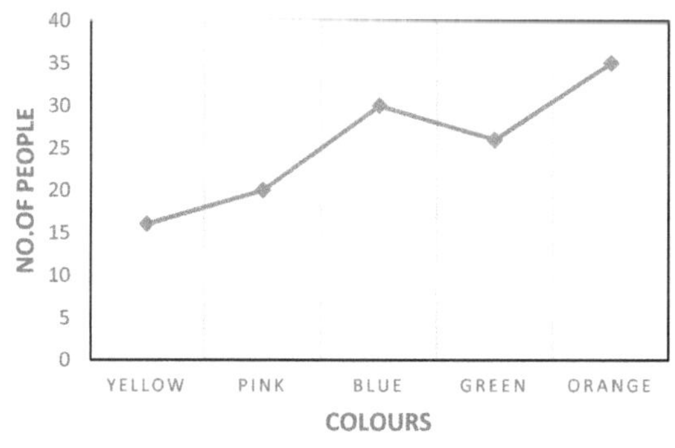

Example 5:

A bookshop made a line graph of the number of books it sold each week during a certain period. Based on the information provided in the above line graph, find how many fewer books were sold in week 8 than in week 7.

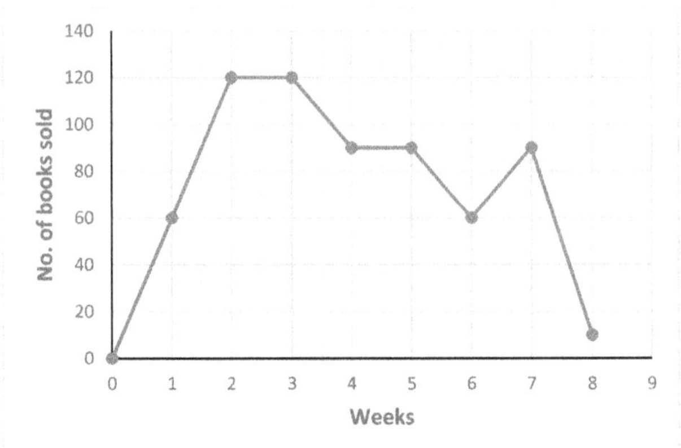

Solution:

Number of books sold in week 7 = 90
Number of books sold in week 8 = 10
So, the difference = 80
Therefore, there were 80 fewer books sold in week 8 as compared to week 7.

Example 6: Read the line graph carefully and answer the following questions:

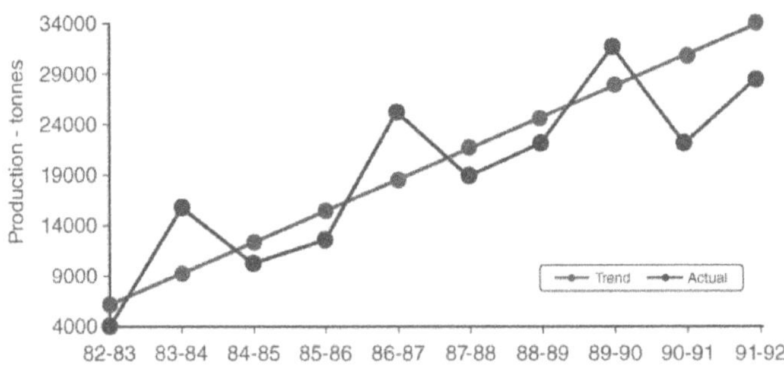

- What was the biggest deviation between the actual and the trend?

- How many times has actual production increased by more than 50% compared to the previous year?

Solution:

- From the given line graph, it is observed that the greatest deviation between the actual and the trend was in the year 90 – 91.

In that case, the actual value was 21000 and the trend value was 30000.

Therefore, the deviation of the actual value from the trend value is:

$$= \left(-\frac{9000}{30000}\right) \times 100 = -30\%.$$

- Actual production increased by more than 50% over the previous year between the years 83-84 and 86-87, as seen in the graph. As a result, the answer is two times.

- **Tables:** Tables are a common way to represent bivariate data, with one variable in the columns and the other in the rows. Some key aspects of using tables include:
  - Organize data into rows and columns
  - Columns and rows should be clearly labeled with the variable names
  - Variables can be ordered in any way, but ordered meaningfully if possible
  - Can include raw data values, summary statistics like means, or frequencies/counts
  - Provides an overall snapshot of the data and distributions

Example 7: Using the below table, what is the average rate of change of weight with respect to height?

Height (cm)	Weight (kg)
180	73
165	58
170	62
178	69

- **Change in Height:**
  - Subtract the initial height from the final height: 180−165=15 cm

- **Change in Weight:**
  - Subtract the initial weight from the final weight: 73−58=15 kg

- **Average Rate of Change:** Use the formula

$$\textbf{Average Rate of Change} = \frac{\text{Change in Weight}}{\text{Change in Height}} = \frac{15}{15} = 1\text{kg/cm}$$

This indicates that, on average, for every 1 cm increase in height, there is a 1 kg increase in weight based on the data provided in the table.

Two-Way Tables

A two-way table, also known as a contingency table, is a tabular representation of data that categorizes information based on two variables. It allows you to analyze the relationship between two categorical variables and understand how the frequency or count of observations is distributed across different categories. Here's an overview of two-way tables:

Structure of a Two-Way Table:

A typical two-way table is organized with rows and columns, representing the categories of two different variables. Each cell in the table contains the frequency or count of observations falling into a specific combination of categories.

	Category A	Category B	Category C	Total
Group 1	25	15	10	50
Group 2	30	20	25	75
Total	55	35	35	125

In this example, "Group" and "Category" are the two variables, and the numbers in the cells represent the counts of observations falling into each combination.

When analyzing a two-way table, pay attention to the following:

- The **titles of the column(s)**

- The **titles of the row(s)**

- Rows or columns that specify **total values**

Example 8:

Suppose you have a two-way table representing the distribution of students based on their gender (Male or Female) and their preference for a subject (Math, Science, or English). How many female students prefer Math?

	Math	Science	English	Total
Male	25	15	10	50
Female	30	20	25	75
Total	55	35	35	125

Solution:

The number of female students who prefer Math is 30.

Two-way tables are a valuable tool for organizing and interpreting categorical data, making it easier to identify patterns and relationships between variables.

- **Bar Graph:** A bar graph is a common way to visually represent categorical data. It consists of rectangular bars or columns, where the length of each bar corresponds to the frequency or proportion of data within a specific category. Bar graphs are effective for comparing different categories or displaying the distribution of data.

Example 9: In a firm of 406 employees, the percentage of monthly salary saved by each employee is given in the following table. Represent it through a bar graph.

Savings (in percentage)	Number of Employees(Frequency)
20	105
30	199
40	29
50	73
Total	406

Solution:

The given data can be represented as (**Vertical Bar Graphs**)

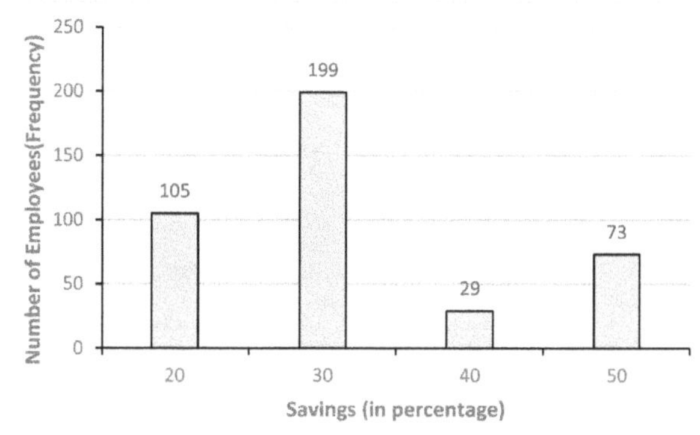

This can also be represented using a horizontal bar graph as follows:

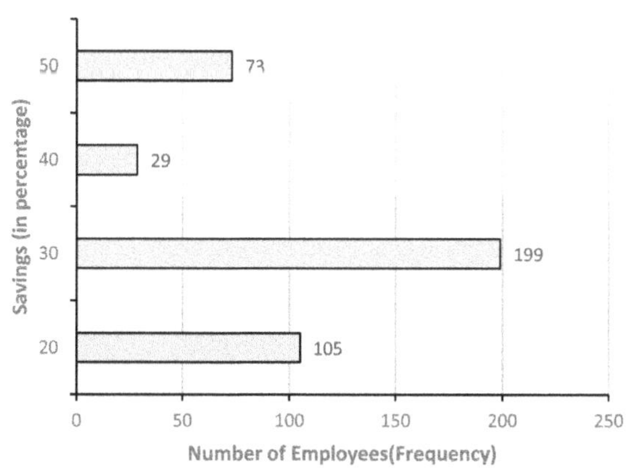

Example 10:

Suppose we have a Vertical Bar Graphs representing the number of years employees have been with a company and their corresponding savings:

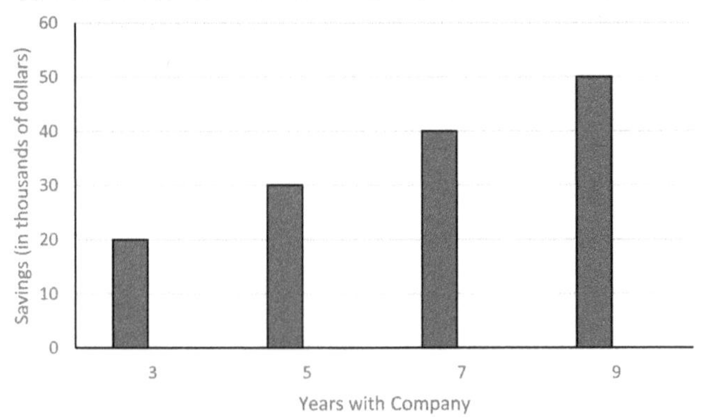

Using the above Bar Graphs, if an employee stays with the company for an additional 2 years, what is the predicted change in savings based on the average rate of change calculated from the provided data?

Solution:

1. **Average Rate of Change:**

   - Calculate the average rate of change in savings per year.

   - $Average\ Rate\ of\ Change\ = \dfrac{Change\ in\ Savings}{Change\ in\ Years}$

   - For the given data:

     - Change in Savings $= 50 - 20 = 30\ thousand\ dollars$

     - Change in Years $= 9 - 3 = 6\ years$

   - Average Rate of Change $= \dfrac{30}{6} = 5$ thousand dollars per year.

2. **Predicted Change in Savings:**

   - Given that an employee stays with the company for an additional 2 years, the predicted change in savings is calculated by multiplying the average rate of change by the additional years.

   - Predicted Change in Savings $= 5 \times 2 = 10$ thousand dollars. For additional 2 years i.e. 11 years stay in company, predicted savings will be $60,000

Example 11: A cosmetic company manufactures 4 different shades of lipstick. The sale for 6 months is shown in the table. Represent it using bar charts.

Month	Sales (in units)			
	Shade 1	Shade 2	Shade 3	Shade 4
January	4500	1600	4400	3245
February	2870	5645	5675	6754
March	3985	8900	9768	7786
April	6855	8976	9008	8965
May	3200	5678	5643	7865
June	3456	4555	2233	6547

Solution:

The graph given below depicts the following data

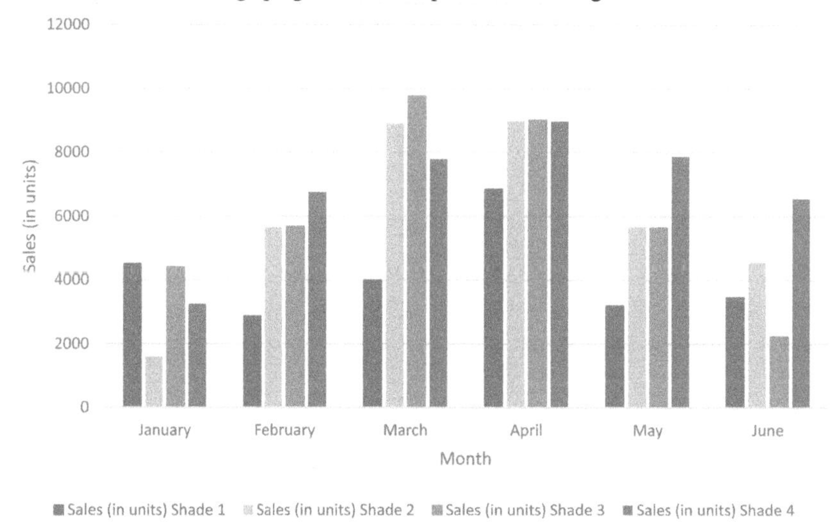

- **In which month did Shade 3 have the maximum sales ?**

  Solution: The maximum sales for Shade 3 occurred in the month of **March**, with 9768 units sold.

- **In which month did Shade 4 have the maximum increase in sales ?**
  Solution: calculate the monthly increases in sales for Shade 4:

  January to February: $6754 - 3245 = 3509$ units

  February to March: $7786 - 6754 = 1032$ units

  March to April: $8965 - 7786 = 1179$ units

  April to May: $7865 - 8965 = -1100$ units (decrease)

  May to June: $6547 - 7865 = -1318$ units (decrease)

The maximum increase occurred from **January to February** with an increase of 3509 units.

- Therefore, the answer is **February.**

Example 12: The variation of temperature in a region during a year is given as follows. Depict it through the graph (bar).

Month	Temperature
January	-6°C
February	-3.5°C
March	-2.7°C
April	4°C
May	6°C
June	12°C
July	15°C
August	8°C
September	7.9°C
October	6.4°C
November	3.1°C
December	-2.5°C<

Solution: As the temperature in the given table has negative values, it is more convenient to represent such data through a horizontal bar graph.

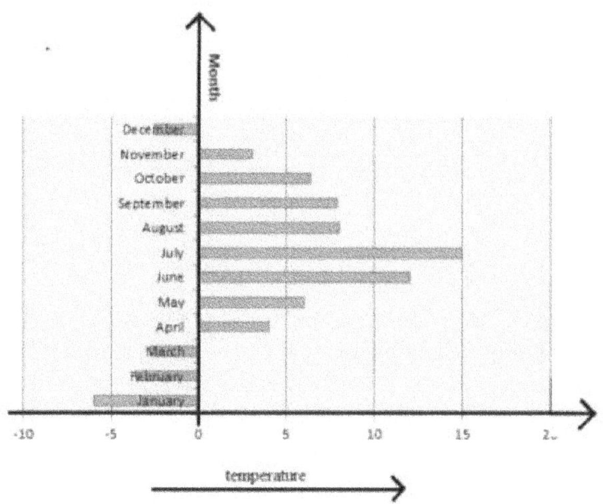

- **How many months did the temperature drop below zero ?**
  Solution:
  The months with temperatures below zero are January, February, March, and December. Therefore, there are **4 months** in which the temperature dropped below zero.
- **Which month experienced the maximum rate of change ?**
  Solution:
  To calculate the rate of change for each month, we can use the formula:

$$Rate\ of\ Change = \frac{Change\ in\ Temperature}{Original\ Temperature} \times 100\%$$

- **January to February:** Rate of Change $= \frac{-3.5-(-6)}{-6} \times 100\% \approx 41.67\%$

- **February to March:** Rate of Change $= \frac{-2.7--3.5}{-3.5} \times 100\% \approx 22.86\%$

- **March to April:** Rate of Change $= \frac{4--2.7}{-2.7} \times 100\% \approx 248.15\%$

- **April to May:** Rate of Change $= \frac{6-4}{4} \times 100\% = 50\%$

- **May to June:** Rate of Change $= \frac{12-6}{6} \times 100\% = 100\%$

- **June to July:** Rate of Change $= \frac{15-12}{12} \times 100\% \approx 25\%$

- **July to August:** Rate of Change $= \frac{8-15}{15} \times 100\% \approx -46.67\%$

- **August to September:** Rate of Change $= \frac{7.9-8}{8} \times 100\% \approx -1.25\%$

- **September to October:** Rate of Change $= \frac{6.4-7.9}{7.9} \times 100\% \approx -18.99\%$

- **October to November:** Rate of Change $= \frac{3.1-6.4}{6.4} \times 100\% \approx -51.56\%$

- **November to December:** Rate of Change $= \frac{-2.5-3.1}{3.1} \times 100\% \approx -180.65\%$

These are the calculated rates of change for each month based on the temperature data. Negative values indicate a decrease in temperature, and positive values indicate an increase.

So correct answer is **April**

Histogram: A histogram is a graphical representation of the distribution of a dataset. It provides a visual summary of the frequency or probability distribution of a set of continuous or discrete data. Histograms are commonly used to understand the underlying shape of a dataset, identify patterns, and observe the central tendency. Let's create an example histogram:

Example 13: The below histogram shows the weekly wages of workers at a construction site:

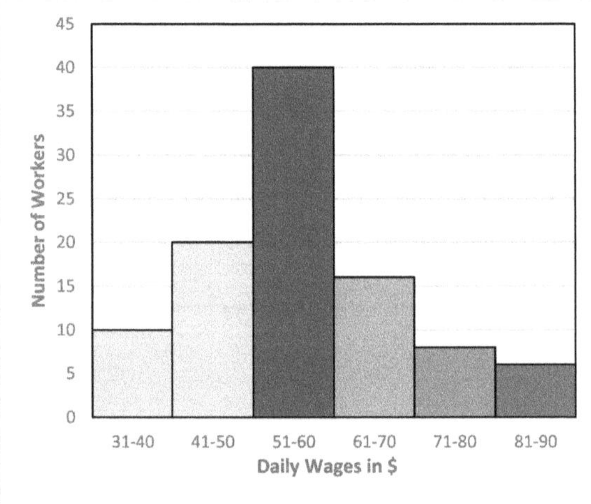

Answer the following questions:

- How many workers get wages of $61-70?
- Construct a frequency distribution table.
- How many workers get daily wages not exceeding $70 ?

Solution:

- 16 workers
- frequency distribution table

Daily Wages in $	Number of Workers
31-40	10
41-50	20
51-60	40
61-70	16
71-80	8
81-90	6

- The sum the number of workers in the categories with wages up to $70:

$$10 + 20 + 40 + 16 = 86$$

Therefore, 86 workers get daily wages not exceeding $70.

Example 14: The time taken (in seconds) by 25 students to solve a problem was:

17, 20, 24, 26, 27, 30, 38, 34, 40, 35, 47, 41, 44, 49, 45, 48, 44, 54, 50, 60, 58, 58, 63, 55, 20.

Solution:bLet us make a grouped frequency table for the given data:

Time Taken (in seconds)	Number of Students
10-19	1
20-29	5
30-39	4
40-49	8
50-59	5
60-69	2

The histogram can be plotted as

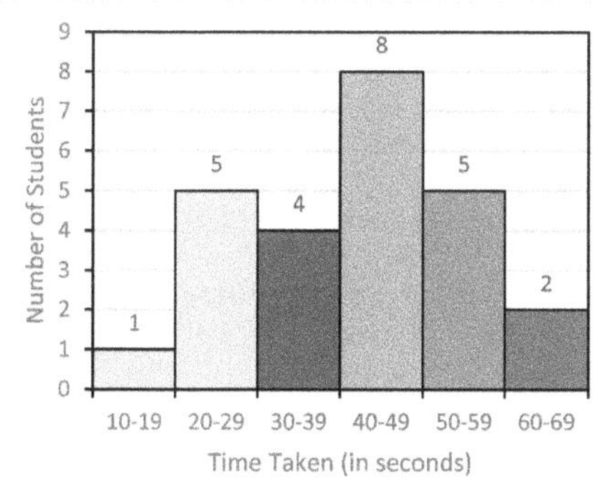

:

Practice Questions

1. Sally spent 5 hours studying for an exam. Based on the line of best fit in the scatterplot below, approximate what exam score would you predict for Sally?

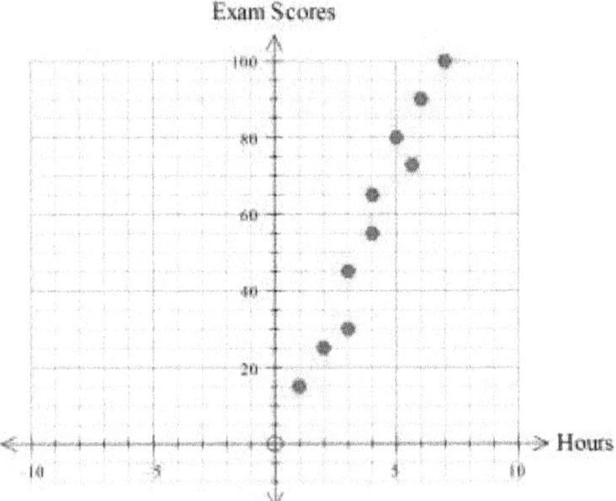

2. The scatterplot shows the average price per square foot of a house in the United States each year for several years. A line of best fit for the data is also shown.

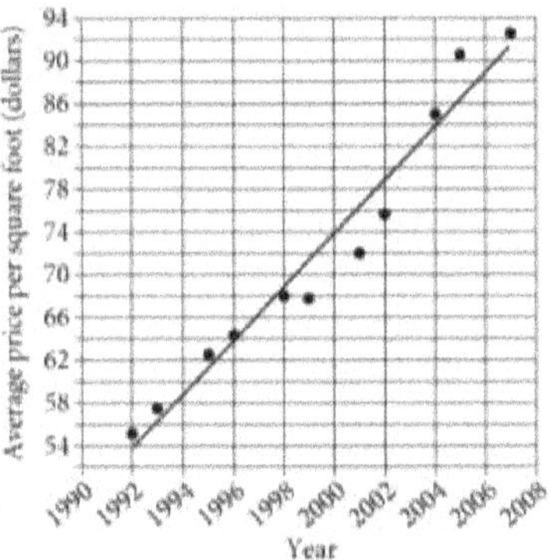

The Line of best fit predicted that the average price per square foot in 2001 would be $76. What is the difference between the predicted value and the actual average price per square foot in 2001?

3. The scatterplot shows 10 values from a data set. Which of the following equations is the most appropriate linear model for the data shown?

(a) $Y = 9 + \left(\frac{3}{10}\right) x$

(b) $Y = 9 - \left(\frac{3}{10}\right) x$

(c) $Y = \left(\frac{6}{5}\right) x$

(d) $Y = \left(\frac{3}{8}\right) x$

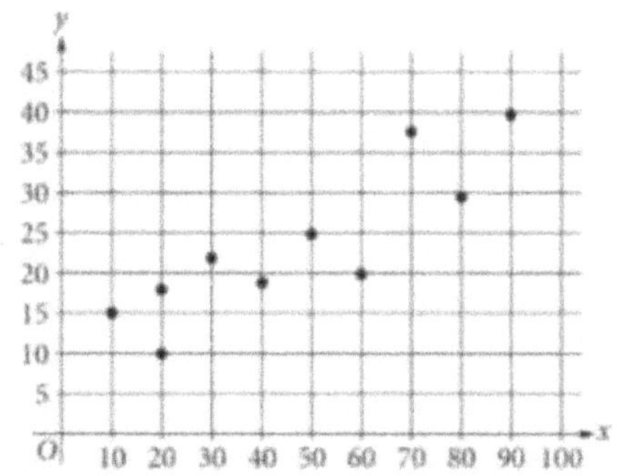

4. had visited a zoo recently and had collected the following data. How can Laurell use a scatter plot to represent this data?

5. The meteorological department has collected the following data about the temperature and humidity in their town. Refer to the table given below to find the approximate humidity at a temperature of 60 degrees Fahrenheit.

Temperature (Degree Fahrenheit)	Humidity(%)
45	60
62	48
77	40
97	30
118	20
122	18

6. The following table shows the number of apple trees planted by the gardener of a school in different years. Draw the bar graph to represent the data.

Years	Number of Apple Trees
2005	150
2006	220
2007	350
2008	150
2009	300
2010	380

7. Observe the given horizontal bar graph which shows the baking of cakes in a bakery from Monday to Saturday. Find out the day on which the maximum number of cakes were baked. Also, find the number of cakes baked on that day.

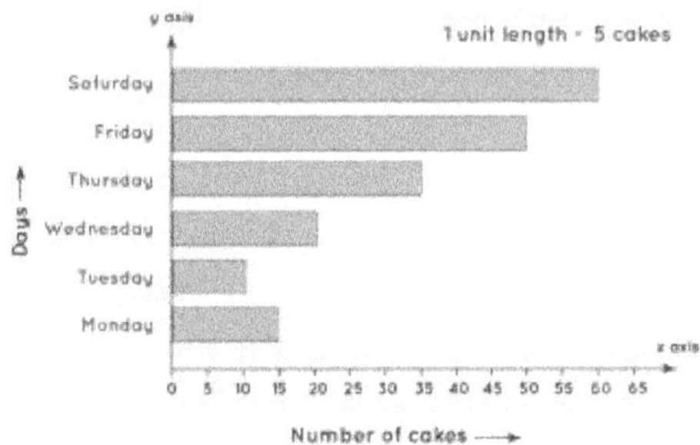

8. The table below displays the number of bicycles produced at a factory from 1998 to 2002.

Year	No. of Bicycles Manufactured
1998	800
1999	600
2000	900
2001	1100
2002	1200

(a) Create a bar graph to represent this information. Select your preferred scale.

(b) Which year had the greatest number of bicycles produced?

(c) Which year had the least number of bicycles produced?

9. The bar graph below depicts the number of students in various classes at a school.

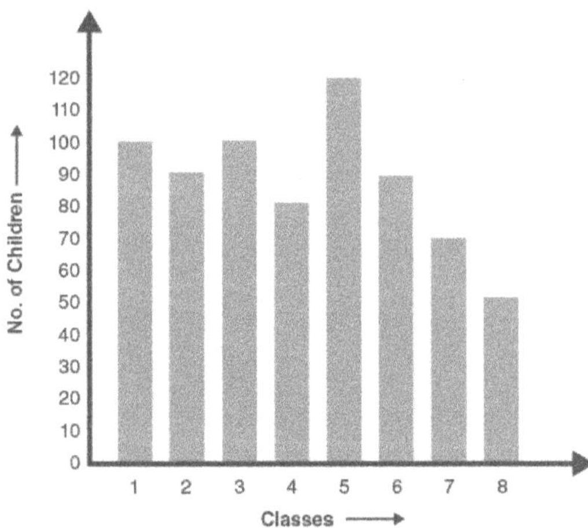

Answer the below questions using the bar graph provided.

(a) The total number of students in each class.

(b) The overall number of students from grades 6 to 8.

(c) The overall number of students from grades 1 to 8.

(d) The number of students in a class on average.

10. Given below is the frequency distribution of the heights of 50 students in a class:

Class Interval	140-145	145-150	150-155	155-160	160-165
Frequency	8	12	18	10	5

Draw a histogram representing the above data.

11. The following histogram shows the number of literate females in the age group of 10 to 40 years in a town:

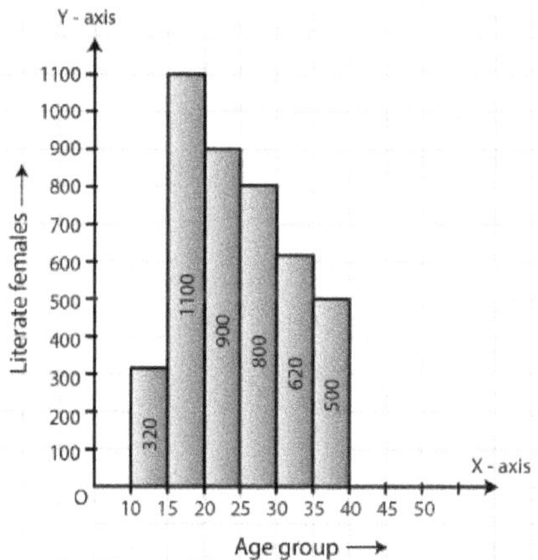

(a) Write the age group in which the number of literate females is the highest.
(b) What is the class width?
(c) What is the lowest frequency?
(d) In which age group are literate females the least?

12. The weekly wages (in $) of 30 workers in a factory are given below:

830, 835, 890, 810, 835, 836, 869, 845, 898, 890, 820, 860, 832, 833, 855, 845, 804, 808, 812, 840, 885, 835, 835, 836, 878, 840, 868, 890, 806, 840

Mark a frequency table with intervals as 800-810, 810-820 and so on, using tally marks.

Also, draw a histogram and answer the following questions:
(a) Which group has the maximum number of workers?
(b) How many workers earn $ 850 and more?
(c) How many workers earn less than $ 850?

13. The below graph shows the annual profit percentage earned by the company during the years 1995 to 2000. what is the average profit earned during the years 1995 to 2000?

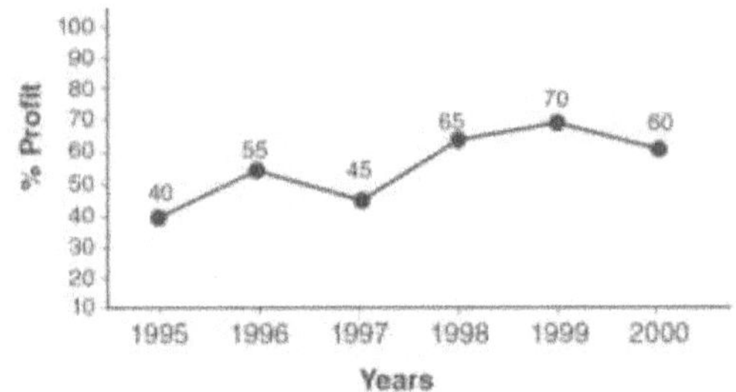

14. The table below shows the number of books sold by a bookstore over a period of five months.

Month	Books Sold
January	120
February	85
March	150
April	110
May	130

What is the average number of books sold per month during this five-month period?

15. The following line graph shows the number of visitors to a national park over a six-month period. During which month did the park have approximately 25,000 visitors?

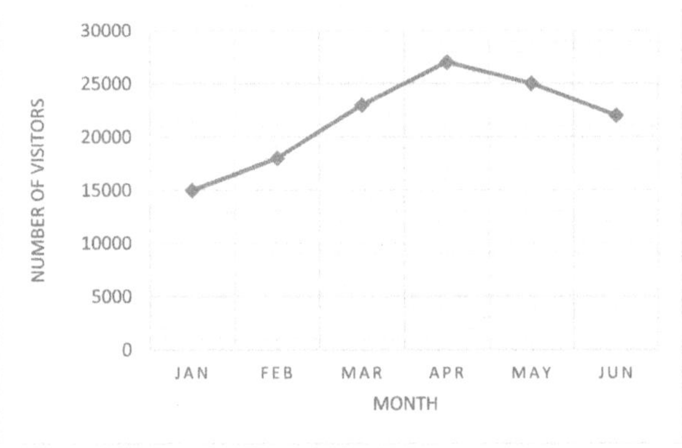

16. The bar graph below displays the favorite colors of 50 students. How many more students chose blue as their favorite color than red?

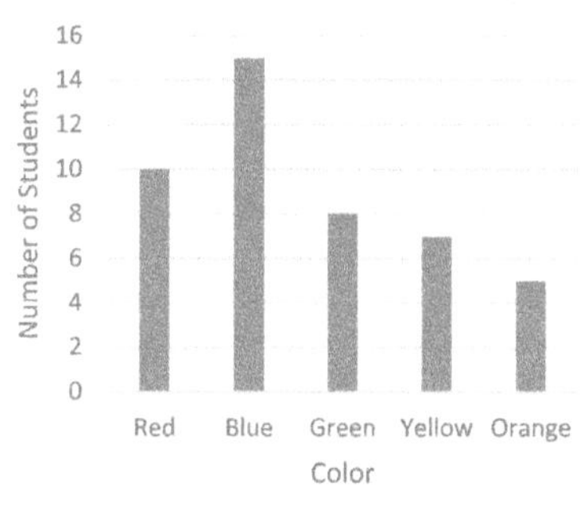

17. The following table represents the number of hours spent by a group of students on various activities in a week.

Activity	Hours Spent
Studying	10
Sleeping	56
Socializing	12
Exercising	8
Working	14

What percentage of the total time spent in a week is allocated to sleeping?

18. The data below shows heart rate and blood pressure measurements for 10 patients. Which graph should illustrate the relationship between these two variables?

Patient	Heart Rate	Blood Pressure
1	68	120
2	72	118
3	70	125
4	78	130
5	75	135
6	62	110
7	80	140
8	65	115
9	71	122
10	60	100

19. The table below shows points scored per game by 5 basketball players. Which graph should be used to compare their scoring averages?

Player	Points per game
Anna	12
Becca	8
Carlos	10
Diego	15
Emma	20

20. Thomas took his body temperature every day for the past 7days. The results are shown in the graph. What was Thomas's body temperature on day 4?

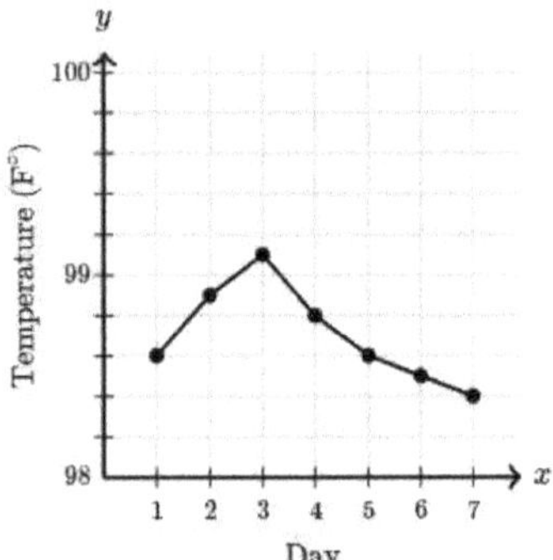

Answer

1. 80
2. $4
3. a
4.

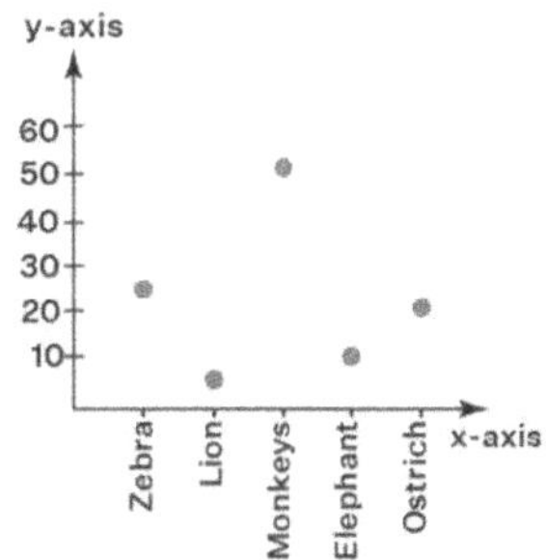

5. The humidity at a temperature of 60 degrees Fahrenheit is 50%.
6.

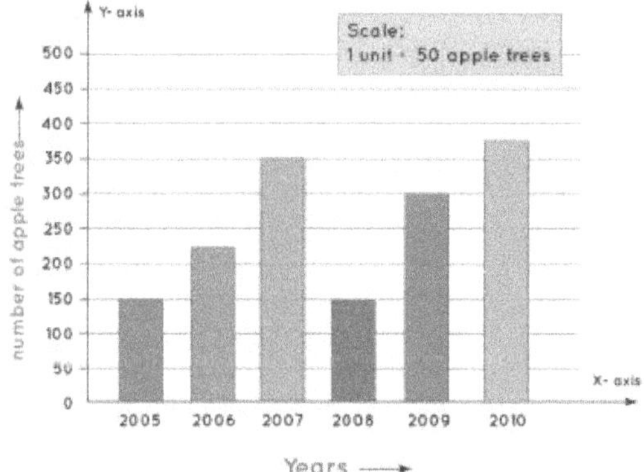

7. Saturday; 60 cakes
8. (a)

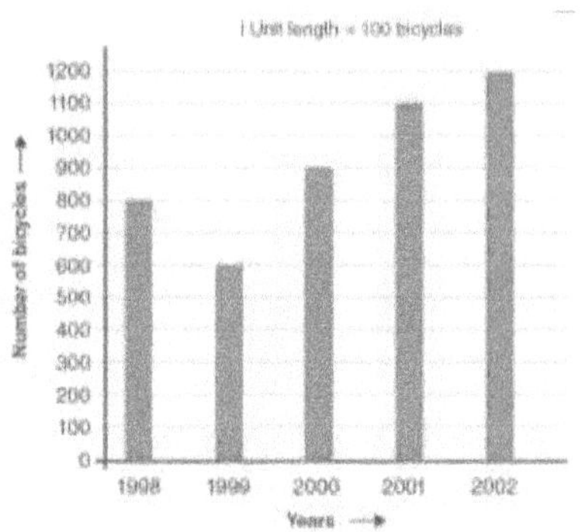

(b) The year 2002 is depicted by the bar with the highest height. As a result, the highest number of bikes, i.e., 1200, was sold in 2002.

(c) The year 1999 is illustrated by the bar with the shortest height. As a result, in 1999, a minimum of 600 cycles were sold.

9. (a) In Class 1, there are 100 students.

   In Class 2, there are 90 students.

   In Class 3, there are 100 students.

   In Class 4, there are 80 students.

   In Class 5, there are 120 students.

   In Class 6, there are 90 students.

   In Class 7, there are 70 students.

   In Class 8, there are 50 students.

   (b) 210
   (c) 700 students
   (d) 87.5

10.

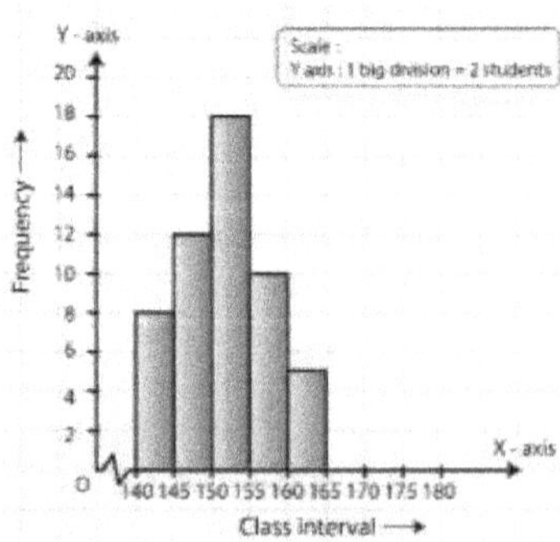

11. (a) 15–20 years.
(b) The class intervals are 10–15, 15–20, 20–25, 30–35 and 35–40. Hence, the class width is 5.
(c) 320.
(d) 10–15 years.

12.

Wages (in $)	No. of workers
800-810	3
810-820	2
820-830	1
830-840	9
840-850	5
850-860	1
860-870	3
870-880	1
880-890	1
890-900	4
Total	30

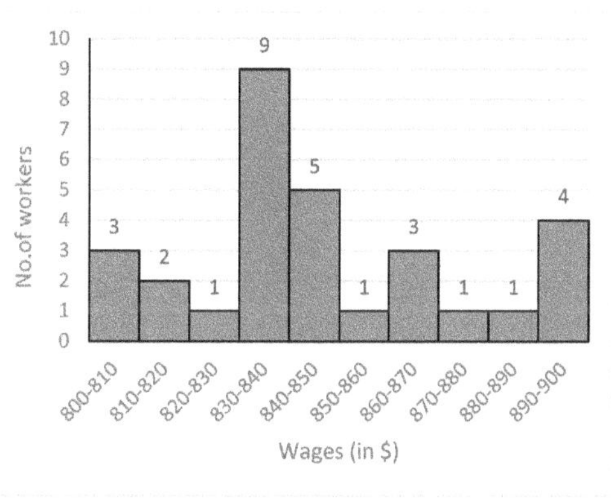

(a) Maximum workers are in the wage group 830-840.
(b) Number of workers getting $ 850 and more are 1+3+1+14=10.
(c) Number of workers getting less than $850 are 3+2+1+9+5=20
13. 335 / 6 years = 55.83333
14. 120
15. May
16. 5 more students chose blue as their favorite color than red.
17. 56%
18. Scatterplot
19. Bar graph
20. 98.8 F°

Lesson 4: Probability and Conditional Probability

Probability: Probability is a measure that quantifies the likelihood of an event occurring. It is expressed as a number between 0 and 1, where 0 indicates impossibility, 1 indicates certainty, and values between 0 and 1 represent degrees of likelihood.

The probability of an event can be calculated using the following formula:

$$P(A) = \frac{\text{Total Number of Possible Outcomes}}{\text{Number of Favorable Outcomes}}$$

In this formula:

- $P(A)$ is the probability of event A.

- The "Number of Favorable Outcomes" is the number of outcomes that make the event A happen.

- The "Total Number of Possible Outcomes" is the total number of different outcomes that could occur.

Probability of Single Events

Sample Space (S):

- The set of all possible outcomes of a random experiment or process.

- Denoted as S, the sample space includes every possible result of an experiment.

Event (E):

- A subset of the sample space, representing a specific outcome or a collection of outcomes.

- Denoted as E, an event can be a single point in the sample space or a combination of points.

Simple Event:

- An event that consists of a single outcome in the sample space.

- For example, rolling a die and getting a 3.

Compound Event:

- An event that consists of more than one outcome.

- For example, rolling a die and getting an even number (2, 4, or 6).

Mutually Exclusive (Disjoint) Events:

- Two events that cannot occur simultaneously, meaning they have no outcomes in common.

- If events A and B are mutually exclusive, $A \cap B = \emptyset$.

Independent Events:

- Two events, A and B, are independent if the occurrence of one does not affect the occurrence of the other.

- For independent events, $P(A \cap B) = P(A) \times P(B)$

Conditional Event:

- An event whose probability depends on or is conditioned on another event occurring. Denoted $P(A \mid B)$.

Dependent Events:

- Two events, A and B, are dependent if the occurrence of one affects the occurrence of the other.

- For dependent events, $P(A \cap B) = P(A) \times P(B \mid A)$.

Complementary Event (A'):

- The complement of event A, denoted as A', includes all outcomes not in A.

- $P(A') = 1 - P(A)$.

Impossible Event:

- An event with no outcomes in the sample space.

- P(impossible event) = 0.

Certain Event:

- An event that includes all outcomes in the sample space.

- P(certain event) = 1.

Probability rules and axioms

Probability of an Event $(0 \leq P(A) \leq 1)$:

- The probability of any event A is a number between 0 and 1, inclusive.

Example: If you roll a fair six-sided die, the probability of getting a 3 (event A) is $P(A) = \frac{1}{6}$

Complement Rule $P(A') = 1 - P(A)$:

- The probability of the complement of an event A is 1 minus the probability of A.

Example 1: If the probability of rain tomorrow (event A) is $P(A) = 0.3$.

Then the probability of no rain $P(A') = 1 - 0.3 = 0.7$

Examples 2:

1. **Coin Toss:**

   - P(Heads) = 0.5: This means there are two equally likely outcomes (heads or tails), and each has a 0.5 probability of occurring.

2. **Dice Roll:**

- $P(6) = \frac{1}{6}$: In a fair six-sided die, there is one favorable outcome (rolling a 6) out of six possible outcomes.

- $P(Odd) = \frac{1}{2}$: Half of the outcomes (1, 3, 5) are odd,

  so the probability of rolling an odd number is $\frac{3}{6} = \frac{1}{2}$

3. **Deck of Cards:**

- $P(Ace) = \frac{4}{52} = \frac{1}{13}$ There are four Aces in a standard deck of 52 cards, so the probability of drawing an Ace is 1 in 13.

- $P(Red) = \frac{26}{52} = \frac{1}{2}$: Half of the cards in a deck are red, so the probability of drawing a red card is 1 in 2.

4. **Spinner:**

- $P(Blue) = \frac{1}{4}$: If there are four colors on the spinner and each is equally likely, the probability of landing on blue is 1 in 4.

- $P(Number > 2) = \frac{2}{4} = \frac{1}{2}$: If there are two numbers greater than 2 on the spinner, the probability of landing on a number greater than 2 is 1 in 2.

5. **Weather Forecast:**

- $P(Rain) = 0.3$: There is a 30% chance of rain tomorrow.

- $P(Sunny) = 0.7$: There is a 70% chance of a sunny day.

6. **Card Game:**

- $P(King\ or\ Queen) = \frac{8}{52} = \frac{2}{13}$: There are four Kings and four Queens in a deck, so the probability of drawing a King or Queen is 2 in 13.

- $P(Spade) = \frac{13}{52} = \frac{1}{4}$: There are 13 spades in a deck, so the probability of drawing a spade is 1 in 4.

Relative Frequency: Relative frequency is an empirical measure that describes the proportion of times an event occurs in a series of trials or observations. It is often expressed as a fraction or a percentage. The relative frequency of an event A is calculated as the ratio of the number of times A occurs to the total number of trials or observations.

$$\text{Relative Frequency of A} = \frac{\text{Total Number of Trials or Observations}}{\text{Number of Times A Occurs}}$$

Note: Relative frequency is also commonly referred to as experimental probability, particularly when calculated based on observed outcomes in an experiment or real-world scenario.

Conditional Probability

Conditional probability is the probability of an event occurring given that another event has already occurred.

Key Aspects of Conditional Events:

- **Notation:**

    - $P(B \mid A)$ denotes the probability of event B given that event A has occurred.

- **Interpretation:**

    - The probability of event B is assessed in the context where event A is known or has already occurred.

- **Formula:**

    - The formula for conditional probability is given by $P(B \mid A) = \frac{P(A \cap B)}{P(A)}$

Example 3: A bag contains 4 red marbles, 3 green marbles, and 5 blue marbles. If a marble is randomly drawn from the bag, find:

a) The probability that the selected marble is red.

b) The probability that the selected marble is not green.

c) The relative frequency of selecting a blue marble if 20 marbles are drawn with replacement.

Solutions:

a) Probability of red marble:

- Number of favorable outcomes: 4 red marbles

- Total possible outcomes: $4 + 3 + 5 = 12$ marbles

- $P(red) = \frac{4}{12} = \frac{1}{3}$

b) Probability of not green:

- Number of not green outcomes: 4 reds + 5 blues = 9

- Total possible outcomes: 12

- $P(not\ green) = \frac{9}{12} = \frac{3}{4}$

c) Relative frequency of blue marble:

- Let's assume 15 blue marbles were selected out of 20 draws

- $Relative\ frequency = \frac{Number\ of\ times\ event\ occurred}{Total\ trials} = \frac{15}{20} = \frac{3}{4} = 75\%$

Example 4 : In a bag, there are 5 red balls and 3 green balls. If one ball is randomly selected without replacement, what is the probability that the first ball chosen is red and the second ball chosen is also red?

Solution:

The probability of the first ball being red is 5/8 (5 red balls out of 8 total balls). If the first ball is red, there are now 7 balls left, with 4 being red. So, the probability of the second ball being red is 4/7.

The probability of both events happening is the product of their individual probabilities:

P(First red and Second red) = P(First red) × P(Second red)

$$= \frac{5}{8} \times \frac{4}{7}$$

$$= \frac{20}{56}$$

Simplifying, we get:

$$= \frac{5}{14}$$

Two-way frequency tables are commonly used to organize data in situations where there are two categorical variables. These tables help calculate probabilities and relative frequencies of various events based on the given data.

Let's consider a simple example with a two-way frequency table:

Suppose we are studying the relationship between gender and whether or not students participate in a school club. The data is organized in a two-way frequency table:

	Club Member	Not a Club Member	Total
Male	20	15	35
Female	25	40	65
Total	45	55	100

In this table:

- The rows represent the gender (Male or Female).

- The columns represent the club participation (Club Member or Not a Club Member).

- The numbers in the cells represent the frequencies (counts) of individuals falling into each category.

Now, let's use this table to calculate probabilities and relative frequencies:

1. **Probability of being a Club Member given that the person is Male:**

$$P(\text{Club Member} \mid \text{Male}) = \frac{\text{Number of Club Members who are Male}}{\text{Total Number of Males}} = \frac{20}{35}$$

2. **Relative Frequency of being a Club Member given that the person is Female:**

Relative Frequency of Club Member | Female =

$$\frac{\text{Number of Club Members who are Female}}{\text{Total Number of}} = \frac{25}{65}$$

3. **Probability of being Not a Club Member:**

4. $P(\text{Not a Club Member}) = \dfrac{\text{Number of Not Club Members}}{\text{Total Number of Individuals}} = \dfrac{55}{100}$

5. **Joint Probability of being Female and a Club Member:**

$$P(\text{Female and Club Member}) = \frac{\text{Number of Females who are Club Members}}{\text{Total Number of Individuals}} = \frac{25}{100}$$

Example 5: A bag contains 3 red, 5 blue, and 2 green marbles. A marble is randomly drawn and its color recorded, then replaced in the bag. This is done 15 times. The results are shown in the frequency table:

	Red	Blue	Green	Total
Draw 1	1	3	1	5
Draw 2	0	2	3	5
Draw 3	1	2	2	5
Total	2	7	6	15

Based on the table, calculate:

a) The theoretical probability of drawing a blue marble

b) The relative frequency of drawing a red marble

c) The probability of drawing a green marble on the 3rd draw

Solutions:

a) $P(blue) = \dfrac{7}{15}$

b) Relative frequency of red $= \dfrac{\text{Number of red drawn}}{\text{Total draws}} = \dfrac{2}{15}$

c) P(green on 3rd draw) $= \dfrac{2}{5} = 0.4$

Example 6:

Consider two events:

- Event A: Drawing an ace from a deck of cards.

- Event B: Drawing a king from the remaining cards after drawing an ace.

$P(A)$ is the probability of drawing an ace, and $P(B|A)$ is the probability of drawing a king given that an ace has already been drawn.

- $P(A) == \frac{4}{52} = \frac{1}{13}$ (there are 4 aces in a deck of 52 cards).

- $P(B \mid A) = \frac{4}{51}$ (since there are 51 cards remaining after drawing an ace).

Example based on conditional probability using a two-way frequency table:

Example 7: A company conducted a survey to analyze the preferences of its employees regarding two training programs: Program A and Program B. The data collected is organized into the following two-way frequency table:

	Program A	**Program B**	**Total**
Department X	40	10	50
Department Y	30	20	50
Total	70	30	100

Conditional Probability:

(a) What is the probability that an employee selected at random is from Department X?
(b) Given that an employee is from Department Y, what is the probability that they prefer Program A?
(c) Calculate the conditional probability that an employee prefers Program B given that they are from Department X.

Solution:

(a) Probability that an employee selected at random is from Department X:
$$P(\text{Department X}) = \frac{\text{Total in Department X}}{\text{Grand Total}} = \frac{50}{100} = 0.5$$

(b) Given that an employee is from Department Y, probability that they prefer Program A: $P(\text{Program A} \mid \text{Department Y})$
$$= \frac{\text{Number of employees from Department Y who prefer Program A}}{\text{Total in Department Y}} = \frac{30}{50} = 0.6$$

(c) Conditional probability that an employee prefers Program B given that they are from Department X:
$P(\text{Program B} \mid \text{Department X})$
$$= \frac{\text{Number of employees from Department X who prefer Program B}}{\text{Total in Department X}} = \frac{10}{50} = 0.2$$

Example 8: The incomplete table below shows the distribution of age and gender for 32 people who entered a tennis tournament.

	Under 30	**30 or older**	**Total**
Male	3		12
Female			20
Total	8	24	32

(a) If a tennis player is chosen at random, what is the probability that the player will be either a male under age 30 or a female aged 30 or older?

Solution: Complete the Table:

	Under 30	30 or older	Total
Male	3	9	12
Female	5	15	20
Total	8	24	32

From the completed table:

- Number of Males under 30: 3

- Number of Females 30 or Older: 15

P(Male under 30 or Female 30 or Older)
$$= \frac{\text{Number of Males under 30} + \text{Number of Females 30 or Older}}{\text{Total Number of Players}}$$

- P(Male under 30 or Female 30 or Older) $= \frac{3+15}{32}$
- P(Male under 30 or Female 30 or Older) $= \frac{18}{32}$

(b) To find the probability that the player will be a female, given that a player 30 year or older is selected.

$$P(\text{Female} \mid 30 \text{ or Older}) = \frac{\text{Number of Females 30 or Older}}{\text{Total Number of Players 30 or Older}}$$

From the completed table:

- Number of Females 30 or Older: 15

- Total Number of Players 30 or Older: 24

- $P(Female \mid 30\ or\ Older) = \frac{15}{24}$

Practice Question:

1. An urn contains 3 red marbles, 4 green marbles, and 5 blue marbles. If a marble is randomly selected, what is the probability it will be red?

2. A bag contains 4 purple balls, 5 orange balls, and 6 yellow balls. If two balls are randomly selected from the bag, without replacement, what is the probability that both balls will be yellow?

3. An experiment has outcomes A, B, C, and D with probabilities 0.3, 0.1, 0.4, and 0.2 respectively. What is the probability of NOT obtaining outcome C?

4. There is a 0.6 probability that it will rain today. If it does not rain today, the probability of rain tomorrow is 0.2. What is the probability that it will rain neither today nor tomorrow?

5. A spinner has 4 equal sections numbered 1-4. It is spun twice. What is the probability that it lands on 4 both times?

6. A basketball player makes 70% of free throw attempts. If he takes 3 free throws, what is the
probability he will make the 3 throws ?

7. A jar contains 5 red balls and 2 green balls. Two balls are randomly selected, one at a time. What is the probability the second ball drawn is green, given the first ball was red?

8. A survey of 100 high school students asked about their preferred music genres and whether they play a musical instrument. The results are summarized in the following two-way frequency table:

	Plays an Instrument	Does Not Play an Instrument	Total
Pop	25	30	55
Rock	18	27	45
Total	43	57	100

Given that a student plays an instrument, what is the probability that they prefer pop music?

9. The table below shows the distribution of a group of 120 college students by gender and major.

	Economics	History	Music
Male	24	20	19
Female	18	22	17

(a) If one student is randomly selected from the group, what is the probability that the student is a History major?

(b) If a male student is selected at random, which of the following is closest to the probability that he is a Music major?

(c) If one student is randomly selected from the group what is the probability that the student is a male Economics major?

(d If a Music major is selected at random, which of the following is closest to the probability that the student is a female?

10. A summer camp has 18 boys and 12 girls signed up for 3 different activities - swimming, archery, and hiking. The registrations are shown below:

	Swimming	Archery	Hiking
Boys	7	4	7
Girls	5	3	4

If one camper is chosen randomly, what is the probability they are a girl signed up for archery?

11. A bag contains 4 red, 3 green, and 5 yellow marbles. After randomly drawing marbles 12 times, the results were recorded:

	Red	Green	Yellow
Draw 1	2	1	3
Draw 2	1	2	2

What is the relative frequency of drawing red?

12. The incomplete table below shows the distribution of age and gender for 40 participants in a chess tournament.

	Under 25	25 or Older	Total
Male	12	?	24
Female	?	8	16
Total	?	?	?

(a) If a chess player is chosen at random, what is the probability that the player will be either a male under age 25 or a female aged 25 or older?

(b) If a person is selected at random from the 25 or older player group, what is the probability that the person is a female?

13. An animal shelter has dogs and cats available for adoption. The incomplete table below shows the distribution by age group:

	Under 1 year	1-3 years	Over 3 years	Total
Dogs	5	?	11	28
Cats	?	8	6	19
Total	15	?	?	47

If an animal is chosen randomly for adoption, what is the probability it will be either a dog under 1 year or a cat over 3 years?

14. Is New York-style Pizza Your Favorite?

	Yes	No
New Yorker	93	7
Non-New Yorker	33	17

Frank asked both New Yorkers and non-New Yorkers the question "is New York-style pizza your favorite?" The responses are summarized in the table. According to the table, how many New Yorkers responded?

15.

	Have pets	Do not have pets
Have children	57	53
Do not have children	68	22

A sociologist interviewed 200 married couples in their 30s. The table summarizes whether or not the couples have children, pets, both, or neither.

(a) According to the table, how many couples have both pets and children?
b) If a married couple with children is selected at random, what is the probability that they do not have pets?
c) If a married couple with no pets is selected at random, what is the probability that they do not have children?
d) If a married couple is selected at random, what is the probability that they do not have children ?

16. An urn contains 3 red marbles and 5 blue marbles. If a marble is drawn at random, what is the probability it is red?
17. A spinner has 5 equal sections labeled A-E. If the spinner is spun twice, what is the probability that it lands on A both times?
18. A six-sided die is rolled 3 times. What is the probability that the rolls are 2, 3, and 5 in any order?
19. A bag contains 4 green balls, 3 blue balls, and 5 red balls. If two balls are drawn at random without replacement, what is the probability that both balls are red?
20. A box contains 8 red balls and 6 green balls. Two balls are drawn without replacement. What is the probability that the first ball drawn is red and the second ball drawn is green?

Answer:

1. 3/12=1/4
2. (6/15) x (5/14) = 1/7
3. 0.6
4. 0.4 x 0.8 = 0.32
5. 1/16
6. 0.7 x 0.7 x 0.7 = 0.343
7. 2/6
8. 25/43.
9. (a) 42/120 (b)0.302 (c)24/120 (d) 0.472
10. $\frac{3}{30} = \frac{1}{10}$
11. 3/11
12.

	Under 25	25 or Older	Total
Male	12	12	24
Female	8	8	16
Total	20	20	40

(a)$\frac{12+8}{40} = \frac{1}{2}$ (b) $\frac{8}{20} = \frac{2}{5}$

13. 11/47
14. 100
15. (a) 57 (b) 68/125 (c) 22/75 (d) 90/200
16. 3/8
17. (1/5) * (1/5) = 1/25.
18. (1/6) * (1/6) * (1/6) = 1/216.
19. (5/12) * (4/11) = 20/132.
20. (8/14) *(6/13)

Lesson 5: Distributions and Measures of Center and Spread

One-variable data distribution:

One-variable data is data that consists of observations on a single characteristic or variable collected from a group of individuals.

For example, consider the scores received by 100 students on a math test. This would be considered one-variable data since there is only one type of measurement (math score) recorded for each student. The single variable (math score) can take on different values for each individual student.

Describing Distributions:

- Shapes of distributions: Recognizing and interpreting symmetrical, skewed, and bimodal distributions.

- Outliers: Identifying and understanding the impact of outliers on measures of center and spread.

- Variability: Analyzing the range and variability within a distribution.

Measures of Center:

Mean:

- Calculation: Sum all values in the data set and divide by the number of values.

- Interpretation: Represents the "average" value in the data set. However, it can be sensitive to outliers (extreme values) that skew the calculation.

- Example: Consider the dataset of exam scores: 75, 80, 85, 90, and 120.

$$\text{Mean} = \frac{(75 + 80 + 85 + 90 + 120)}{5} = 90$$

Example 1: Suppose you have a dataset representing the ages of a group of people, but one age is missing. The given dataset is:

25,30,22,28,___,35,26,29

The mean age of this group is given as 28. To calculate the missing value, you can use the formula for the mean:

$$\text{Mean} = \frac{\text{Sum of all values}}{\text{Number of values}}$$

The sum of the ages is $25 + 30 + 22 + 28 + \_\_ + 35 + 26 + 29$, and the number of values is 8 (ignoring the missing value). The mean is given as 28. Let missing value is x

$$28 = \frac{25 + 30 + 22 + 28 + x + 35 + 26 + 29}{8}$$

Now, solve for the missing value:

$$(25 + 30 + 22 + 28 + x + 35 + 26 + 29) = 28 \times 8$$

$$(25 + 30 + 22 + 28 + x + 35 + 26 + 29) = 224$$

$$x = 224 - (25 + 30 + 22 + 28 + 35 + 26 + 29)$$

$$x = 224 - 195$$

$$x = 29$$

So, the missing value is 29. Therefore, the completed dataset is:

$$25, 30, 22, 28, \mathbf{29}, 35, 26, 29$$

Median:

- Calculation: Arrange the data in ascending order and identify the middle value (if odd number) or the average of the two middle values (if even number).

- Interpretation: Represents the value that divides the data set in half (50% below, 50% above). Less sensitive to outliers than the mean.

- Example: Using the same dataset of exam scores: 75, 80, 85, 90, and 120.

  When arranged in order: 75, 80, 85, 90, 120.

  Median $=$ 85, which is the middle value.

Example 2: The histogram below shows the distribution of exam scores for a class of 30 students. Each bar represents the number of students who earned a score within the specified range.

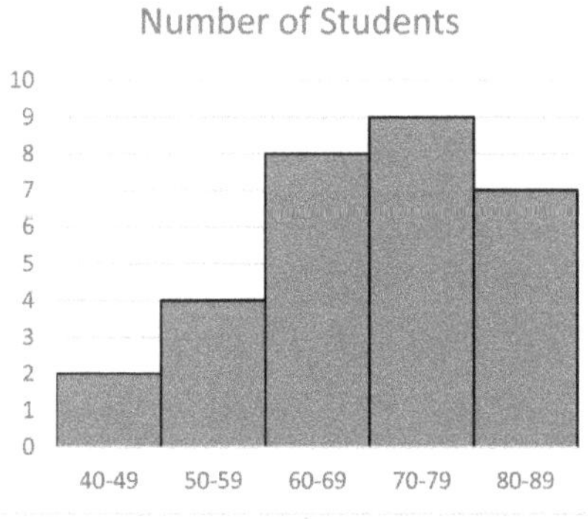

Based on the histogram, could the following pairs of values be the mean and median scores for the class?

a) Mean = 68, Median = 69

b) Mean = 72, Median = 75

c) Mean = 65, Median = 64

d) Mean = 75, Median = 60

Solution

Mean : We can calculate a minimum and maximum mean, and leverage same to arrive at the range for the mean.

Minimum mean (assuming worst case):

$$\frac{(40*2)+(50*4)+(60*8)+(70*9)+(80*7)}{30}=\frac{1950}{30}=65$$

Maximum mean (assuming best case):

$$\frac{(49*2)+(59*4)+(69*8)+(79*9)+(89*7)}{30}=\frac{2220}{30}=74$$

So we can see from above, that mean will be in the 65-74 range.

Median : In the set of 30 students, if we place scores in order, then we are looking at the average of 15th and 16th score.

Placing the scores in order -

2 students : 40-49

6 students : 40-59

14 students : 40-69

23 students : 40-79

30 students : 40-89

So we can see from above, that the first 14 scores are between 40-69.

So the 15th and 16th score i.e. the median will be in the 70-79 range

So the correct answer is **a,** since this is the only choice where range for median and mean are satisfied.

Mode:

- Calculation: Identify the value that appears most frequently in the data set.

- Interpretation: Represents the most common value, but not necessarily the "typical" value, especially for multimodal distributions (with multiple peaks).

- Example: Consider the dataset of exam scores: 75, 80, 85, 85, and 90.

  The mode is 85, as it appears most frequently.

No Mode Example: Consider the following dataset representing the number of goals scored by a football team in each of their last 7 matches:

2,1,3,4,6

In this dataset, no single value appears more frequently than others. Each value occurs only once, and therefore, there is no mode. This situation is common in datasets where each value is unique, and there is no clear "most common" value.

Multiple Modes Example: let's consider a dataset representing the number of hours students spend studying per week:

8,5,10,8,10

In this dataset, the value 8 and value 10 occurs 2 times. So this data set has 2 modes - the numbers 8 and 10.

Measures of Spread:

Measures of spread quantify the extent to which data values deviate from the central tendency, providing insights into the variability within a dataset. Common measures include:

Range:

- **Definition:** The difference between the maximum and minimum values in a dataset.

- **Calculation:** Range = Maximum Value − Minimum Value

Interquartile Range (IQR):

- **Definition:** The range of the middle 50% of the data, calculated as the difference between the third quartile (Q3) and the first quartile (Q1).

- **Calculation:** IQR = Q3 − Q1

The "Interquartile Range" is from Q1 to Q3:

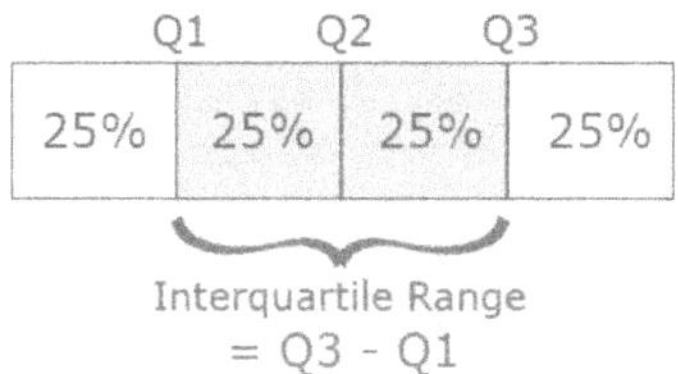

Variance and Standard Deviation:

- **Definition:** Measures the average squared deviation of each data point from the mean. The standard deviation is the square root of the variance.

- **Calculation:** Variance $(\sigma^2) = \dfrac{\sum_{i=1}^{n}(x_i-\bar{x})^2}{N}$

Standard Deviation :

A standard deviation (or σ) is a measure of how dispersed the data is in relation to the mean. Low, or small, standard deviation indicates data are clustered tightly around the mean, and high, or large, standard deviation indicates data are more spread out.

A standard deviation close to zero indicates that data points are very close to the mean, whereas a larger standard deviation indicates data points are spread further away from the mean.

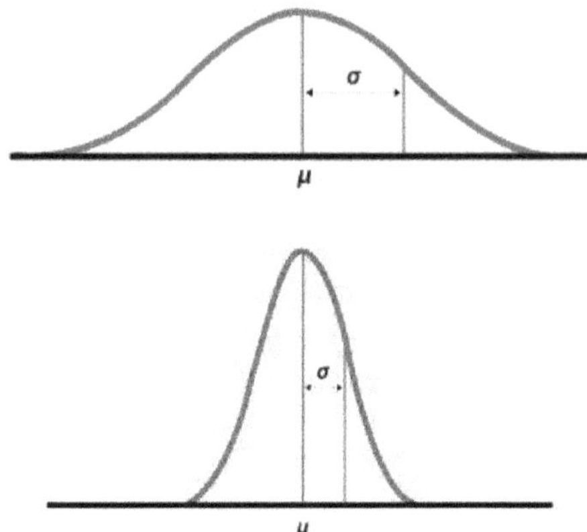

- In the image, the curve on top is more spread out and therefore has a higher standard deviation, while the curve below is more clustered around the mean and therefore has a lower standard deviation

- Standard Deviation$(\sigma) = \sqrt{\text{Variance}}$

Relation between Cluster and Standard deviation

Low Standard Deviation and Tight Clusters:

- When the standard deviation is low, it indicates that the data points in a dataset are close to the mean. In other words, the values are tightly clustered around the mean.

- Low standard deviation suggests that there is little variability or spread in the data. The majority of data points are close to the average, forming a tight cluster.

High Standard Deviation and Wide Clusters:

- Conversely, when the standard deviation is high, it indicates that the data points are more spread out from the mean.

- High standard deviation suggests a greater degree of variability in the data. Data points are scattered over a wider range, leading to wider clusters or a more dispersed distribution.

Example 3: Consider two datasets representing the number of hours spent studying for two groups of students:

- **Dataset A:** 10, 12, 11, 10, 12

- **Dataset B:** 5, 15, 10, 20, 5

In both datasets, the mean is 11. However, Dataset A has a lower standard deviation than Dataset B. In Dataset A, the values are close to the mean, forming a tight cluster, leading to a low standard deviation. In Dataset B, the values are more spread out from the mean, forming a wider cluster, resulting in a higher standard deviation.

Example 4: Consider two datasets of student test scores:

Dataset 1: {81, 85, 83, 82, 84}

The mean here is 83, and the standard deviation is 1.64.

Notice the test scores are all very close to the mean value of 83. There is tight clustering around this mean. And this is reflected in the low standard deviation value of 1.64.

Dataset 2: {70, 90, 50, 95, 80}

The mean here is also 83 (coincidence). But the standard deviation is 16.9, much higher.

Here the test scores range from 50s to 90s, varying greatly from the mean. There is not much clustering - the data is quite spread out from the mean. This results in the high standard deviation of 16.9.

So for the first dataset with tight clustering, the standard deviation was low. And for the second dataset with lower clustering (more spread), the standard deviation was high.

This demonstrates again that as clustering increases, standard deviation decreases. And vice versa - less clustering means a higher deviation.

The Effects of Outliers

Outliers, those data points that significantly deviate from the rest of the dataset, can have a substantial impact on various measures of central tendency like standard deviation, mean, and median. Here's how:

Standard Deviation: Outliers increase standard deviation. Standard deviation calculates how far data points are from the mean. Outliers are data points much further from the mean, which directly increases the standard deviation. Removing outliers reduces the spread of data and lowers the standard deviation.

Mean: Outliers can skew the mean. The mean calculates the average of all data points. Extreme outliers that are much higher or lower than other data points can pull the mean towards them. Removing outliers eliminates this skew and shifts the mean to be more representative of the majority of data.

Median:
The median is fairly resistant to outliers among measures of central tendency. The median represents the middle value when the data is sorted numerically. As long as an outlier does not directly fall into the center point, it does not shift the median value much if at all. Removing or including outliers has little direct effect on the median in most cases.

Here's a table summarizing the impact of outliers:

Measure	Impact of Outliers
Standard deviation	Increases significantly
Mean	Pulls towards the outlier
Median	Little to no effect

Example 5 : Let's examine what can happen to a data set with outliers. For the sample data set:

1, 1, 2, 2, 2, 2, 3, 3, 3, 4, 4

We find the following mean, median, mode, and standard deviation:

Mean = 2.58

Median = 2.5

Mode = 2

Standard Deviation = 1.08

If we add an outlier to the data set:

1, 1, 2, 2, 2, 2, 3, 3, 3, 4, 4, 400

The new values of our statistics are:

Mean = 35.38

Median = 2.5

Mode = 2

Standard Deviation = 114.74

As you can see, having outliers often has a significant effect on your mean and standard deviation. Because of this, we must take steps to remove outliers from our data sets.

An outlier is a value that is very different from the other data in your data set. This can skew your results.

Coefficient of Variation (CV):

- **Definition:** Measures the relative variability of a dataset, expressed as a percentage. It is the ratio of the standard deviation to the mean.

- **Calculation:** $CV = \left(\frac{\text{Standard Deviation}}{\text{Mean}}\right) \times 100$

Example 6 : A dataset of test scores for five students to find the variance and standard deviation for the given dataset

Student	Test Score
A	78
B	85
C	92
D	88
E	95

Step 1: Calculate the Mean (μ): Mean $(\mu) = \frac{78+85+92+88+95}{5} = \frac{438}{5} = 87.6$

Step 2: Calculate the Squared Differences from the Mean:
Squared Differences: Differences:, , , ,

Student	Test Score (x)	$(x_i - \bar{x})^2 = (x_i - 87.6)^2$
A	78	$(78 - 87.6)^2 = 73.96$
B	85	$(85 - 87.6)^2 = 2.56$
C	92	$(92 - 87.6)^2 = 20.25$
D	88	$(88 - 87.6)^2 = 0.16$
E	95	$(95 - 87.6)^2 = 54.76$
Total	**438**	**151.69**

- Variance $(\sigma^2) = \frac{\sum_{i=1}^{n}(x_i-\bar{x})^2}{N} = \frac{151.69}{5} = 30.34$

- Standard Deviation$(\sigma) = \sqrt{\text{Variance}} = \sqrt{30.34} = 5.50$

Practice Question:

1. A survey recorded the ages of 10 individuals: 22, 25, 28, 35, 40, 42, 50, 55, 60, 65. Calculate the mean age.
2. A dataset has a mean of 48 and a median of 50. What does this suggest about the distribution of the data?
3. Given a dataset of exam scores: 78, 85, 92, 88, 95, calculate the range.
4. The data set {2, 3, 6, 7, 10} has a mean of 5.6 and a standard deviation of 3.2. What is the variance of this data set?
5. Susan collected the following exam scores: 82, 75, 68, 81, 84, 90. What is the median exam score?
6. The number of pages read per week by students in a class were: 55, 23, 47, 55, 31. If a student read 38 pages last week, how many standard deviations above or below the mean did they read?
7. If a data set has 9 values with a mean of 45 and a standard deviation of 5, what is the sum of all 9 values?
8. If the third quartile of a data set is 85 and the lower quartile is 55, which measure cannot be determined?
9. If a dataset has a standard deviation of 6 and a mean of 30, calculate the coefficient of variation (CV) as a percentage.
10. A dataset has a mean of 60 and a standard deviation of 8. If a new data point is added with a value of 85, how will this impact the mean and standard deviation?
11. For a dataset with a mode of 40, explain the interpretation of the mode in the context of the data.
12. A data set has a mean of 45 and a standard deviation of 5. If all values in the set are increased by 3, what will be the new standard deviation?
13. The distribution of scores on a math test has a mean of 82 and a standard deviation of 6. If Zara scored 3 standard deviations below the mean, what was her math test score?
14. If a data set has 9 values with a mean of 7 and a standard deviation of 2, what is the sum of the squared differences of each value from the mean?
15. Oscar ran a fundraiser that received 85 donations. He found that the average donation amount was $34.12, and the median donation amount was $10. Which of the following situations could explain the difference between the mean and median donation amounts?
16.

Thousands of Law Degrees Conferred Annually in
the United States

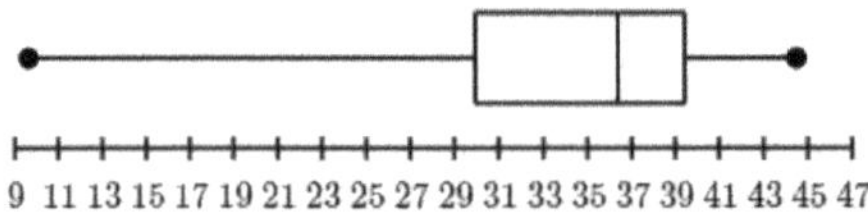

The box plot depicts the numbers of law degrees (JD or LL.B), in thousands, conferred each year in the United States over a span of 49 years. No two years had duplicate numbers of degrees conferred. If the next year, there were 46 thousand degrees conferred, how would that affect the range, mean, and median of the numbers?

17. Farmer John took a sample of 10 piglets from a litter and their weights (kg) are shown below. Based on this sample, which measure is best represented?
1.13, 1.25, 1.36, 1.48, 1.52, 1.38, 1.20, 1.66, 1.33, 1.44.

18. If the average (arithmetic mean) of b and 2 is equal to the average of b, 3, and 4, what is the value of b?

19. A violinist practices 1 hour a day from Monday through Friday. How many hours must she practice on Saturday in order to average 2 hours a day for the 6-day period?

20. The average (arithmetic mean) of two numbers is 3n-4. If one of the numbers is n, then the other number is:

21. Jerry's average (arithmetic mean) score on the first three of four tests is 85. If Jerry wants to raise his average by 2 points, what score must he earn on his fourth test?

22. In a certain course, Lily received an average (arithmetic mean) score of 82 for her first 2 tests, 76 for her third test, and 92 for her fourth test. What grade must she receive on her next test if she wants an average (arithmetic mean) of 86 for all 5 tests?

23. 15 movie theaters average 600 customers per theater per day. If 6 of the theaters close down but the total theater attendance stays the same, what is the average daily attendance per theater among the remaining theaters?

24. If the average of 27-x, x-8, and 3x+ 11 is y, what is the average of 2y and 2y/3in terms of x?

25. George drives the first 30 miles of a trip at a constant rate of 40 miles per hour. If he drives the remaining 75 miles of the trip at a constant rate of 50 miles per hour, what is his average speed for the entire trip?

26. Blaire, Chen, Erin, Liz, and Mauro all participate in a 1-mile race. The average (arithmetic mean) for the times of all girls is 6.5 minutes. If the average time for Blaire, Chen, and Erin is 6.7 minutes, what is the average time for Liz and Mauro?

27. What is the median of the modes in the dataset (-5,4,3,7,2,1,3,4,5,-1,7,8,-4,2,6)?

Answer

1. 44.2
2. The mean and median being close suggests that the distribution is approximately symmetric.
3. 17
4. 10.24
5. 81.5
6. Mean is 42.2, so deviation from mean is 4.2
7. 405
8. Mean
9. 20%
10. The mean will increase, and the standard deviation will also increase.
11. The mode of 40 suggests that this value occurs most frequently in the dataset.
12. It will remain unchanged, as changing all the values by adding/subtracting a constant shifts the distribution and the mean, but does not affect variability/spread; so the standard deviation stays the same
13. 58 ,The mean is 82 and Zara scored 3 SD below the mean. 3 SD is $3 * 6 = 18$. $82 - 18 = 58$.
14. 36
15. There were a few donations that were much larger than the rest.
16. The range, median, and mean would all increase.
17. The median weight of piglets from this litter.
18. 8
19. 7 hours.
20. $5n - 8$
21. To raise his 4-test average to 87, Jerry needs a score of 93 on the fourth test.
22. Lily needs a 98 on her 5th test.
23. 1000 customers per theater.
24. $\frac{(40+4x)}{3}$
25. George's average speed for the entire trip is 140/3 or approximately 46.67 miles per hour.
26. 6.2 minutes.
27. the median of the modes in the given dataset is 5.5.

Lesson 6: Data Inferences & Statistical Claims

Introduction to Data Inferences:

Definition: Data inference is a statistical process used to draw conclusions about a population by analyzing information obtained from a representative sample of that population. It involves making educated predictions or generalizations based on a subset of data.

Population and Sample:

Population: The entire group under investigation.

Sample: A subset of the population chosen for analysis. It should be *representative* and *random*, to ensure accurate inferences.

Examples:

- If a medical researcher studies a sample of patients and finds a particular treatment effective for 80% of them, they might infer that the treatment is likely effective for around 80% of all patients with similar conditions.

- In a marketing survey, if 60% of a sample prefers a certain brand of detergent, an inference could be made that approximately 60% of the entire target market shares this preference.

Calculate the Sample Proportion:

- When you take a random sample from a population, the sample proportion can be used to estimate the population proportion, since a representative random sample should have similar characteristics to the overall population

$$\text{Estimate} = \text{Sample proportion} * \text{Population}$$

Example 1: if you survey a random sample of 100 voters and find that 40% prefer Candidate A, you can estimate the proportion in the overall population of voters that prefer Candidate A as:

$$\text{Estimate} = \text{Sample proportion} * \text{Population}$$

In formulas:

$$Estimate = \hat{p} * N$$

Where:

$\hat{p}$ = Sample proportion (0.4 in this example)

N = Population size

So if there were 20,000 voters total, the estimated number that prefer Candidate A would be:

Estimate = 0.4 * 20,000 = 8,000

Statistical Claims:

Statistical claims are assertions or statements derived from the analysis of numerical data using statistical methods. These claims aim to provide insights, draw inferences, or make predictions about a population based on information gathered from a sample. Statistical claims play a crucial role in research, decision-making, and policy formation, offering a quantitative basis for understanding and interpreting various phenomena.

Key components of statistical claims include point estimates, confidence intervals, and measures of uncertainty, such as margin of error

Importance of Evaluating Statistical Claims

- Statistics can be powerful tools, but also misused or misinterpreted
- Faulty statistics can mislead and spread inaccurate information
- Checking methodology helps determine validity and relevance of claims
- Helps identify improperly applied or biased statistical analyses
- Prevents spreading false claims not properly supported by data
- Critical evaluation promotes sound science and informed decision making
- Allows for identifying exaggerations or distortions of actual findings
- Ensures statistical significance correlates to real-world significance
- Key part of information and data literacy skills

Evaluating statistical claims carefully is vital to assess their trustworthiness and prevent the spread of misinformation based on misused or invalid statistics. Critical analysis helps extract factual meaning from numbers and data.

Components of a Statistical Claim

A. Point Estimate

- The single value that represents the statistic of interest (e.g. mean, percentage)

B. Confidence Interval

- Range of values likely to contain the true population parameter

C. Margin of Error

- How far the point estimate may deviate from the true value

D. Sample Size

- Number of subjects/data points included in analysis

E. Level of Confidence

- Probability the confidence interval contains the true parameter (often 95%)

Key Concepts in Evaluating Statistical Claims

A. Understanding Confidence Levels

- **Definition:**
    - Confidence levels express the degree of certainty or assurance that a calculated confidence interval contains the true population parameter. Common confidence levels include 90%, 95%, and 99%.

- **Interpretation:**
    - A 95% confidence level, for example, implies that if the same sampling process were repeated many times, the calculated confidence interval would encompass the true parameter in approximately 95% of those cases.

- **Significance:**
    - Higher confidence levels result in wider confidence intervals, reflecting greater certainty. However, a balance is needed, as excessively high confidence levels may lead to overly broad intervals.

B. Interpreting Margin of Error

- **Definition:**
    - The margin of error quantifies the potential variability or imprecision associated with a point estimate. It is expressed as a percentage and indicates the range within which the true population parameter is likely to fall.

- **Calculation:**
    - The margin of error is influenced by factors such as the sample size and the desired level of confidence. Larger sample sizes and higher confidence levels result in smaller margins of error.

- **Impact on Precision:**
    - A smaller margin of error indicates higher precision, as it narrows the range of possible values for the true parameter. Conversely, a larger margin of error signifies greater variability in the estimate.

- **Calculation of Range:**
    - The range is established by adding and subtracting the margin of error from the point estimate. This creates an interval within which we can be reasonably confident the true population parameter lies.
    - Range = Estimate $\pm$ Margin of Error

C. Considering Sample Size

- **Role in Precision:**
  - Sample size is a critical determinant of the precision of a statistical claim. Larger sample sizes generally lead to more accurate point estimates and narrower confidence intervals.

- **Influence on Margin of Error:**
  - Increasing the sample size tends to decrease the margin of error, enhancing the reliability of the estimate. Smaller sample sizes may result in larger margins of error and greater uncertainty.

- **Generalizability:**
  - Adequate sample sizes are essential for the generalizability of results to the broader population. Insufficient sample sizes may lead to biased or unreliable estimates.

D. **Population Variability:** Population variability refers to the degree of diversity or dispersion present in a population with respect to a specific characteristic or variable. It is a measure of how much individual values in a population differ from the population mean (average) or from each other.

Here are a few key points related to population variability:

- **Standard Deviation:**
  - The standard deviation (σ) is a measure of how spread out values are in a population.

$$\sigma = \sqrt{\frac{\sum(X_i - \mu)^2}{N}}$$

  - Where X_i represents each individual data point, μ is the population mean, and N is the total number of data points.
  - Standard deviation is a common measure of population variability. It quantifies the average distance between each data point in the population and the mean. A larger standard deviation indicates greater variability, while a smaller one indicates less variability.
- **Coefficient of Variation (CV):**

  - CV is the ratio of the standard deviation to the mean, expressed as a percentage.

$$CV = \left(\frac{\sigma}{\mu}\right) \times 100$$

  - CV is the ratio of the standard deviation to the mean, expressed as a percentage. It is a relative measure of variability that allows for comparisons between populations with different means.

- **Impact on Margin of Error:**

- The margin of error is influenced by the variability in a population. The margin of error represents the range within which the true population parameter is likely to fall. It is calculated based on the standard deviation and the desired level of confidence.

- **Larger Variability, Larger Margin of Error:**

  - When the population is more variable (higher standard deviation), the range of potential values for the parameter is larger. Consequently, to achieve a given level of confidence and a smaller margin of error, a larger sample size is needed.

- **Smaller Variability, Smaller Margin of Error:**

  - Conversely, when the population is less variable (lower standard deviation), the potential range of values is smaller. In this case, a smaller sample size may be sufficient to achieve the same level of confidence with a smaller margin of error.

Example 2:

Suppose a poll reports a 45% approval rating for a political candidate with a margin of error of $\pm 3\%$. The range would be: Range $= 45\% \pm 3\% = (42\%, 48\%)$

This means we can be reasonably confident that the true approval rating falls within the range of 42% to 48%

Example 3: In a recent survey of 700 randomly selected registered voters in the town of Rivertown, 540 expressed support for increasing funding for the town's mental health services. Based on the survey results, approximately how many of Rivertown's 25,000 registered voters are estimated to be in favor of increasing funding for the town's mental health services?

Solution: Given that

- Sample Size $(n) = 700$ (the number of surveyed registered voters)

- Sample Proportion $(\hat{p}) = \frac{540}{700}$ (the proportion in favor in the sample)

- Population Size $(N) = 25{,}000$ (the total number of registered voters in Rivertown)

Using the formula: $p = (\hat{p}) \times \text{Population Size}$

Substitute the values: $p = \frac{540}{700} \times 25{,}000$

Calculate this expression to find the estimated number of voters in favor of increasing funding for mental health services in Rivertown:

$p \approx 0.7714 \times 25{,}000$

$p \approx 19{,}285$

So, based on the survey results, it's estimated that approximately 19,285 of Rivertown's 25,000 registered voters are in favor of increasing funding for the town's mental health services.

Example 4: Emma conducted a survey of a random sample of members of a fitness club about their dietary habits. From the sample data, she estimated that 62% of club members follow a balanced diet, with a margin of error of 4%. What is the most appropriate conclusion about all members of the fitness club, based on the given estimate and margin of error?

Solution: Given information:

- Sample Estimate ($\hat{p}$): 62%

- Margin of Error (MOE): 4%

The confidence interval is calculated by subtracting the margin of error from the estimate to get the lower bound and adding the margin of error to the estimate to get the upper bound.

Lower Bound $= \hat{p} - \text{MOE} = 62\% - 4\% = 58\%$

Upper Bound $= \hat{p} + \text{MOE} = 62\% + 4\% = 66\%$

So, the estimated range is approximately 58% to 66%. This means that based on the survey, we can estimate with a 95% confidence level that the true proportion of fitness club members following a balanced diet is within this range.

Therefore, the most appropriate conclusion is:

"Approximately 58% to 66% of all fitness club members follow a balanced diet."

8. Sampling methods and their implications

- **Simple random sampling** - This involves selecting a sample at random from the population, giving each individual an equal probability of being chosen. It helps minimize sampling bias and provides representative data on the population as a whole. Simple random sampling allows for making statistically valid inferences. However, it can be difficult to implement for large populations.
- **Stratified sampling** - The population is divided into distinct subgroups (strata) based on characteristics like age, gender, income etc. Random sampling is then conducted within each strata to ensure representation. This helps capture diversity and facilitates analysis of differences between groups.
  However, it requires clear stratification criteria and adequate sample sizes within subgroups.
- **Cluster sampling** - The population is divided into clusters based on natural groupings, and random samples are drawn from selected clusters. This is logistically easier but risks missing variability across clusters. Findings may only apply to the specific clusters sampled. Clustering effects also need to be accounted for in analysis.
- **Convenience sampling** - Samples are collected from the most accessible parts of the population. This is easy to implement but risks severe sampling bias and cannot be generalized. Groups not in the sampling frame are completely missed. Findings only describe the convenience sample itself.

- **Voluntary response sampling** - Participation is open to all volunteers from the target population. This is prone to bias as certain types of people are more likely to volunteer. Those with strong opinions or motivations are over-represented. Generalizability is very limited.
- **Undercoverage bias** -Undercoverage bias occurs when certain segments of the target population are systematically excluded or underrepresented in the sampling frame. This can skew results away from the true values for the overall population.

Causes include:

- Excluding groups due to accessibility, geography, language barriers, etc.

- Using outdated lists that miss newly eligible members of the population.

- Relying only on listed phone numbers and missing cell phone-only users.

Under coverage biases the sample away from the missed groups' characteristics. Claims based on these samples lack generalizability and may reinforce disparities.

- **Nonresponse bias** -Nonresponse bias happens when a significant portion of the selected sample does not respond or participate. This can distort results if those responding differ from initial non respondents.

Causes include:

- Inability to contact selected individuals.

- Refusals to participate in the survey.

- Differences in engagement between groups.

Since reasons for nonresponse are often unknown, it is hard to quantify the resulting bias. Higher response rates minimize potential nonresponse bias in survey claims.

Example 5: In a study on the lengths of frogs in a pond, a random sample of 50 American bullfrogs was caught and tagged, ensuring that none were measured more than once. The sample revealed that 40% of the American bullfrogs were shorter than 7 inches. Based on the sample data, what conclusion can be drawn about the lengths of American bullfrogs in the pond?

Solution:

- **Sample Selection:**

  - A sample of 50 American bullfrogs was chosen randomly from all the American bullfrogs in the pond. Random sampling helps ensure that the selected frogs are representative of the entire population of bullfrogs in the pond.

- **Observation in the Sample's**

- Within this randomly selected sample, it was observed that 40% of the American bullfrogs are shorter than 7 inches. This percentage is based on the measurements taken from the 50 frogs in the sample.

- **Inference to the Population:**
  - Since the sample was chosen randomly, and the observed characteristic (being shorter than 7 inches) is known for this sample, we can reasonably infer that this percentage is reflective of the entire population of American bullfrogs in the pond.

- **Conclusion:**
  - Therefore, the conclusion drawn is that approximately 40% of all American bullfrogs in the pond are estimated to be shorter than 7 inches. This inference is made by extrapolating the observed percentage from the sample to the entire population, assuming the random selection process ensures representativenes.

Correlation and Causality

Correlation: Correlation is a statistical measure that describes the extent to which two variables change together. If one variable tends to go up when the other goes up, there is a positive correlation. If one variable tends to go down when the other goes up, there is a negative correlation.

Correlation Coefficient: The correlation coefficient, often denoted as r, quantifies the strength and direction of the linear relationship between two variables. It ranges from -1 (perfect negative correlation) to 1 (perfect positive correlation), with 0 indicating no correlation.

Causality: Causality implies a cause-and-effect relationship between two variables. If changes in one variable reliably produce changes in another, there may be a causal relationship.

Criteria for Causation: Establishing causation requires meeting criteria such as temporal precedence (cause precedes effect), correlation, and ruling out alternative explanations.

Difference between correlation and causation:

- Correlation refers to a relationship between two variables, where they either increase or decrease together. It does not imply that one variable causes the other. Causation refers to a cause-and-effect relationship, where one variable directly leads to changes in the other variable.

Controlled Experiments:

Study Design:

- **Random Assignment:** Participants are randomly assigned to different conditions, including a control group.

- **Manipulation:** One or more variables are manipulated to observe their effect.

Data Collection:

- **Data Measurement:** Collect quantitative or qualitative data based on the study's objectives.

- **Controlled Conditions:** Keep conditions consistent across groups, except for the manipulated variable.

Data Analysis:

- **Comparisons:** Analyze differences between the experimental and control groups.

- **Statistical Tests:** Use statistical tests to determine if observed differences are statistically significant.

Drawing Conclusions:

- **Causation:** If there is a significant difference between the groups, causation may be inferred, suggesting that the manipulated variable had an effect.

- **Internal Validity:** Assess the internal validity of the study design to ensure that the observed effects are genuinely due to the manipulated variable.

Example 6: In a drug trial, if the experimental group shows a statistically significant improvement compared to the control group, the conclusion may be drawn that the drug has a positive effect. However, external validity and potential confounding variables must be considered.

Example 7: A community organization conducted a survey of 600 senior citizens aged 65 and above to gauge their opinions on increasing funding for local senior centers. The survey revealed that the majority of seniors in the sample supported increased funding. Based on these results, which of the following populations in the community is most likely to share a similar opinion on increasing funding for senior centers?

(a) Adults aged 25-35
(b) Teenagers aged 13-18
(c) Residents with no affiliation to senior centers
(d) Senior citizens aged 65 and above
(e) Middle-aged individuals aged 40-50

Solution: The survey conducted by the community organization targeted senior citizens aged 65 and above to gather their opinions on increasing funding for local senior centers. The majority of seniors in the sample expressed support for increased funding. Therefore, the population most likely to share a similar opinion on this matter would be:

(d) Senior citizens aged 65 and above

Practice question

1. Jason conducted a survey among employees in a company to estimate the proportion who prefer remote work. His findings suggest 85% preference with a margin of error of 2%. What can be concluded about the entire workforce's preference for remote work based on this estimate and margin of error?

2. Maria conducted a survey on a college campus to estimate the proportion of students who participate in extracurricular activities. Her estimate is 48%, with a margin of error of 5%. What is the most appropriate conclusion about the participation of all students in extracurricular activities based on this estimate and margin of error?

3. In a survey of 600 randomly selected registered voters in the town of Carrington, 65% expressed support for increasing funding for mental health services. If the original estimate of the total registered voters in Carrington who support increased funding was 15,448, and the sample proportion changed to 85%, what would be the new estimate of the registered voters in Carrington who support increased funding?
   (a) 19,586
   (b) 20,201
   (c) 24,000
   (d) 21,217

4. A researcher collecting information about 800 randomly selected software engineers concluded that the median annual salary for software engineers in the United States at the time of the study was between $70,000 and $120,000, with a 95% confidence level. Which of the following could represent the median annual salary, based on the same sample, for software engineers in the United States with a 90% confidence level?
   (a) 67,000 to $123,000
   (b) $65,000 to $125,000
   (c) $68,000 to $122,000
   (d) $72,000 to $118,000.

5. A university administrator collected data on the GPAs of a random sample of 150 students. Based on this sample, he concluded that the median GPA for students at the university was between 3.2 and 3.6, with a 95% confidence level. Which of the following intervals could represent the median GPA, based on the same sample of 150 students, with a 90% confidence level?
   (a) 3.1 to 3.7
   (b) 3.0 to 3.8
   (c) 2.9 to 3.9
   (d)3.3 to 3.5

6. A survey of 100 students at Jefferson High School concluded that the average amount of time students spend on homework per night is 3.5 hours. Which of the following statements is true about this survey?
   (a) The results can be reliably generalized to all high school students, since 100 is a large sample size.
   (b) The survey likely underestimates average homework time because the sample only included one school.

(c) Since students self-reported homework time, the estimate could be inflated due to exaggeration.

(d) The findings are highly precise given the large sample and can be generalized nationally.

7. Researchers conducted a study observing 500 patients who took a new antidepressant medication. They found depression symptoms improved in 320 patients. The researchers concluded the medication definitively cures depression. The conclusion is most likely flawed owing to which reason?

    (a) The sample size was too small at only 500 patients.

    (b) Correlation does not imply causation regarding the medication's effects.

    (c) The symptoms should have been measured over a longer time period.

    (d) There was no control group for comparison to account for placebo effects.

8. A medical study found that eating chocolate daily was correlated with lower blood pressure. The study concluded that chocolate consumption helps reduce blood pressure. Which of the following, if true, would most weaken this conclusion?

    (a) The study was conducted with a small sample size of 50 participants.

    (b) Participants who consumed more chocolate also exercised regularly.

    (c) The researchers failed to account for subjects' weight and diet.

    (d) Subjects were aware they were part of a study on chocolate.

9. Researchers conducting an exit poll at 120 polling places across a state reported candidate Jones leading candidate Smith by 8 percentage points in the governor's race, with a 3% margin of error at 95% confidence. What is the best conclusion based on this exit poll?

    (a) Jones has definitively won the election by 8 points state-wide.

    (b) Jones is likely ahead state-wide but his lead could be as low as 5 points or as high as 11 points.

    (c) The exit poll cannot provide useful information with such a high margin of error.

    (d) With 95% confidence, there is only a 3% chance that Jones is not ahead by 8 points.

10. A medical study found that people who consumed 3 or more alcoholic drinks per day had higher blood pressure on average than non-drinkers. Which additional information would be most important to determine the validity of inferring causation from this association?

    (a) The distribution of blood pressure measurements among the subjects

    (b) Whether subjects were taking medications that affect blood pressure

    (c) If the study controlled for diet, exercise, family history, and other factors

    (d) The number of subjects in the study who consumed 3 or more drinks per day

11. An ice cream company randomly selected 100 participants to test their new line of ice cream. For the study, each participant was given a pint of the new ice cream. The results showed that 98%of the participants reported enhanced moods after consuming the ice cream.

    (a) Did the study have a control group?

    (b) Do the results of the study show that consuming the new ice cream is associated with reports of enhanced moods in the study participants?

    (c) Do the results of the study show that the new ice cream is more effective at enhancing the moods of people than other ice cream brands?

12. A skincare company conducted a study with 150 participants to evaluate the effectiveness of their new moisturizer. Each participant used the moisturizer daily for six weeks. The results showed that 80% of participants reported improved skin hydration during the study.

(a) Did the study have a control group?

A) Yes, there was a group that did not use the new moisturizer.

B) No, all participants used the new moisturizer.

(b) Do the results of the study suggest that using the new moisturizer is associated with improved skin hydration in the study participants?

A) Yes, as 80% of participants reported improved skin hydration.

B) No, there is no information about skin hydration in the participants.

(c) Do the results of the study indicate that the new moisturizer is more effective at enhancing skin hydration compared to other moisturizers on the market?

A) Yes, since the study focused specifically on the new moisturizer.

B) No, the study design does not allow for a direct comparison with other moisturizers.

13. A wildlife researcher conducted a study on the population of deer in a forest. A random sample of 60 deer was captured, and it was found that 25% of them had antlers with more than six points. Which of the following conclusions is best supported by the sample data?

(a) Approximately 25% of all deer in the forest have antlers with more than six points.

(b) Approximately 25% of all animals in the forest have antlers with more than six points.

(c) The average number of points on antlers for all deer in the forest is approximately six.

(d) The majority of all animals in the forest have antlers with more than six point.

14. A research study aimed to assess the impact of a new exercise regimen on weight loss. 400 participants were randomly selected from a population of individuals seeking weight loss solutions. Half of the participants were randomly assigned to follow the new exercise regimen, while the other half did not engage in any specific exercise routine. The results showed that participants who followed the new exercise regimen experienced a significant reduction in weight compared to those who did not exercise. Based on the design and results of the study, which of the following is an appropriate conclusion?

(a) The new exercise regimen is likely to result in weight loss for anyone who follows it.

(b) The new exercise regimen is better than all other available weight loss methods.

(c) The exercise regimen is likely to contribute to weight loss for individuals seeking weight loss solutions.

(d) None of the conclusions are appropriate.

15. Hannah conducted a survey on a random sample of residents in Texas to gather information about their preferences for renewable energy sources. The results of the survey are most representative of which of the following populations?

(a) Texas residents

(b) Houston, Texas residents

(c) Texas residents aged 25 to 35

(d) Houston, Texas residents aged 25 to 35

Answer

1. With a 95% confidence level, we estimate that between 83% and 87% of the entire workforce prefers remote work, derived from an 85% estimate with a 2% margin of error.
2. We are 95% confident that the proportion of all students participating in extracurricular activities is likely to be within the range of 43% to 53%, based on a 48% estimate with a 5% margin of error.
3. (b)
4. (d) $72,000 to $118,000.
5. (d) 3.3 to 3.5
6. (c)
7. (b)
8. (b)
9. (b)
10. (c)
11. (a) No, (b) Yes (c) No
12. (a) No, (b) Yes (c) No
13. (a)
14. (c)
15. (a)

Part (IV)
Geometry and Trigonometry

1. Area and Volume Formulas; Word Problems
2. Lines, Angles, and Triangles, Congruent and Similar Triangles
3. Right Triangles and Trigonometry
4. Circles - Unit Circles, Angles/Arc, Equation

Area is a measure of the amount of space enclosed by a two-dimensional shape. It is a fundamental concept in geometry and is expressed in square units. The formula for calculating the area depends on the type of shape.

For common geometric shapes:

Name of the shape	Image of the Shape	Area Formula
Rectangle		$Area = Length \times Width$ $Area = l \times w$
Square		$Area = Side^2$ $Area = a^2$
Triangle		$Area = \dfrac{1}{2} \times Base \times Height$ $Area = \dfrac{1}{2}bh$
Parallelogram :		$Area = Base \times Height$ $Area = l \times h$
Trapezoid		$Area = \dfrac{1}{2} \times (Base1 + Base2) \times Height$ $Area = \dfrac{1}{2} \times (a + b) \times h$
Circle:		$Area = \pi \times Radius^2$ $Area = \pi r^2$

Volume:

Volume is a measure of the three-dimensional space occupied by a solid object. It is expressed in cubic units. The formulas for calculating the volume of common three-dimensional shapes are as follows:

Name of the shape	Image of the Shape	Volume Formula
Cube		$Volume = Side^3$ $Volume = a^3$
Cuboid (Rectangular Prism)		$Volume = Length \times Width \times Height$ $Volume = lwh$
Cone:		$Volume = \dfrac{1}{3} \times \pi \times Radius^2 \times Height$ $Volume = \dfrac{1}{3}\pi r^2 h$
Cylinder:		$Volume = \pi \times Radius^2 \times Height$ $Volume = \pi r^2 h$
Sphere		$Volume = \dfrac{4}{3}\pi\, Radius^3$ $Volume = \dfrac{4}{3}\pi r^3$

| Pyramid | 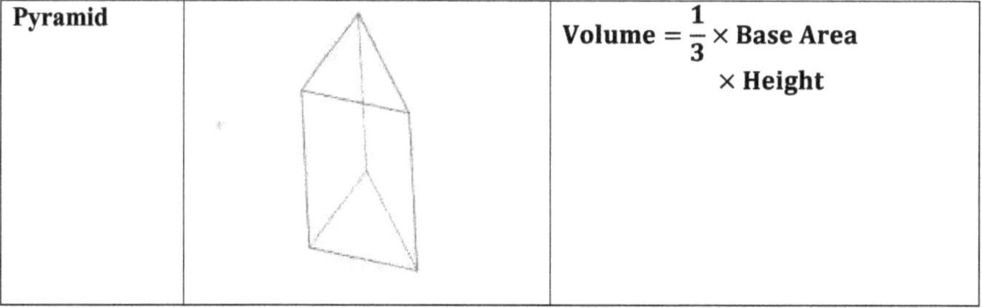 | $\text{Volume} = \dfrac{1}{3} \times \text{Base Area} \times \text{Height}$ |

Example 1: A puzzle box is shaped like a rectangular prism and has a volume of 240 cubic inches. If the puzzle box has a length of 10 inches and a width of 8 inches, what is the height of the puzzle box in inches?

Solution :

The puzzle box is shaped like a rectangular prism

It has a volume of 240 cubic inches

It has a length of 10 inches

It has a width of 8 inches

To find the height, we can use the formula for volume of a rectangular prism:

$$\text{Volume} = \text{Length} \times \text{Width} \times \text{Height}$$

Substituting the given values:

$$240 \text{ cubic inches} = 10 \text{ inches x } 8 \text{ inches x Height}$$

$$240 = 80 \times \text{Height}$$

$$\text{Height} = 240/80$$

$$\text{Height} = 3 \text{ inches}$$

Therefore, if the puzzle box has a volume of 240 cubic inches, a length of 10 inches, and a width of 8 inches, then its height must be 3 inches

Example 2: A pyramid has a square base with a side length of 8 centimeters. The height of the pyramid is 3/4 as long as the side length of its base.

Solution: The pyramid has a square base

The side length of the square base is 8 cm

The height of the pyramid is 3/4 the side length of the base

The side length of the base is 8 cm

$$\frac{3}{4} \text{ of } 8 \text{ cm is } \left(\frac{3}{4}\right) * 8 = 6 \text{ cm}$$

Therefore, the **height of the pyramid is 6 cm**

Now, to find the volume of a pyramid, we use the formula:

$$Volume = \left(\frac{1}{3}\right) \times Base\ Area \times Height$$

The base is a square with side length 8 cm

So the base area is:

$$Base\ area = side^2$$

$$Base\ area = 8^2 = 64\ cm^2$$

The height is 6 cm

Plugging this into the volume formula:

$$Volume = \left(\frac{1}{3}\right) 64\ cm^2\ 6\ cm$$

$$Volume = 128\ cm^3$$

Therefore, the volume of the pyramid with a square base of side length 8 cm and a height of 3/4 the base side length is $128\ cm^3$.

Example 3: A medicine bottle is in the shape of a right circular cylinder. If the volume of the bottle is $144\,\pi$ cubic centimeters, what is the diameter of the base of the bottle, in centimeters?

Solution:

Volume (V) $= 144\pi$ cm^3

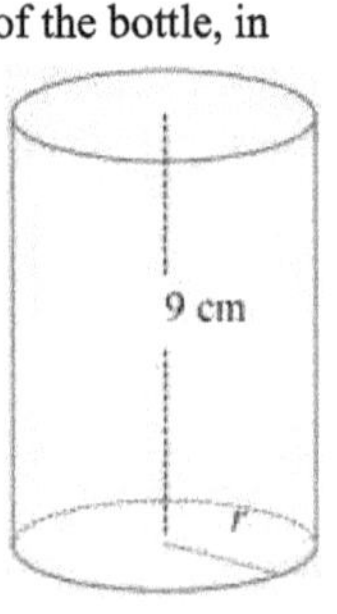

Formula for cylinder volume is $V = \pi r^{2h}$

Height (h) $= 9$ cm

Substitute into formula:

$$144\pi = \pi r^2(9)$$

Divide both sides by π:

$$144 = r^2(9)$$

Divide both sides by 9:

$$16 = r^2$$

Take square root:

$$\sqrt{16} = r$$

So r $= 4$ cm

Diameter $= 2r$

Therefore, diameter $= 2 * 4 = 8$ cm

Reference Information

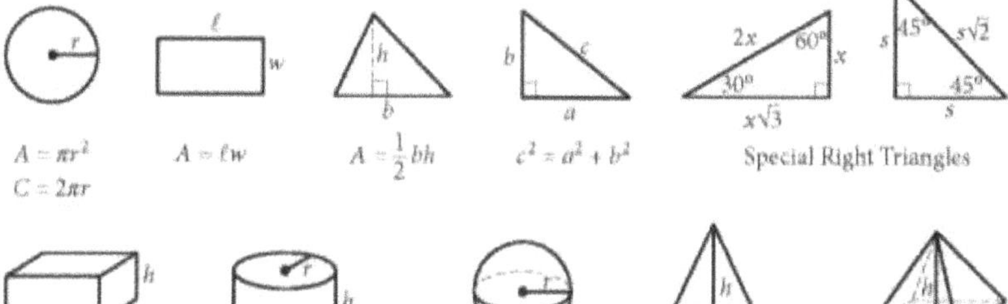

$A = \pi r^2$

$C = 2\pi r$

$A = \ell w$

$A = \frac{1}{2}bh$

$c^2 = a^2 + b^2$

Special Right Triangles

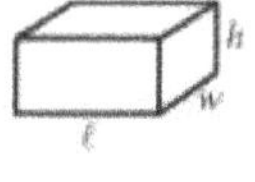

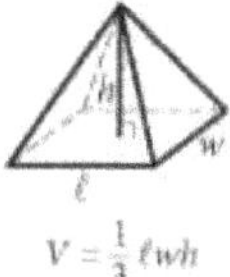

$V = \ell wh$

$V = \pi r^2 h$

$V = \frac{4}{3}\pi r^3$

$V = \frac{1}{3}\pi r^2 h$

$V = \frac{1}{3}\ell wh$

The number of degrees of arc in a circle is 360.

The number of radians of arc in a circle is 2π.

The sum of the measures in degrees of the angles of a triangle is 180.

Practice question:

1. Find the area of each figure.

(a)

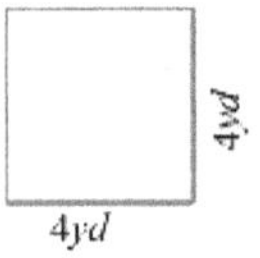

4 yd
4 yd

(b)

3cm
10cm

(c)

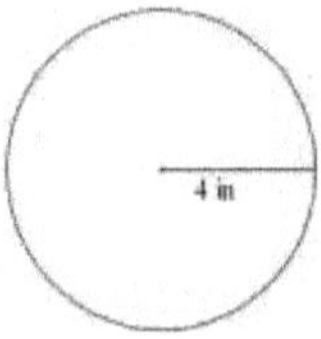

4 in

(d)

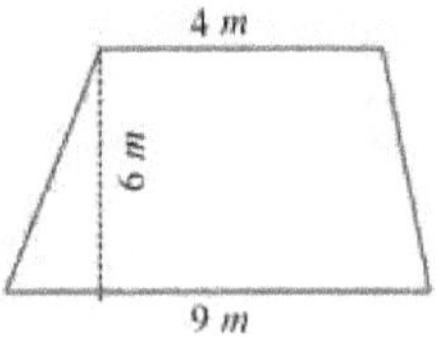

4 m
6 m
9 m

(e)

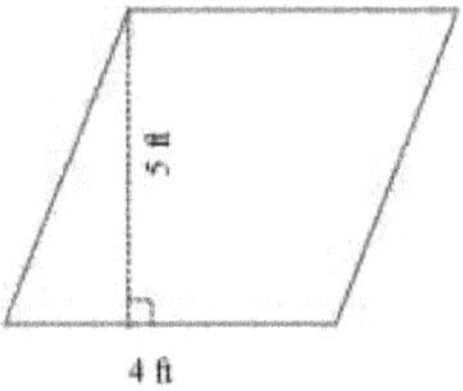

5 ft
4 ft

(f)

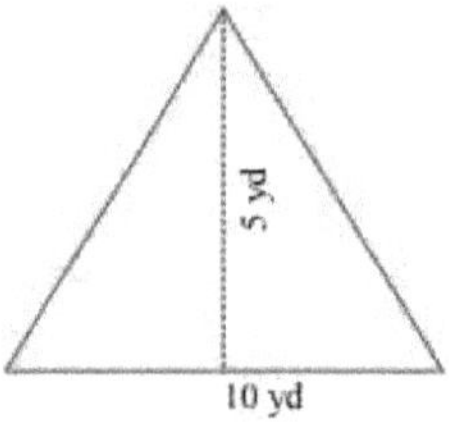

5 yd
10 yd

2. Find the exact volume of each shape.

(a)

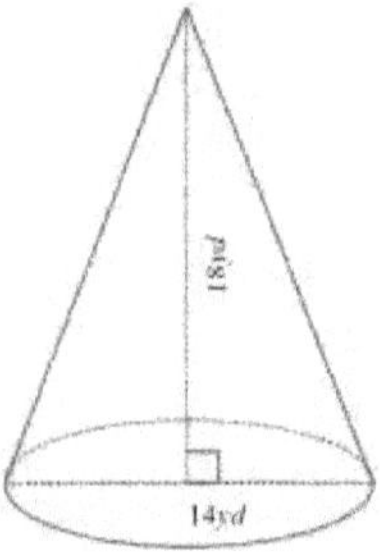

18 yd
14 yd

(b)

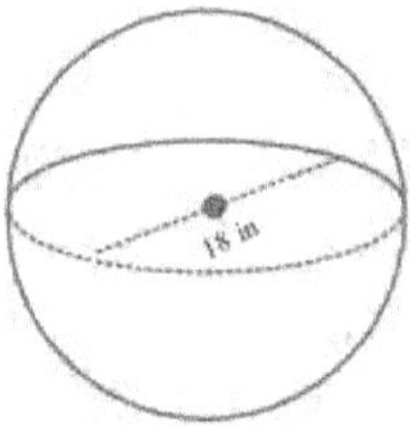

18 in

(c)

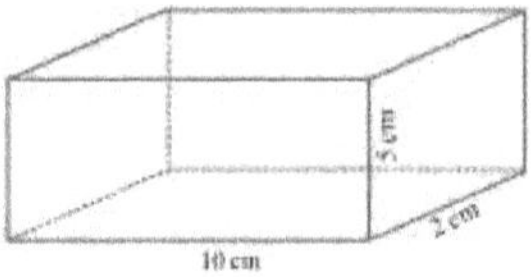

5 cm
2 cm
10 cm

(d)

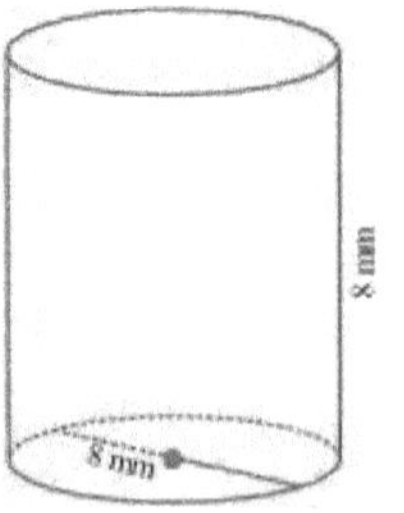

8 mm
8 mm

(e)

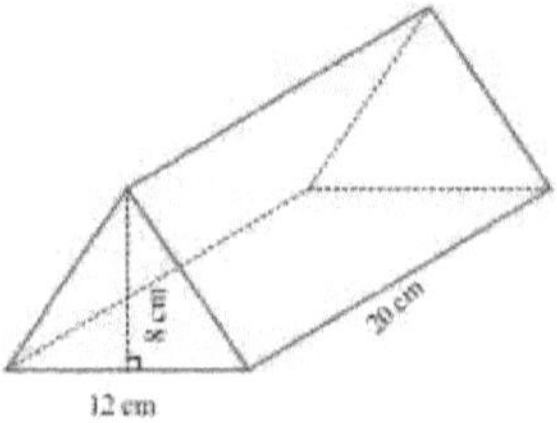

8 cm
12 cm
30 cm

(f)

15 in

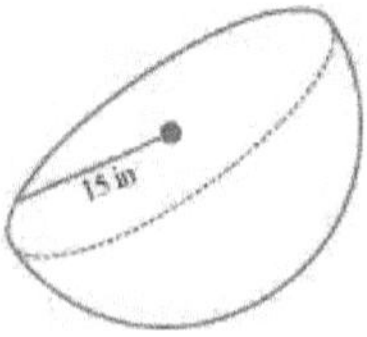

3. A canal is 300 cm wide and 120 cm deep. The water in the canal is flowing at a speed of 20 km/h. How much area will it irrigate in 20 minutes if 8 cm of standing water is desired?

4. Two cones have their heights in the ratio 1 : 3 and radii in the ratio 3 : 1. What is the ratio of their volumes?

5. A cubical ice-cream brick of edge 22 cm is to be distributed among some children by filling ice-cream cones of radius 2 cm and height 7 cm up to its brim. How many children will get the ice cream cones?

6. Three cubes of a metal whose edges are in the ratio 3:4:5 are melted and converted into a

   single cube whose diagonal is $12\sqrt{3}$ cm. Find the edges of the three cubes.(Note that diagonal of a cube with side s is given by $s\sqrt{3}$)

7. Find the number of solid spheres each of diameter 6 cm that can be made by melting a solid metal cylinder of height 45 cm and diameter 4 cm.

8. 2 cubes each of volume 64 cm^3 are joined end to end. Find the surface area of the resulting cuboid.

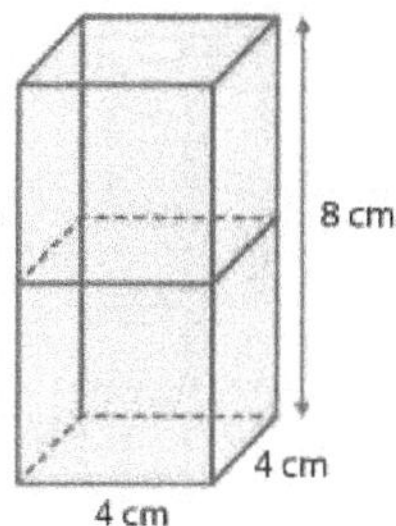

9. A solid toy is in the form of a hemisphere surmounted by a right circular cone. The height of the cone is 2 cm, and the diameter of the base is 4 cm. Determine the volume of the toy. If a right circular cylinder circumscribes the toy, find the difference between the volumes of the cylinder and the toy. (Take $\pi = 3.14$)

10. A spherical glass vessel has a cylindrical neck 8 cm long, 2 cm in diameter; the diameter of the spherical part is 8.5 cm. By measuring the amount of water it holds, a child finds its volume to be 345 cm^3. Check whether she is correct, taking the above as the inside measurements, and $\pi = 3.14$.

11. Metallic spheres of radii 6 cm, 8 cm and 10 cm, respectively, are melted to form a single solid sphere. Find the radius of the resulting sphere.

12. A horse is tied to a pole with 28 m long string. Find the area where the horse can graze.

13. A steel wire when bent in the form of a square, encloses an area of 121 cm^2. If the same wire is bent in the form of a circle, find the area of the circle.

14. The radii of the two circles are 8 cm and 6 cm, respectively. Find the radius of the circle having its area equal to the sum of the areas of two circles.

15. The area of a circle inscribed in an equilateral triangle is 154 cm^2. Find the perimeter of the triangle.

16. 2.2 cubic dm of brass is to be drawn into a cylindrical wire of 0.25 cm in diameter. Find the length of the wire. (1 dm = 10 cm).

17. How many spherical lead shots of diameter 4 cm can be made out of a solid cube of lead whose edge measures 44 cm?

Answer:

1. (a) 16 yd^2 (b) 30cm^2 (c) 16π in^2 (d) 69m^2 (e) 20 ft^2 (f) 25 yd^2
2. (a) 294π ft^3 (b) 972π in^3 (c) 100 cm^3 (d) 128π mm^3 (e) 960 cm^3 (f) 2250π in^3
3. 300,000 sq meters
4. 3 : 1
5. 363 children will get the ice cream cones.
6. The edges of the three cubes are 6 cm, 8 cm and 10 cm
7. n = 5
8. 160 cm^2
9. 25.12 cm^3
10. 346.67 cm^3
11. 12 cm
12. 2464 m^2
13. 154 cm^2.
14. 10 cm.
15. 72.7 cm
16. 448 m.
17. 2541

Lesson 2: Lines, Angles, and Triangles, Congruent and Similar Triangles

Line: A straight, continuous path extending indefinitely in both directions.

Line Segment: A part of a line with two endpoints.

Ray: A portion of a line that starts at one point and extends infinitely in one direction.

Types of Lines:

- **Parallel Lines:** Lines that never intersect and remain equidistant from each other.

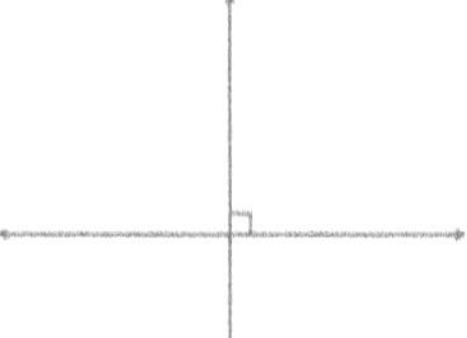

- **Perpendicular Lines:** Lines that intersect at a right angle (90 degrees).

- **Transversal Line:** A line that intersects two or more parallel lines.

Angles are the shape that is formed when the endpoints of two rays meet at a single point. They are measured in degrees (°) or radians. A complete rotation is equal to an angle of 360 degrees. It is represented by the symbol '∠'.

For example, ∠AOC is formed when lines AB and CD intersect with each other.

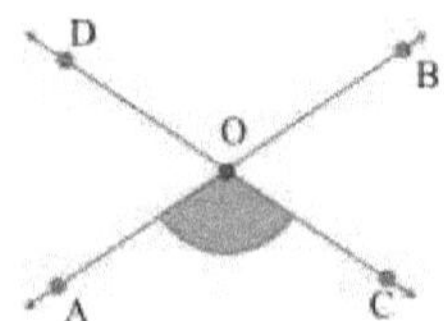

Types of Angles:

- **Acute Angle:** Less than 90 degrees.

- **Right Angle:** Exactly 90 degrees.

- **Obtuse Angle:** More than 90 degrees but less than 180 degrees.

- **Reflex Angle:** Angle is between 180 degrees and 360 degrees.

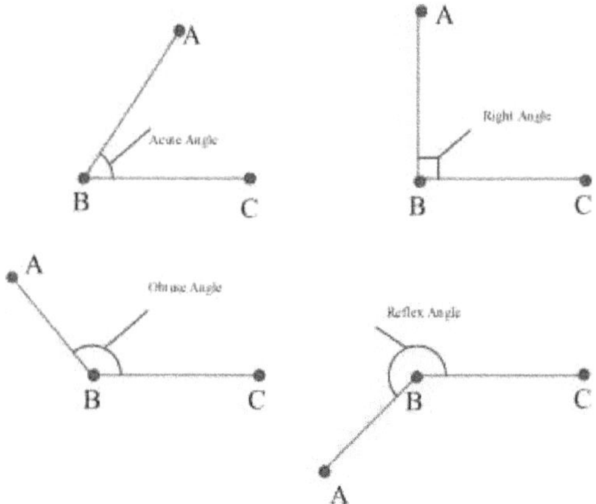

Angles formed between two intersecting lines

Vertically Opposite Angles

When two lines intersect each other, then 4 angles are formed.

- At the point of intersection, angles situated opposite to each other are referred to as vertically opposite angles.
- Vertically opposite angles consistently possess equal measures.
  $\angle A = \angle B$
  $\angle C = \angle D$

Angles formed by a transversal line

- **Corresponding angles:** These are the angles that are in the same position relative to the transversal. Corresponding angles formed transversal are *congruent* (equal in measure).

Corresponding angles

- $\angle 1$ & $\angle 5$
- $\angle 2$ & $\angle 6$
- $\angle 3$ & $\angle 7$
- $\angle 4$ & $\angle 8$

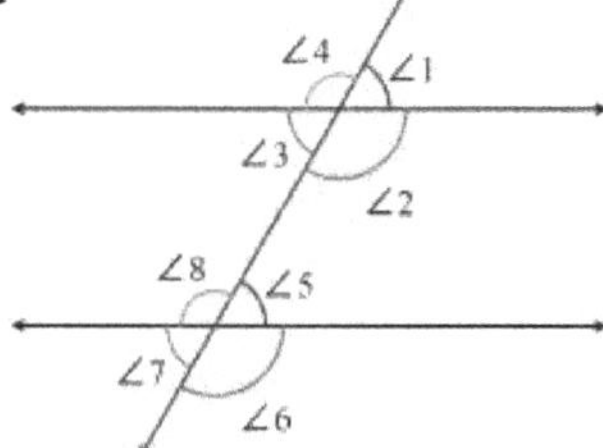

- **Alternate interior angles**: These angles are between the two lines, on alternate sides of the transversal. Alternate interior angles formed by parallel lines cut by a transversal are *congruent.*

  Alternate interior angles:
  - $\angle 2$ & $\angle 8$
  - $\angle 3$ & $\angle 5$

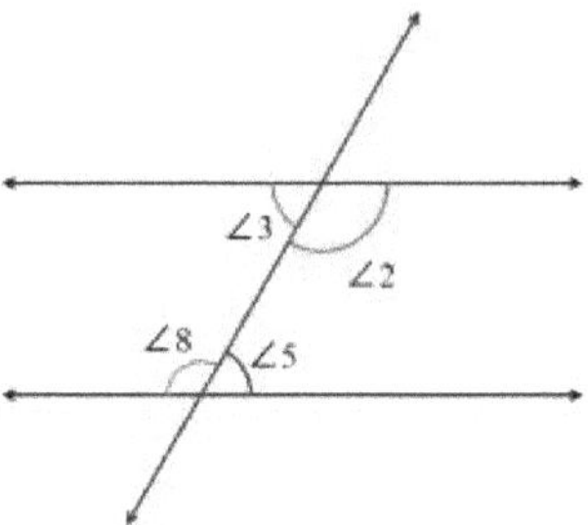

- **Alternate exterior angles**: These angles are outside the two lines, on alternate sides of the transversal. Alternate exterior angles formed by parallel lines cut by a transversal are *congruent.*

  Alternate exterior angles
  - $\angle 1$ & $\angle 7$
  - $\angle 4$ & $\angle 6$

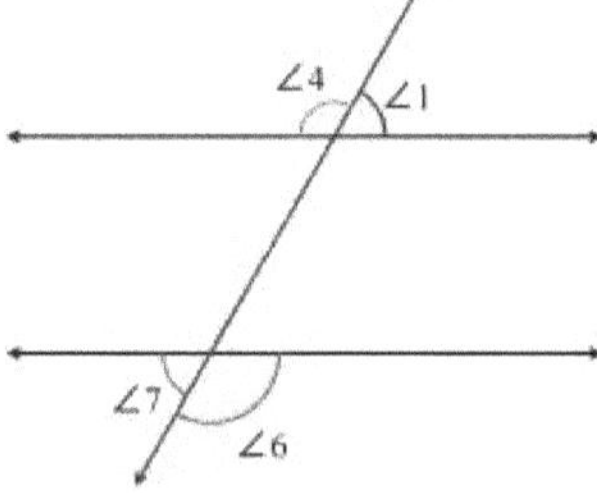

- **Same-side (consecutive) interior angles**: These angles are between the two lines, on the same side of the transversal. They are *supplementary* (In the diagram, angles 3 and 2 are same-side interior angles.

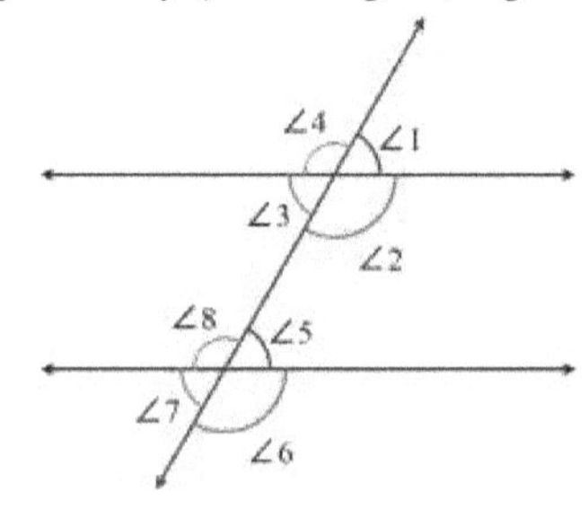

Example 1: In the figure, l ∥ m and a line t intersect lines l and m at P and Q, respectively. Find the sum 2a + b.

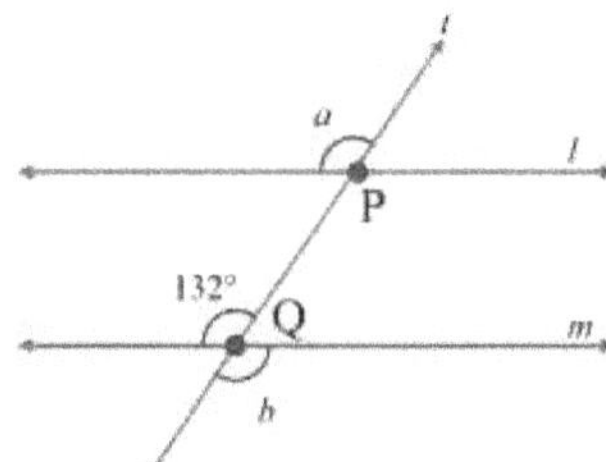

Solution :

Based on the information given:

- l and m are parallel lines

- Line t intersects l at point P, forming angle a

- Line t intersects m at point Q, forming angle b

- Angles a and b are corresponding angles, since they are formed by the transversal t crossing parallel lines l and m

We know that corresponding angles formed when a transversal crosses parallel lines are congruent.

Therefore: $a = b = 132^o$

To find the sum $2a + b$: $2a + b = 2(a) + b = 2a + a\ (since\ a = b) = 3a$

So the sum $2a + b = 3a = 3\ (132^0) = 396^0$

Example 2: In the figure, if AB ∥ DE, ∠ BAC = 35° and ∠ CDE = 53°, find ∠ DCE.

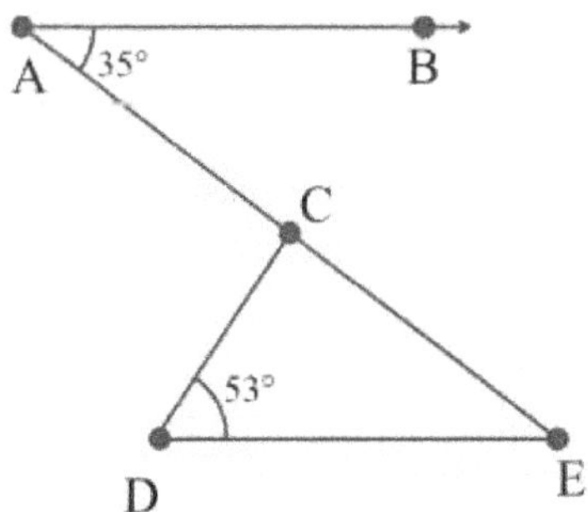

Solution:

AE is a transversal since AB ∥ DE.

Here, ∠BAC and ∠AED are alternate interior angles.

Hence, ∠BAC = ∠AED

∠BAC = 35° {given}

$\angle AED = 35°$

Now consider the triangle CDE.

We know that the sum of the interior angles of a triangle is 180°.

$\therefore \angle DCE + \angle CED + \angle CDE = 180°$

Substituting the values, we get;

$\angle DCE + 35° + 53° = 180°$

$\angle DCE = 180° - 35° - 53° = 92°$

Triangles:

Definition: A triangle is a three-sided polygon with three angles and three sides.

1. **Types of Triangles:**

    - **Scalene Triangle:** All sides and angles are different.

    - **Isosceles Triangle:** Two sides and two angles are equal.

    - **Equilateral Triangle:** All three sides and angles are equal.

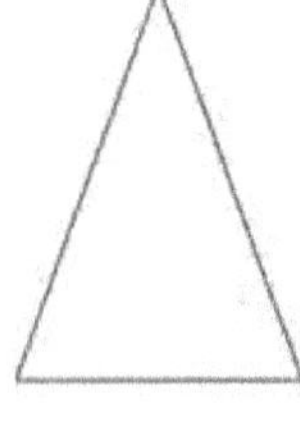

Scalene Triangle

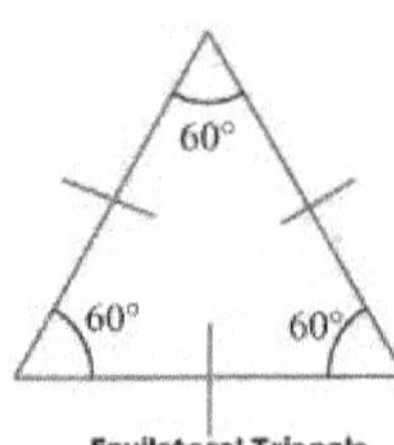

Equilateral Triangle

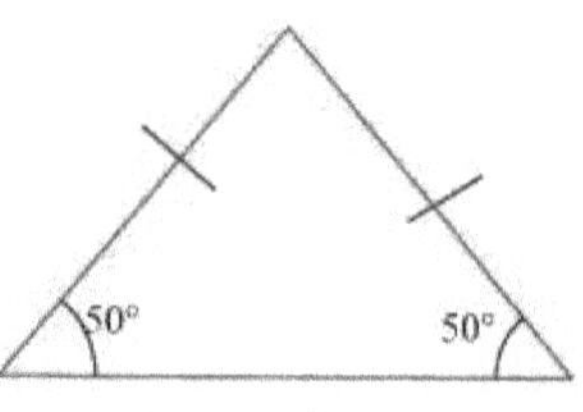

Isosceles Triangle

2. **Angle Sum Property:**

    - The sum of the interior angles of a triangle is always 180 degrees.

Congruent Triangles:

Definition: Two triangles are congruent if their corresponding sides and angles are equal.

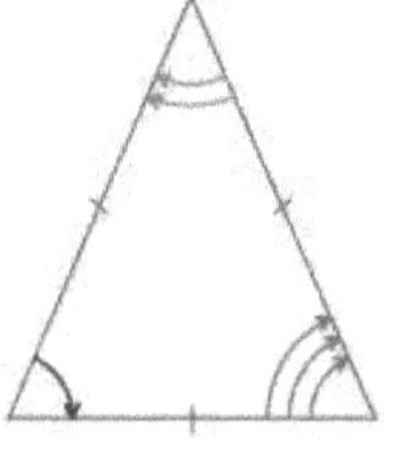

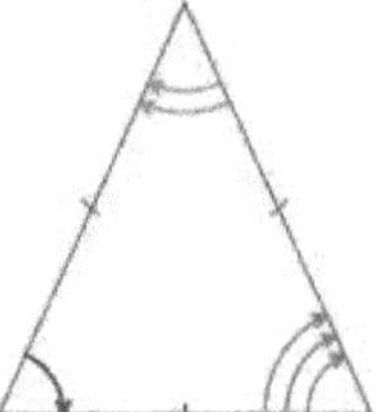

1. **Congruence Criteria:**

- **SSS (Side-Side-Side):** If the three sides of one triangle are equal to the three sides of another triangle.

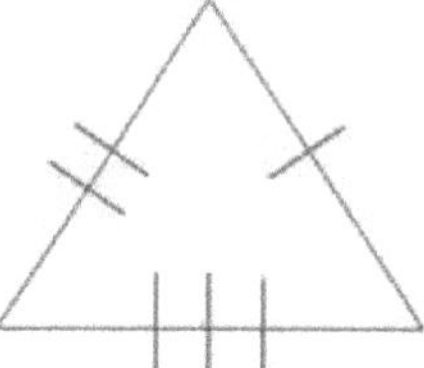 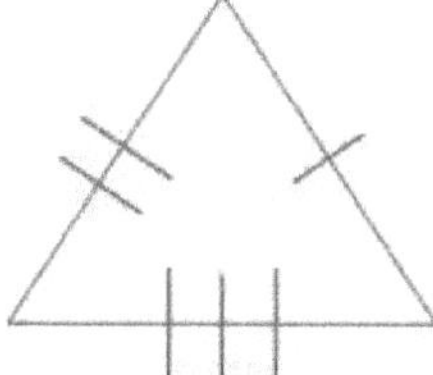

- **SAS (Side-Angle-Side):** If two sides and the included angle of one triangle are equal to two sides and the included angle of another triangle.

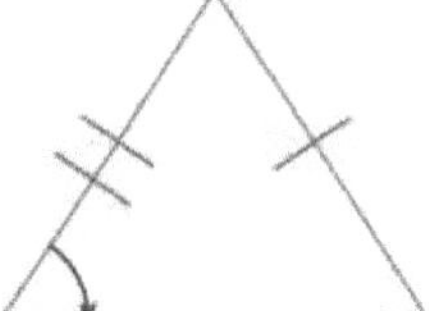 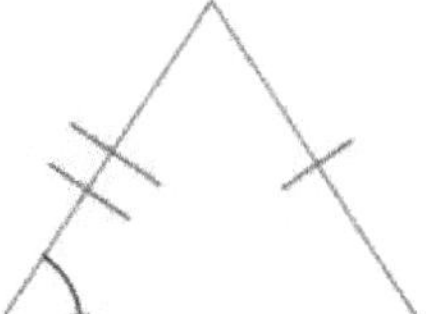

- **ASA (Angle-Side-Angle):** If two angles and the included side of one triangle are equal to two angles and the included side of another triangle.

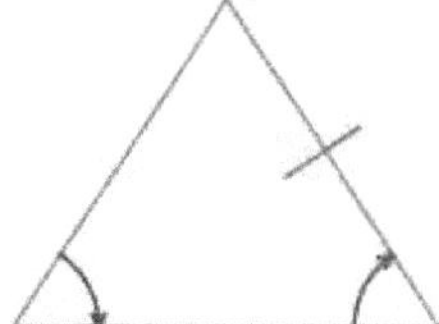 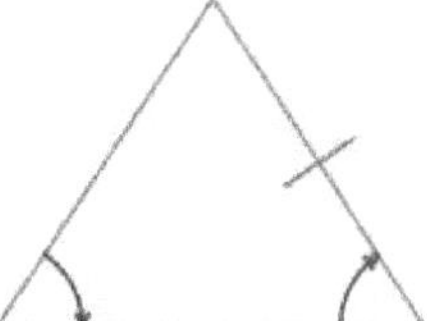

- **Hypotenuse-Leg:** The pair of hypotenuses and another pair of corresponding sides are equal in two right triangles.

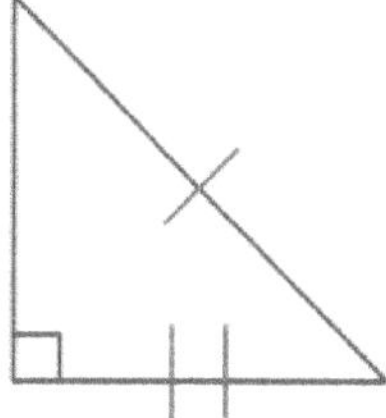 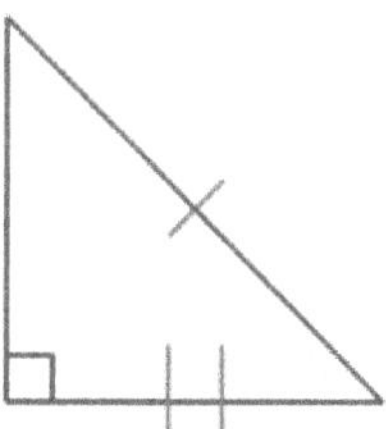

Similar Triangles:

Definition: Two triangles are similar if their corresponding angles are equal, and their corresponding sides are in proportion.

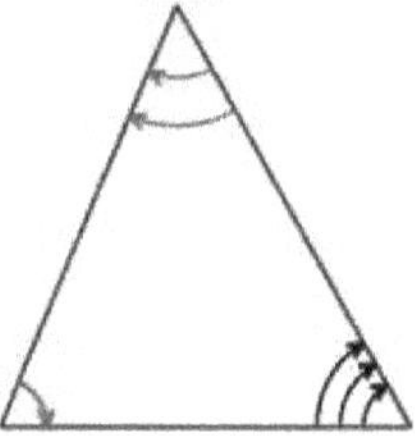
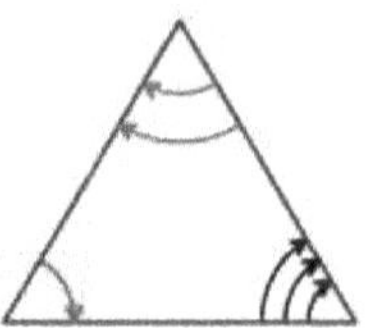

1. **Similarity Criteria:**

   - **AA (Angle-Angle):** If two angles of one triangle are equal to two angles of another t

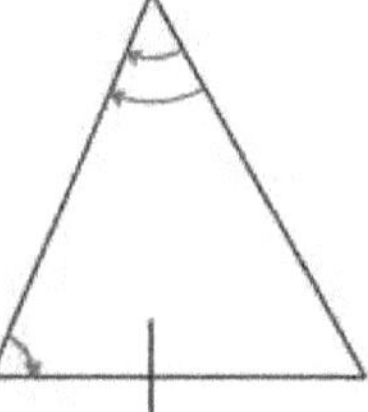
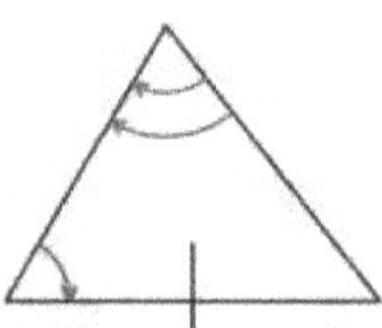

   - **SAS (Side-Angle-Side):** If the ratio of the lengths of the corresponding sides is the same, and the included angles are equal.

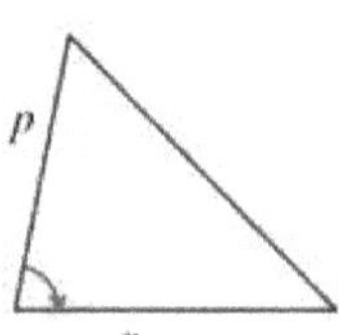

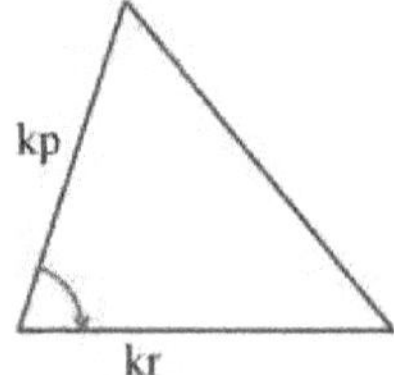

   - **SSS (Side-Side-Side):** If the lengths of all three pairs of corresponding sides are proportional, the triangles are similar.

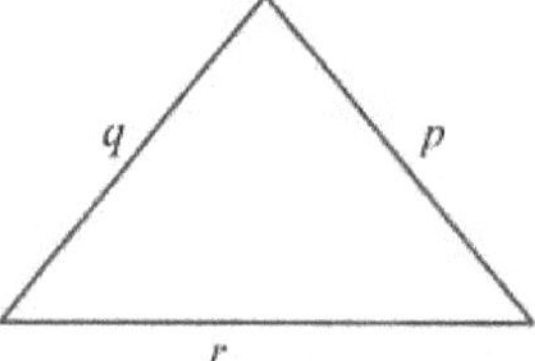

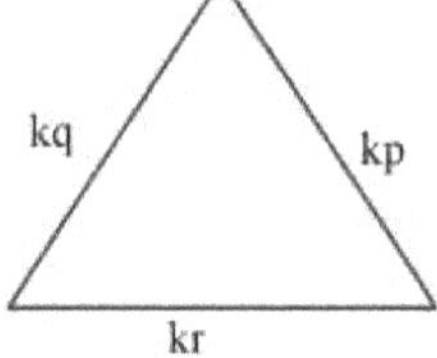

Example 3:

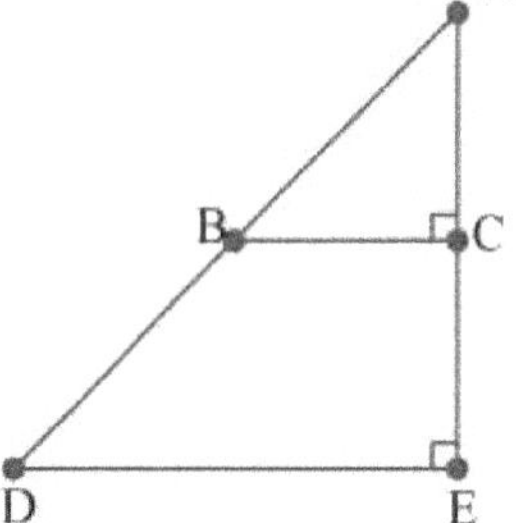

In the above figure, line segment AB measures 10, line segment AC measures 8, line segment BD measures 10, and line segment DE measures 12. What is the perimeter of trapezoid BCDE?

Solution:

Triangles ABC and ADE are similar with a shared right angle at point A, ensuring equal lower-left-hand angles (at points B and D) due to the total angle sum of 180 degrees in a triangle.

For the right triangle ABC, with AC = 8 and AB = 10, determining side BC can be achieved using the Pythagorean triple 3-4-5 side ratio, yielding BC = 6.

Similarly applying the Pythagorean triplet 3-4-5 ratio to the larger triangle ADE (with BD as the hypotenuse, measuring 20), allows the calculation of DE as 12 (twice BC), and CE as 8.

Thus, the dimensions of the parallelogram are determined: BD is 10, BC is 6, CE is 8, and DE is 12, with a total sum of these sides amounting to 36.

Examples 4: The angles of a triangle are in the ratio 2: 3: 4. Find the angles of the triangle.

Solution:

Given that the ratio of angles of a triangle is 2: 3: 4.

Let 2x, 3x, and 4x be the angles of a triangle.

We know that the sum of angles of a triangle is 180°.

So, $2x + 3x + 4x = 180°$

$9x = 180°$

$x = 180°/9 = 20°$

Now,

$2x = 2 \times 20° = 40°$

$3x = 3 \times 20° = 60°$

$4x = 4 \times 20° = 80°$

Therefore, the angles of the triangle are 40°, 60°, and 80°, respective

Practice Question:

1. The ratio of $m\angle AOB$ to $m\angle BOC$ to $m\angle COD$ is $1 : 3 : 2$. What is the measure of $\angle BOD$?

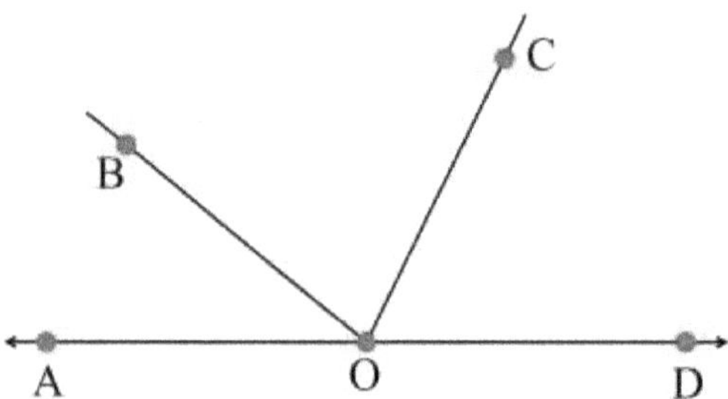

2. In the below figure, line A is parallel to line B and line D is parallel to line E. What is the value of y, in degrees?

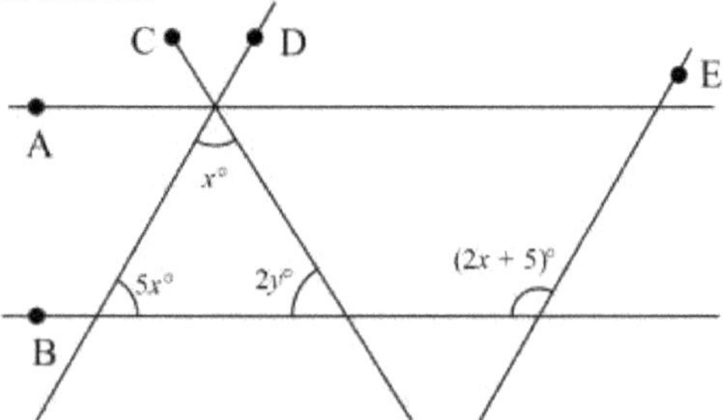

3. Two straight lines intersect to form the angles below. If the measure of angle x is three times the measure of angle y, what is the measure of angle z?

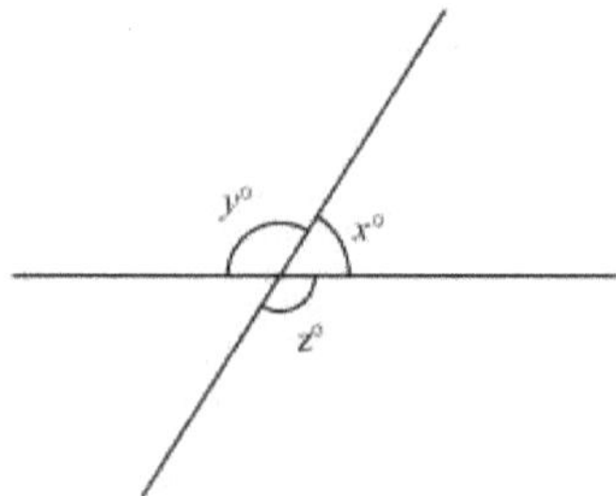

4. What is the value of x in the below figure?

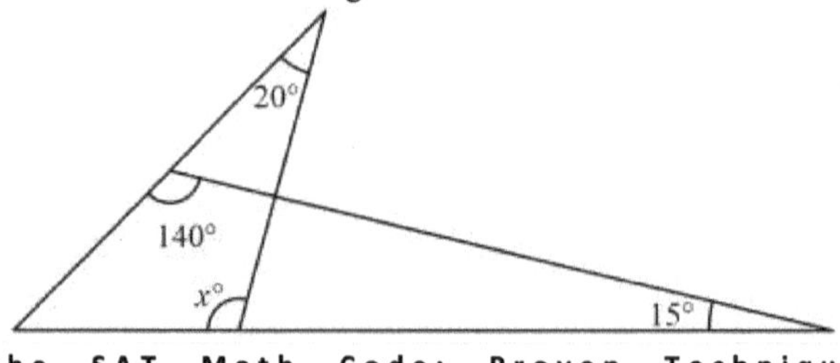

5. In the below figure, lines A and b are parallel. What is the value of x?

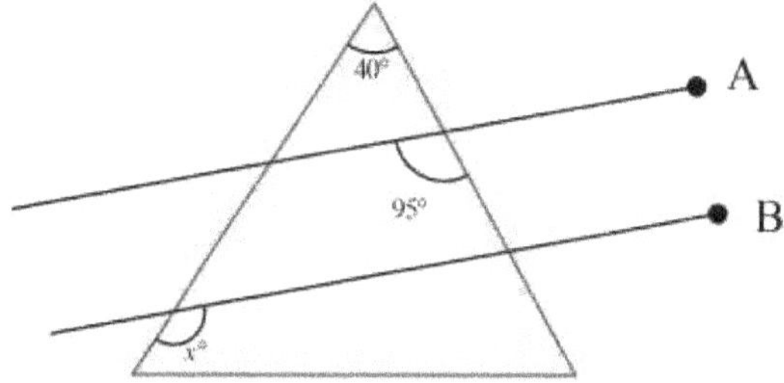

6. In the below diagram, lines x, y, and z all intersect at point A. If m=20 and n=130, what is the value

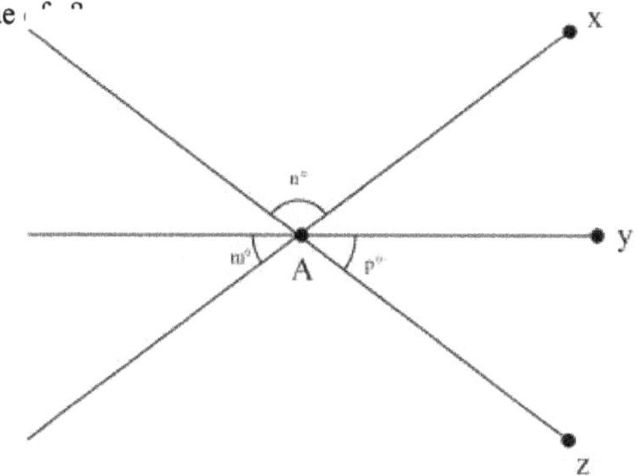

7. On a number line, point D is 2/5 of the way from point C to point E and is located at -2. If C is
   at -10, what is the coordinate of point E ?

8. In the below figure Line A and Line D are parallel. What is the value of $x + y$?

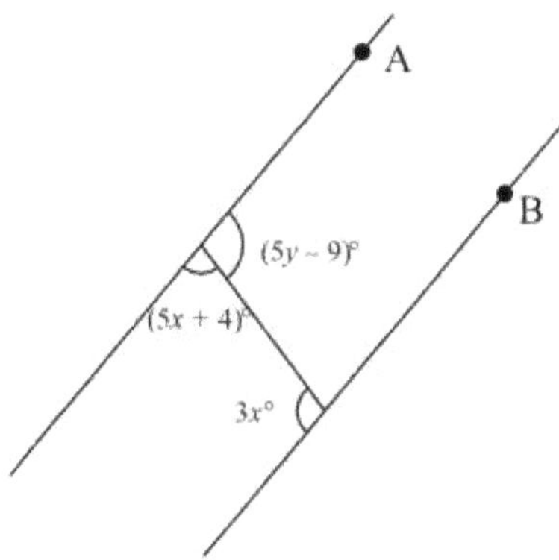

9. Triangles BAC and EDF are shown below. What is the length of side DE?

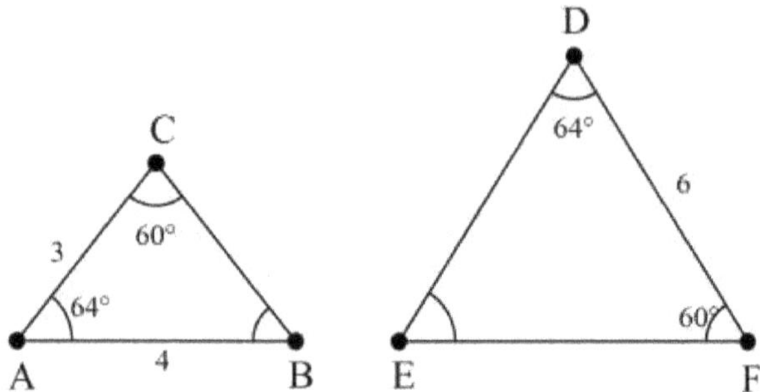

10. In the below figure, line segment DE is parallel to line segment BC. What is the length of side DE?

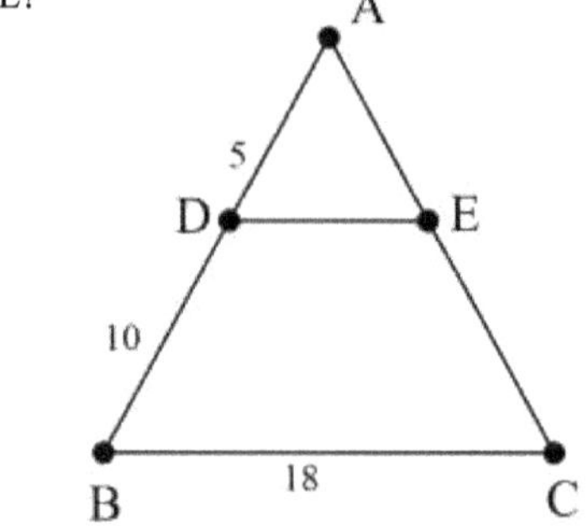

11. Triangles CAB and FDE are shown below. The lengths of their sides are also given. What is equal to the ratio of e to g?

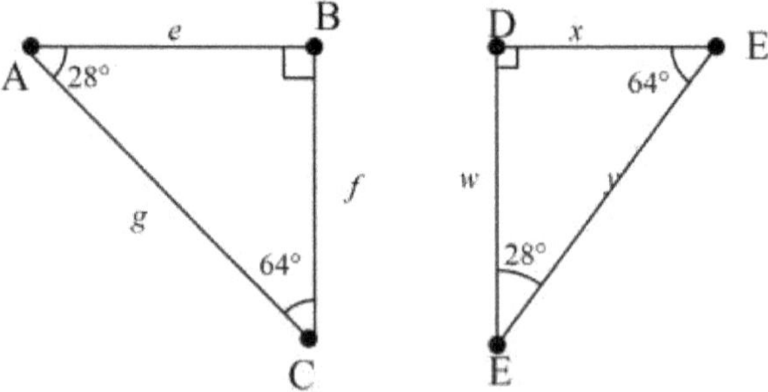

12. In the below diagram $\angle PQR = \angle QRS = \angle RST = 90^o, PQ = QR = RS = 5\ cm\ and\ ST = 1cm.$ Find the length of QU.

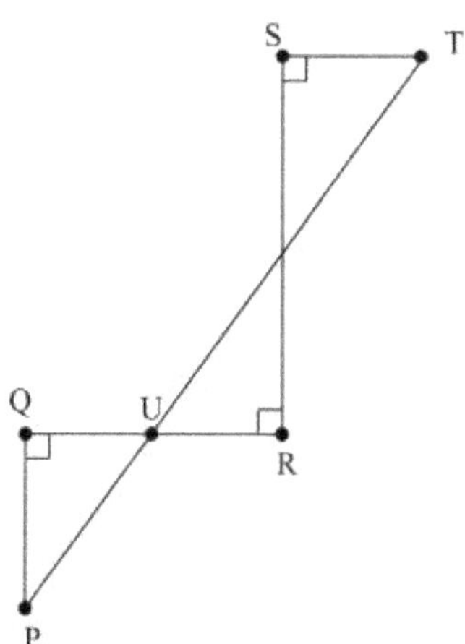

13. State if the triangles in each pair are similar. If so, state how you know they are similar and complete the similarity statement.

(a)

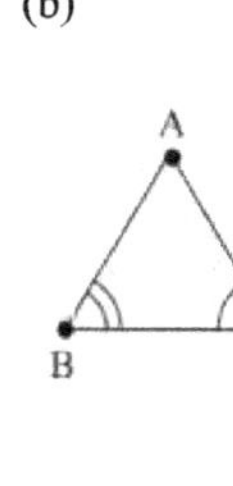

$\triangle ABC \sim$________

(b)

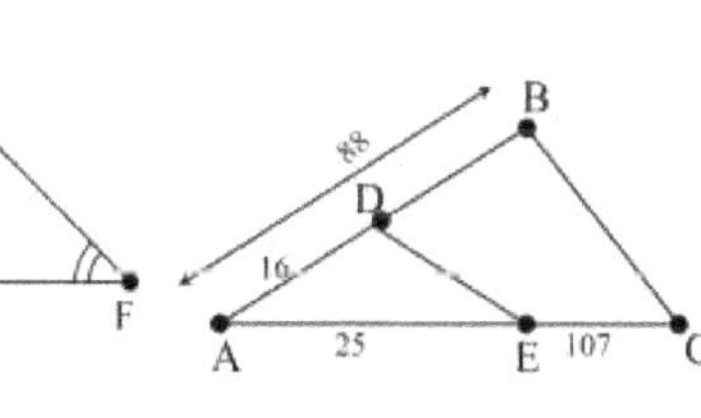

$\triangle ABC \sim$________

(c)

$\triangle ABC \sim$________

(d) 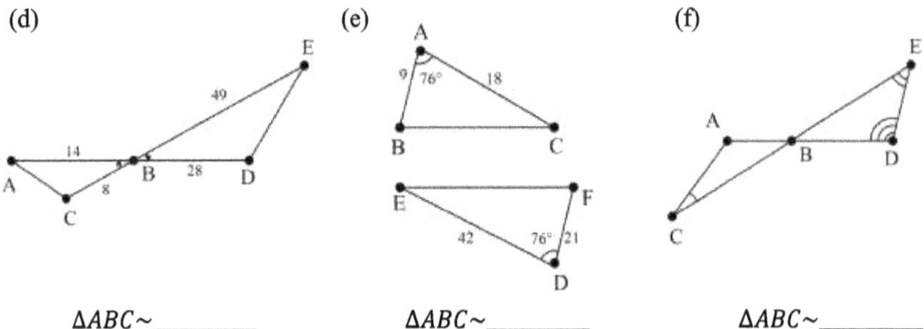

(e)

(f)

$\triangle ABC \sim$__________

$\triangle ABC \sim$__________

$\triangle ABC \sim$__________

14. Find the missing length. The triangles in each pair are similar

(a)

(b)

(c)

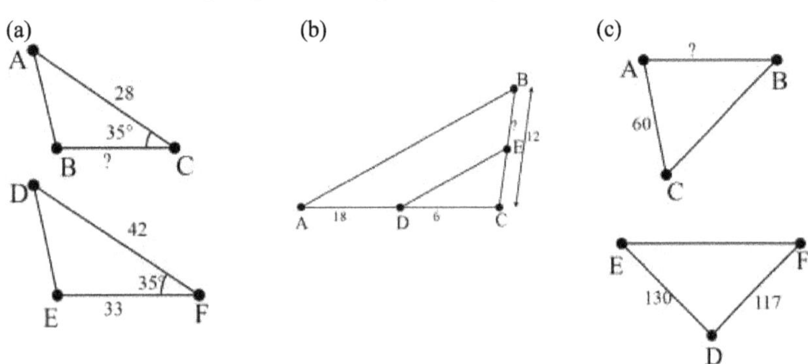

15. Solve for x. The triangles in each pair are similar.

(a)

(b)

(c)

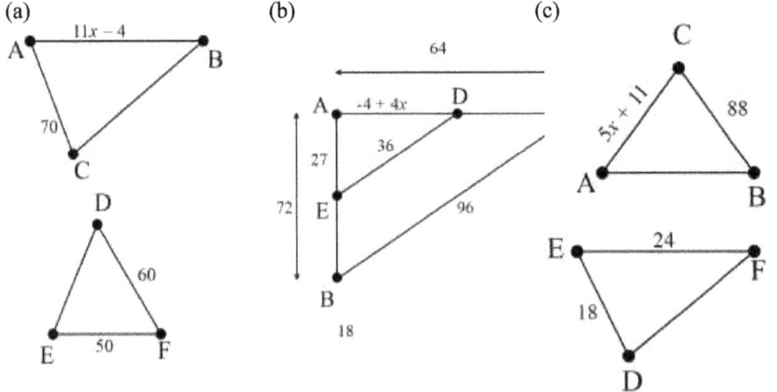

Answer:

1. 150°
2. 15
3. 135 degrees
4. 135 degrees
5. 125 degrees
6. 30
7. 10
8. 37
9. 8
10. 6
11. e/g = w/y.
12. 3
13. (a) Not similar (b) $\triangle ABC \sim \triangle DEf$ (c) $\triangle ABC \neq \triangle ADE$ (d) $\triangle ABC \sim \triangle BDE$ (e) $\triangle ABC \sim \triangle DEF$ (f) $\triangle ABC \neq \triangle BDE$
14. (a) 22 (b) 9 (c) 54
15. (a) 8 (b) 7 (c) 11

Lesson 3: Right Triangles and Trigonometry

Right Triangle: A right triangle is a type of triangle with one angle measuring 90 degrees, known as the right angle. The other two angles are acute (less than 90 degrees). The side opposite the right angle is called the hypotenuse, while the other two sides are referred to as the legs.

Pythagorean Theorem:

The Pythagorean Theorem is a fundamental property of right triangles. It states that in a right triangle, the square of the length of the hypotenuse (c) is equal to the sum of the squares of the lengths of the legs (a and b). Mathematically, this is expressed as $c^2 = a^2 + b^2$.

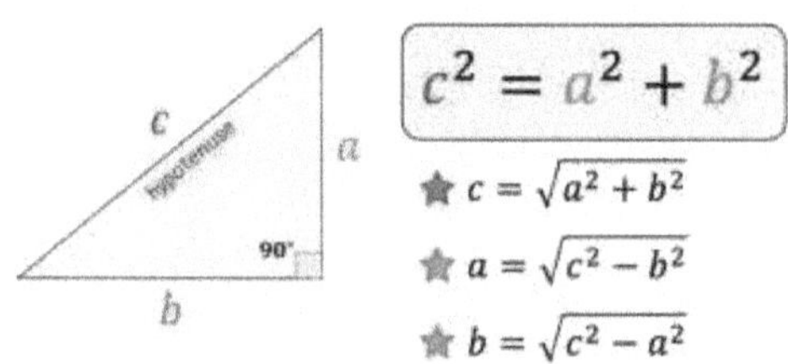

$$c^2 = a^2 + b^2$$

$$\bigstar\ c = \sqrt{a^2 + b^2}$$

$$\bigstar\ a = \sqrt{c^2 - b^2}$$

$$\bigstar\ b = \sqrt{c^2 - a^2}$$

Example 1: In a right triangle, if perpendicular = 8 cm and base = 6 cm, then what is the value of hypotenuse?

Solution : let's solve this step-by-step:

- This is a right triangle

- We are given:

  - Perpendicular side = 8 cm

  - Base side = 6 cm

- We need to find the hypotenuse side

- To find the hypotenuse of a right triangle, we can use the Pythagorean Theorem:

  - $a^2 + b^2 = c^2$

    - Where a and b are the legs, and c is the hypotenuse

- Plugging in the given values:

  - $8^2 + 6^2 = c^2$

  - $64 + 36 = c^2$

  - $100 = c^2$

- Taking the square root of both sides:

- $c = 10$ cm

Therefore, if the perpendicular is 8 cm and the base is 6 cm, the hypotenuse of the right triangle is 10 cm.

Trigonometric Ratios:

Trigonometric ratios are relationships between the angles and sides of a right triangle. The three primary ratios are:

- Sine (sin): $\sin(\theta) = \dfrac{\text{Opposite}}{\text{Hypotenuse}}$
- Cosine (cos): $\cos(\theta) = \dfrac{\text{Adjacent}}{\text{Hypotenuse}}$
- Tangent (tan): $\tan(\theta) = \dfrac{\text{Opposite}}{\text{Adjacent}}$

These ratios are vital in solving trigonometric problems and have applications in various fields.

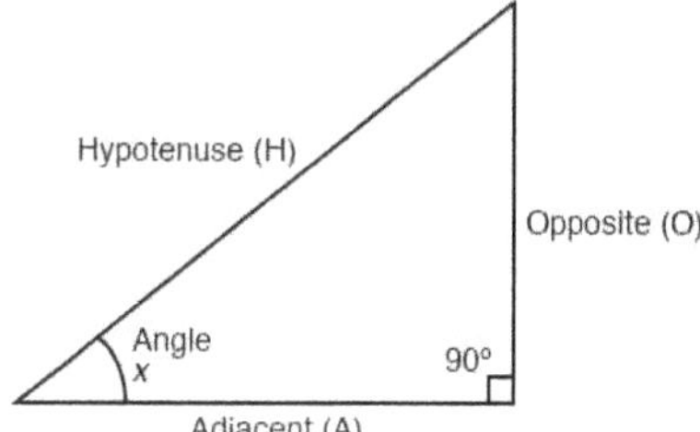

Special Right Triangles:

Special right triangles have well-defined angle measures, leading to specific side relationships. Two common examples are:

- 30-60-90 Triangle: The sides are in the ratio $1 : \sqrt{3} : 2$
- 45-45-90 Triangle: The sides are in the ratio $1 : 1 : \sqrt{2}$.
- **Pythagorean triple triangles**: These triangles have integer side lengths and include examples such as $(3, 4, 5)$, $(5, 12, 13)$, and $(7, 24, 25)$

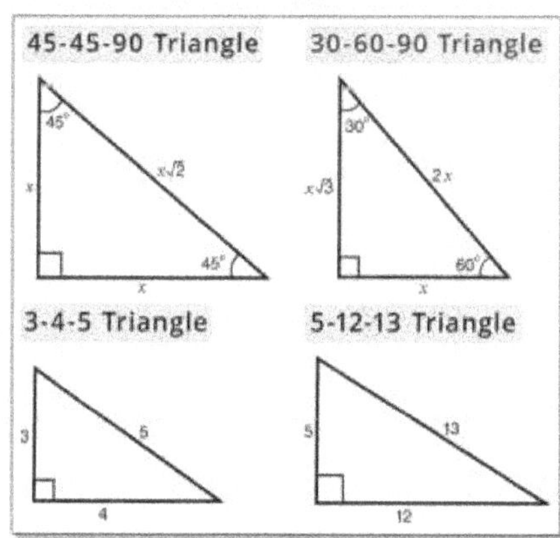

Relation between Sin and Cosine:

- The sine and cosine ratios are related through the Pythagorean Identity. In a right triangle, the sum of the squares of the lengths of the legs is equal to the square of the length of the hypotenuse.

  - Pythagorean Identity: $\sin^2(\theta) + \cos^2(\theta) = 1$

- This identity highlights the relationship between the sine and cosine ratios for any angle in a right triangle.

- Additionally, the tangent ratio can be expressed in terms of sine and cosine:

  - $\tan(\theta) = \dfrac{\sin(\theta)}{\cos(\theta)}.$

Example 2: In a 30-60-90 right triangle, if the hypotenuse is 10, what is the length of the shorter leg?

Solution: For a 30-60-90 right triangle, the ratios of the side lengths are:

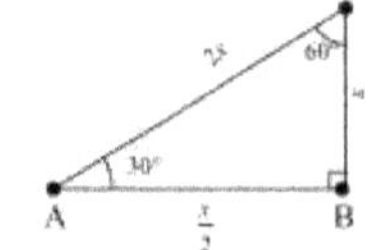

- The hypotenuse is 2x

- The longer leg (opposite the 60° angle) is x

- The shorter leg (opposite the 30° angle) is x/2

In this problem, the hypotenuse is given as 10.

Using the ratios:

- Hypotenuse = 2x = 10

- So, x = 5

- The shorter leg is x/2 = 5/2 = 2.5

Therefore, if the hypotenuse is 10, the length of the shorter leg opposite the 30° angle is 2.5.

Example 3: If cos A = 0.6 in right triangle ABC, what is sin A?

Solution: cos A = 0.6

In a right triangle:

$$\cos A = \frac{\text{adjacent}}{\text{hypotenuse}}$$

$$\sin A = \frac{\text{opposite}}{\text{hypotenuse}}$$

cos and sin are complementary angles. This means:

$$\sin^2 A + \cos^2 A = 1$$

Plugging in the known value:

$(\sin A)^2 + (0.6)^2 = 1 \Rightarrow (\sin A)^2 + 0.36 = 1 \Rightarrow (\sin A)^2 = 0.64$

Taking the square root of both sides:

$\sin A = \sqrt{0.64} \Rightarrow \sin A = 0.8$

Therefore, if $\cos A = 0.6$, then $\sin A = 0.8$.

Example 4: The hypotenuse of a right triangle is 10 units, and one leg is 6 units. What is the measure of the acute angle opposite the leg?

Solution: We're given:

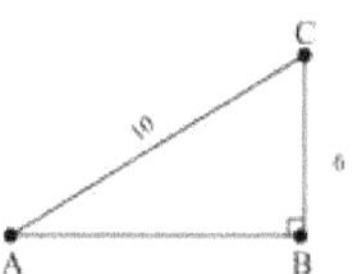

- Hypotenuse is 10 units

- One leg is 6 units

- We need to find:

  - Measure of the acute angle opposite the 6 unit leg

- To find the angle, we can use trig ratios

- Opposite side is 6, hypotenuse is 10

- $\sin(\theta) = \dfrac{opposite}{hypotenuse}$

- $\sin(\theta) = \dfrac{6}{10}$

- $\sin(\theta) = 0.6$

- Take inverse sin:

$$\theta = sin^{-1}(0.6)$$

- Using a calculator:

- $\theta = sin^{-1}(0.6) = 36.87 \; degrees$

Therefore, if the hypotenuse is 10 units and the leg opposite the angle is 6 units, the measure of the acute angle is 36.87 degrees.

The trigonometric identity $sin(A) = cos(90 - A)$ using a right triangle:

Consider a right triangle with an angle A as shown below:

In this triangle:

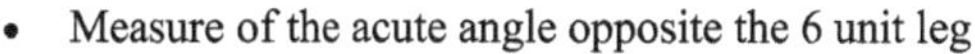

- a is the side adjacent to angle A,

- b is the side opposite angle A,

- c is the hypotenuse.

Now, let's consider the angle 90−A:

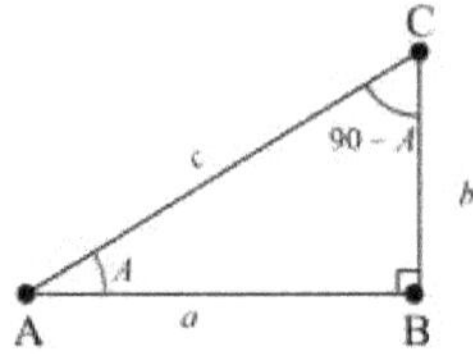

In this triangle:

- a is the side opposite angle $90-A$,

- b is the side adjacent to angle $90-A$,

- c is the hypotenuse.

Now, let's apply the cosine definition:

$$\cos(90 - A) = \frac{b}{c}$$

And the sine definition:

$$\sin(A) = \frac{b}{c}$$

As you can see, $cos(90 - A) = sin(A)$, which verifies the given trigonometric identity.

Now, let's look at the specific example you provided:

$$sin(20) = cos(90 - 20)$$

$$sin(20) = cos(70)$$

A few more examples:

- $Sin(15) = Cos(75)$
- $Sin(25) = Cos(65)$
- $Sin(40) = Cos(50)$
- $Sin(80) = Cos(10)$

Sin Cos Tan Chart

θ	$0°$ (or) 0	$30°$ (or) $\frac{\pi}{6}$	$45°$ (or) $\frac{\pi}{4}$	$60°$ (or) $\frac{\pi}{3}$	$90°$ (or) $\frac{\pi}{2}$
sin θ	0	$\frac{1}{2}$	$\frac{\sqrt{2}}{2}$	$\frac{\sqrt{3}}{2}$	1
cos θ	1	$\frac{\sqrt{3}}{2}$	$\frac{\sqrt{2}}{2}$	$\frac{1}{2}$	0
tan θ	0	$\frac{\sqrt{3}}{3}$	1	$\sqrt{3}$	Not Defined

Angles in The Four Quadrants

The Four Quadrants

The coordinate axes divide the plane into four
quadrants, labeled First, Second, Third and Fourth
as shown. Angles in the third quadrant, for
example, lie between 180° and 270°.

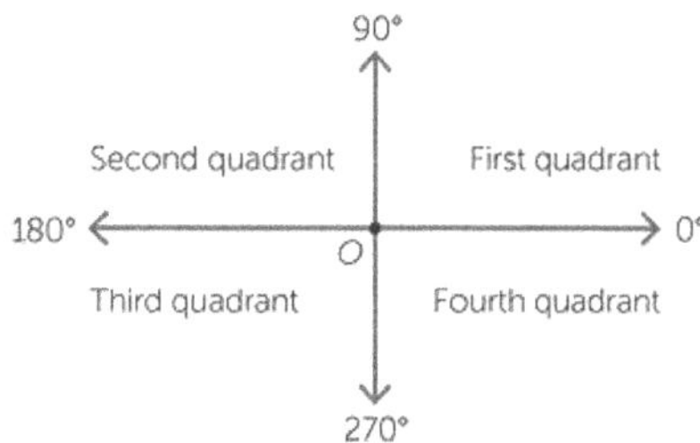

A common way to remember the signs of the three trigonometric ratios (sine, cosine, tangent)
in each quadrant is through the acronym "All Students Take Calculus" and the associated
diagram:

1. **All (All) - Quadrant I:**

   - In the first quadrant, all three
     trigonometric ratios are positive.

2. **Students (Sine) - Quadrant II:**

   - In the second quadrant, only the sine ratio is
     positive.

3. **Take (Tangent) - Quadrant III:**

   - In the third quadrant, only the tangent ratio is positive.

4. **Calculus (Cosine) - Quadrant IV:**

   - In the fourth quadrant, only the cosine ratio is positive.

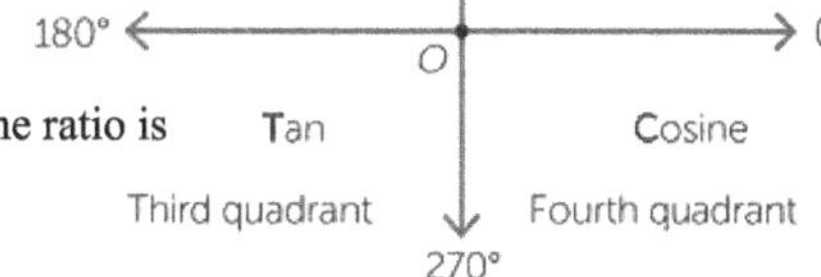

This phrase serves as a mnemonic to help remember which trigonometric ratios are positive
in each quadrant. The first letter of each word corresponds to the first letter of the
trigonometric ratio that is positive in that quadrant.

Example 5: Use the related angle to find the exact value of:

(a) $\sin 120°$ **(b)** $\cos 150°$ **(c)** $\tan 300°$ **(d)** $\cos 240°$

Solution:

(a) The related angle is 60°.

120° is in the second quadrant,

so $\sin 120° = \sin(180 - 60)° = \sin 60° = \dfrac{\sqrt{3}}{2}$.

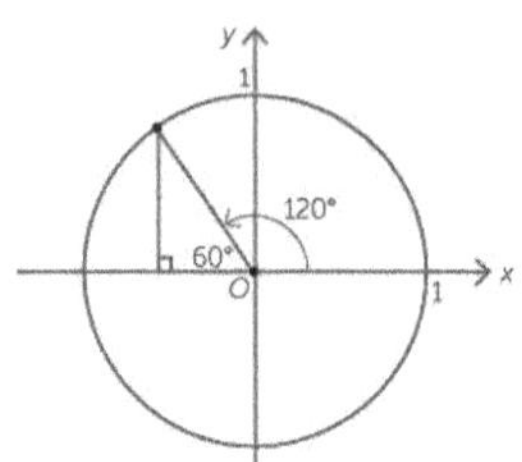

(b) $\cos 150° = \cos(180 - 30)° = -\cos 30° = -\dfrac{\sqrt{3}}{2}$.

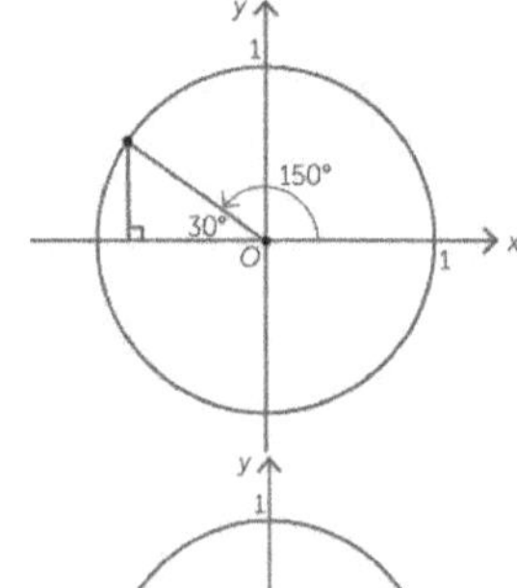

(c) $\tan 300° = \cos(360 - 60)° = -\tan 60° = -\sqrt{3}$

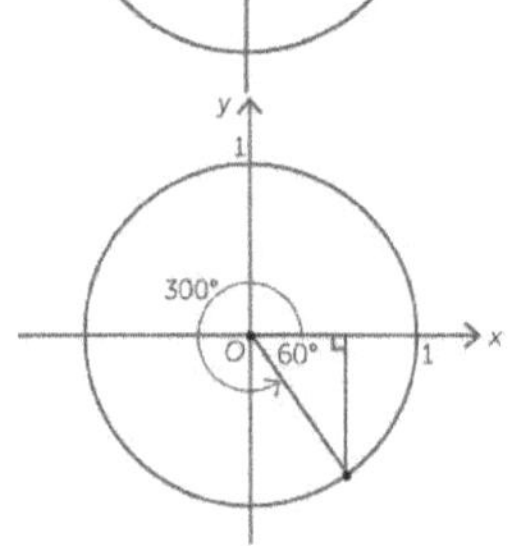

(d) $\cos 240° = \cos(180 + 60)° = -\cos 60° = -\dfrac{1}{2}$

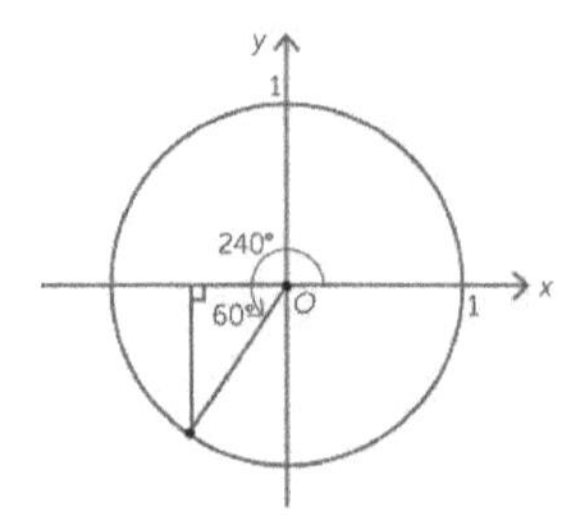

Below information is for reference -

θ (deg.)	θ (rad.)	sin θ		cos θ		tan θ
0	0	0	$\dfrac{\sqrt{0}}{2}$	1	$\dfrac{\sqrt{4}}{2}$	0
30°	$\dfrac{\pi}{6}$	$\dfrac{1}{2}$	$\dfrac{\sqrt{1}}{2}$	$\dfrac{\sqrt{3}}{2}$	$\dfrac{\sqrt{3}}{2}$	$\dfrac{\sqrt{3}}{3}$
45°	$\dfrac{\pi}{4}$	$\dfrac{\sqrt{2}}{2}$	$\dfrac{\sqrt{2}}{2}$	$\dfrac{\sqrt{2}}{2}$	$\dfrac{\sqrt{2}}{2}$	1
60°	$\dfrac{\pi}{3}$	$\dfrac{\sqrt{3}}{2}$	$\dfrac{\sqrt{3}}{2}$	$\dfrac{1}{2}$	$\dfrac{\sqrt{1}}{2}$	$\sqrt{3}$
90°	$\dfrac{\pi}{2}$	1	$\dfrac{\sqrt{4}}{2}$	0	$\dfrac{\sqrt{0}}{2}$	∞
120°	$\dfrac{2\pi}{3}$	$\dfrac{\sqrt{3}}{2}$	$\dfrac{\sqrt{3}}{2}$	$-\dfrac{1}{2}$	$-\dfrac{\sqrt{1}}{2}$	$-\sqrt{3}$
135°	$\dfrac{3\pi}{4}$	$\dfrac{\sqrt{2}}{2}$	$\dfrac{\sqrt{2}}{2}$	$-\dfrac{\sqrt{2}}{2}$	$-\dfrac{\sqrt{2}}{2}$	-1
150°	$\dfrac{5\pi}{6}$	$\dfrac{1}{2}$	$\dfrac{\sqrt{1}}{2}$	$-\dfrac{\sqrt{3}}{2}$	$-\dfrac{\sqrt{3}}{2}$	$-\dfrac{\sqrt{3}}{3}$
180°	π	0	$\dfrac{\sqrt{0}}{2}$	-1	$-\dfrac{\sqrt{4}}{2}$	0

Practice Question:

1. Find the missing side lengths. Leave your answers as radicals in simplest form.

(a) (b) (c) (d)

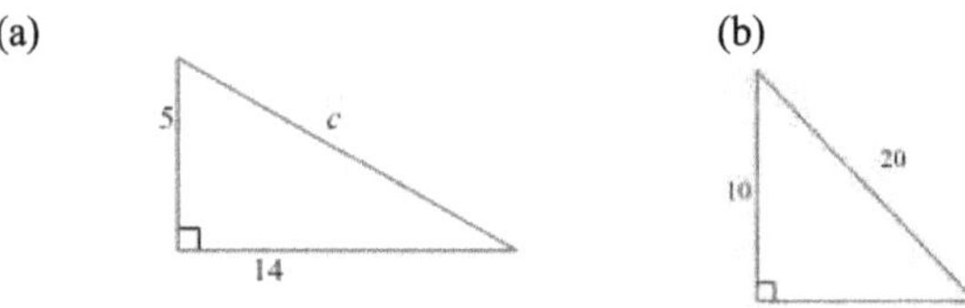

2. For each triangle find the missing length. Round your answer to the nearest tenth. Then find the area and the perimeter.

(a) (b)

3. Find c is the hypotenuse of the right triangle ABC with sides a, b, c

(a) a = 12 ; b = 5;c =_______(b) a=_____b = 40;c =50 (c) a = 15 ;b =____;c = 17

4. Two joggers run 8 miles north and then 5 miles west. What is the shortest distance, to the nearest tenth of a mile, they must travel to return to their starting point?

5. Oscar's dog house is shaped like a tent. The slanted sides are both 5 feet long and the bottom of the house is 6 feet across. What is the height of his dog house, in feet, at its tallest point?

6. To get from point A to point B you must avoid walking through a pond. To avoid the pond, you must walk 34 meters south and 41 meters east. To the nearest meter, how many meters would be saved if it were possible to walk through the pond?

7. A suitcase measures 24 inches long and the diagonal is 30 inches long. How much material is needed to cover one side of the suitcase?

8. Given a right triangle where $sin\theta = \frac{3}{5}$, find the missing side.

9. Given a right triangle where $tan\theta = \frac{17}{18}$, find the missing side.

10. Find the value of x in the triangle below.

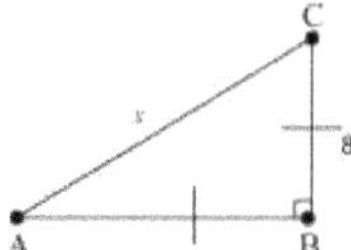

11. In a 45−45−90 triangle, if one leg is 6. What is the measure of the hypotenuse?

12. Find the value of x

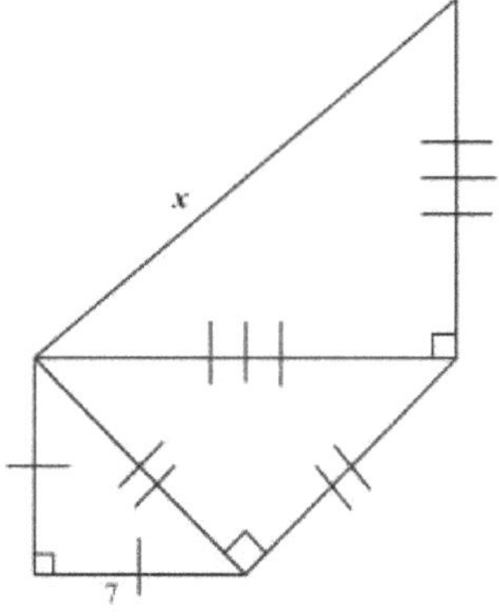

13. In a 30-60-90 triangle, the length of the side opposite the 30○ angle is 5. What is the length of the hypotenuse?
14. A triangle has three angles A, B and C such that B=2A and C=3A. The side opposite to A measures 3 units in length. How long is the side opposite of C?
15. In right triangle ABC, where angle A measures 90 degrees, side AB measures 15 and side AC measures 36, what is the length of side BC?
16. Find the value of each trigonometric ratio. Express your answer as a fraction in lowest terms.

(a) sin C   (b) cos C   (c) tan A   (d) sin C

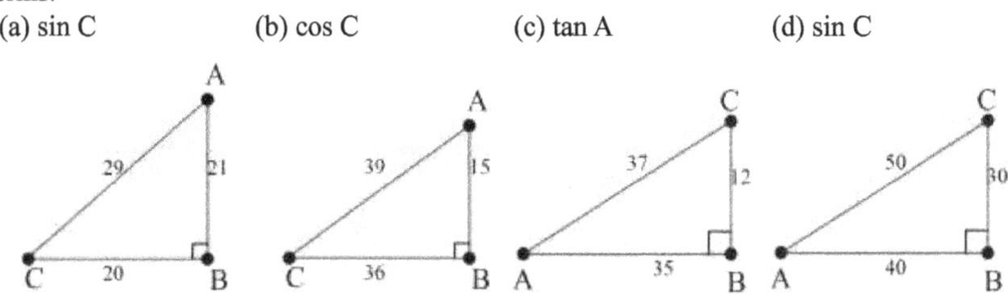

17. In a right triangle, the ratio of the sine and cosine of the smaller angle is 4:5. Find the measure of the smaller angle.
18. In triangle LMN, LM is perpendicular to MN. If $\tan L = \frac{4}{3}$, what is the value of $\cos N$?
19. If $(a + 5) + (b + 5) = 100$, and $\tan a^0 = \frac{2}{3}$, what is the value of $\tan b^0$?

20. The three angles of a right triangle have measures a^0, b^0, and c^0. If $c = 90$ and $\cos a^0 = \frac{3}{5}$, what is $\sin b^0$?

Answer:

1. (a) $a = 4, b = 2\sqrt{2}$ (b) $a = 2\sqrt{3}, b = 2\sqrt{3}$ (c)) $a = 4, b = 2\sqrt{3}$ (d) $a = 8, b = 8$
2. (a) $c = 14.9, Area = 35\ Perimeter = 33.9$ (b)) $c = 17.3, Area = 86.5\ Perimeter = 47.3$
3. (a) c=13 (b)a=30 (c) b=8
4. 9.4 miles
5. 4 feet
6. Hypotenuse=53.3m, Meters saved=21.7m
7. 18 in
8. 4
9. 24.76
10. $8\sqrt{2}$
11. $6\sqrt{2}$
12. $14\sqrt{2}$
13. 10
14. 6
15. 39
16. (a) 21/29 (b) 12/13 (c) 12/35 (d) 3/5
17. $\tan^{-1}(0.8) = 38.6\ degrees$
18. 4/5
19. 3/2
20. 3/5

Lesson 4: Circles - Unit Circles, Angles/Arc, Equation

Circle: A circle is the set of all points in a plane that are a fixed distance (the radius) from a given point (the center).

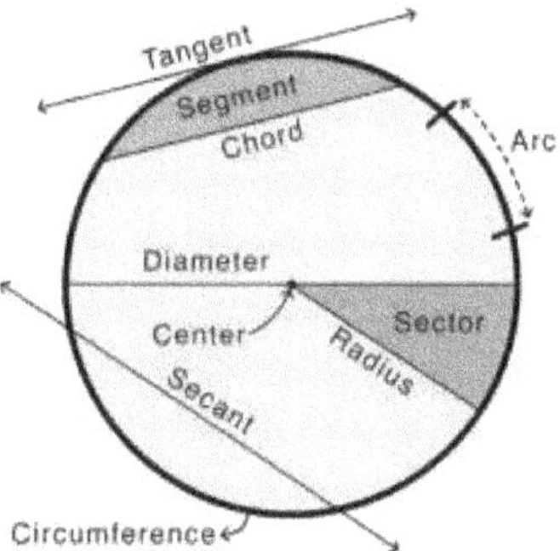

- **Radius:** The radius of a circle is the distance from the center to any point on the circle. It is denoted by "r."

- **Diameter:** The diameter is the longest chord of the circle, passing through the center. It is twice the length of the radius. The diameter is denoted by "d." $d = 2r$

- **Circumference:** The circumference is the perimeter or the distance around the circle. It is given by the formula: $C = 2\pi r$

where π is a mathematical constant approximately equal to 3.14159.

- **Area:** The area of a circle is the region enclosed by the circle. It is given by the formula:

$$A = \pi r^2$$

- **Chord:** A chord is a line segment with both endpoints on the circle.

- **Secant:** A secant is a line that intersects the circle at two distinct points. The line can be extended beyond these points.

- **Sector:** A region bounded by two radii of equal length with a common center.

- **Segment:** The segment of a circle is the region bounded by a chord and the arc subtended by the chord.

- **Tangent:** A tangent is a line that intersects the circle at exactly one point. At the point of intersection, the tangent is perpendicular to the radius.

- **Arc:** An arc is a portion of the circle's circumference. A central angle determines the size of the arc.

- **Central Angle:** A central angle is an angle whose vertex is at the center of the circle, and its sides pass through two points on the circle.

- $Central\ Angle = \dfrac{Length\ of\ the\ Arc}{Radius}$

- **Inscribed Angle:** An inscribed angle is an angle formed by two chords in a circle, with the vertex on the circle.

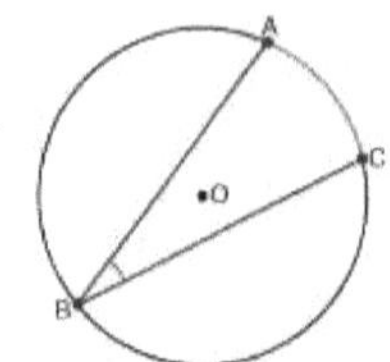

- **Cyclic Quadrilateral:** A cyclic quadrilateral is a four-sided figure whose vertices lie on the circumference of a circle.

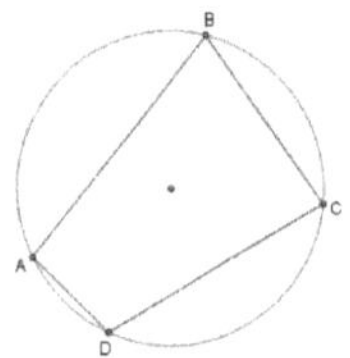

<table>
<tr><th colspan="2">Angles In A Circle</th></tr>
<tr><td>Inscribed angles subtended by the same arc are equal.</td><td></td></tr>
<tr><td>Angles subtended by the diameter (or semi-circle) is 90°.</td><td></td></tr>
<tr><td>Central angle is twice any inscribed angle subtended by the same arc.</td><td></td></tr>
</table>

Example 1: Find the area of a circle with a radius of 9 cm

Solution:

- We are given:

- Radius of the circle = 9 cm
- To find the area of a circle, we use the formula:
  - $Area = \pi \times r^2$
  - Where r is the radius
- Plugging in the given radius:
  - $Area = \pi \times (9\,cm)^2$
  - $Area = \pi \times 81\,cm^2$
- Since $\pi \approx 3.14$
  - $Area \approx 3.14 \times 81\,cm^2$
- Calculate:
  - $Area \approx 254.34\,cm^2$

Therefore, the area of a circle with a radius of 9 cm is approximately 254.34 cm^2.

Example 2: The radius of a circle is 4 inches. Find the circumference

Solution:

- We are given:
  - Radius of the circle = 6 inches
- To find the circumference (C) of a circle, we use the formula:
  - $C = 2\pi r$
  - Where r is the radius
- Substitute the given radius into the formula:
  - $C - 2\pi(6\,inches)$
- Use the value of $\pi \approx 3.14$
  - $C \approx 2(3.14)(6)$
- Calculate:
  - $C \approx 37.68\,inches$

Therefore, the circumference of a circle with radius 6 inches is approximately 37.68 inches.

Measuring Angles in Degrees and Radians:

Degrees

- The full circle is 360°
- Degrees are a familiar unit for measuring angles

- Defined as 1/360 of a full rotation

Radians

- The full circle is 2π radians

- Radians are an alternative unit of angular measure based on the radius of a circle. One radian is the angle subtended when the arc length is equal to the radius.

- $Radians = \frac{Arc\ Length}{Radius}$

- Based on the mathematical constant π

- No fixed upper limit (can be greater than 360°)

Converting between Degrees and Radians

- To convert from degrees to radians: $radians = \left(\frac{degrees}{180}\right) \times \pi$

- To convert from radians to degrees: $degrees = \left(\frac{radians}{\pi}\right) \times 180^0$

- Proportional relationship to convert between radian and degree measures

$$\frac{radian\ measures}{\pi} = \frac{degree\ measures}{180^0}$$

- Some common conversions:

  - $90° = \frac{\pi}{2} radians$

  - $180° = \pi\ radians$

  - $270° = \frac{3\pi}{2} radians$

  - $360° = 2\pi\ radians$

Calculating Arc Lengths and Sector Areas:

- **Arc Length:** The arc length (s) is the distance along the circumference of the circle. It is calculated using the formula: $s = r \times \theta$, where θ is the central angle in radians.

- **Sector Area:** The area of a sector (A) is the region enclosed by an arc and the two radii. It is given by the formula: $A = \frac{1}{2}r^2\theta$, where θ is the central angle in radians.

This also means we can use radian measures to calculate arc lengths and sector areas just like we can with degree measures:

$$\frac{central\ angle}{2\pi} = \frac{arc\ length}{circumference} = \frac{sector\ area}{circle\ area}$$

Example 3: Sam measures the angle in a triangle with the help of a protractor as 60^0. Convert the angle into radian measure.

Solution: Sam measures the angle as 60°

- To convert from degrees to radians, we use the formula:
  - $Radians = \left(\dfrac{Degrees}{180}\right) \times \pi$
- We are given the degrees measure as 60°

- So plugging this into the formula:
  - $Radians = \left(\dfrac{60}{180}\right) \times \pi$
  - $Radians = \left(\dfrac{1}{3}\right) \times \pi$
  - $Radians = \dfrac{\pi}{3}$

Therefore, the angle of 60° converted to radian measure is: π/3 radians

Example 4: Sally marks an arc of length 8 inches and measures its central angle as 120 degrees. What is the radius of the arc?

Solution:

$Arc\ length = r \times \theta$

Where:

- r = radius of the circle
- θ = central angle in radians

In this case, the central angle is given in degrees, so we need to convert it to radians using the conversion factor $\dfrac{\pi}{180}$, since 1 degree is equal to $\dfrac{\pi}{180}$ radians.

Given:

- Arc length s = 8 inches
- Central angle θ = 120 degrees

We can use the formula to find the radius $s = r \times \theta$

$$8 = r \times \dfrac{120\pi}{180}$$

$$8 = r \times \dfrac{2\pi}{3}$$

$$r = \dfrac{8 \times 3}{2\pi}$$

$$r = \dfrac{24}{2\pi}$$

$r = \dfrac{12}{\pi}$ So, the radius of the arc is 12/π inches.

Example 5: George wants to create a garden in the shape of a sector of radius 42 feet and having a central angle of 120 degrees. Calculate the area of the grass which is required to cover the garden.

Solution:

- The garden is in the shape of a sector
- It has:
    - Radius = 42 feet
    - Central angle = 120°
- To find the sector area, we use:
    - $Area\ of\ sector\ =\ \left(\frac{Central\ angle}{360^0}\right) \times \pi \times (Radius)^2$
- Plugging in the values:
    - $Area\ =\ \left(\frac{120°}{360^0}\right) \times \pi \times (42)^2$
    - $Area\ =\frac{1}{3} \times \pi \times 42 \times 42$
    - $Area\ =\frac{1}{3} \times \frac{22}{7} \times 42 \times 42$
    - $Area\ =\ 22 \times 2 \times 42$
    - $Area\ =\ 1848\ square\ feet$

Therefore, the area of the sector is 1848 square feet.

Trigonometric functions using a Unit circle

Unit circle : The unit circle has a radius of 1 unit and is centered at (0,0) on the coordinate plane.

- For an angle θ in standard position on the unit circle:
    - The x-coordinate is defined as cos(θ)
    - The y-coordinate is defined as sin(θ)
- This leads to the following definitions:
    - Cosine function: cos(θ) = x-coordinate on the unit circle
    - Sine function: sin(θ) = y-coordinate on the unit circle

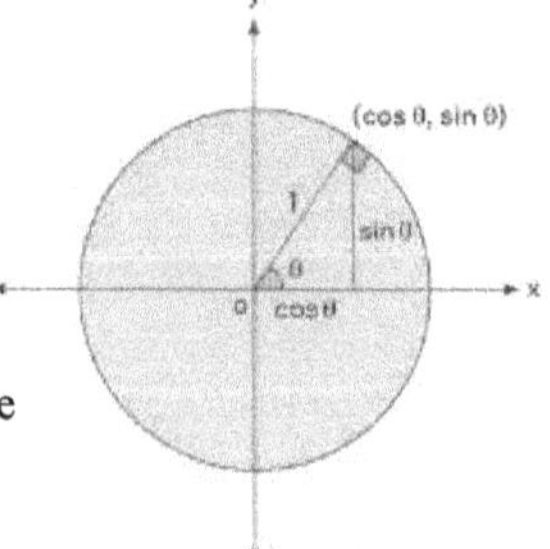

- Tan, sec, csc, cot are defined as ratios:

  - $Tan(\theta) = \dfrac{sin(\theta)}{cos(\theta)}$

  - $Sec(\theta) = \dfrac{1}{cos(\theta)}$

  - $Csc(\theta) = \dfrac{1}{sin(\theta)}$

  - $Cot(\theta) = \dfrac{1}{tan(\theta)} = \dfrac{cos(\theta)}{sin(\theta)}$

- Here is a table of sine and cosine values for some common angles in degrees and radians:

θ	0° (or) 0	30° (or) $\frac{\pi}{6}$	45° (or) $\frac{\pi}{4}$	60° (or) $\frac{\pi}{3}$	90° (or) $\frac{\pi}{2}$
sin θ	0	$\frac{1}{2}$	$\frac{\sqrt{2}}{2}$	$\frac{\sqrt{3}}{2}$	1
cos θ	1	$\frac{\sqrt{3}}{2}$	$\frac{\sqrt{2}}{2}$	$\frac{1}{2}$	0
tan θ	0	$\frac{\sqrt{3}}{3}$	1	$\sqrt{3}$	Not Defined

Example 6 : The circle has center O, and the central angle of the shaded sector measures 225^0. The area of the shaded sector is what fraction of the ar-- -f +h- -i--l-?

(The number of degrees of arc in a circle is 360)

Solution:

- We are given:

  - The circle has center O

  - The central angle of the shaded sector measures 225°

  - The total number of degrees in a circle is 360°

- We want to find:

  - The fraction representing the ratio of the shaded sector area to the total circle area

- To find this, we note:

  - The central angle of the shaded sector is 225° out of the total 360° in the circle

  - The area of a sector is proportional to its central angle

  - Therefore, the fraction representing the shaded area is:

    - $\dfrac{Central\ angle\ of\ shaded\ sector}{Total\ central\ angle\ of\ circle}$

    - $\dfrac{225°}{360°}$

- $\dfrac{5}{8}$

So the area of the shaded sector is 5/8 of the total area of the circle.

Equations of Circles:

The equation of a circle in the Cartesian coordinate system is given by:

$$(x - h)^2 + (y - k)^2 = r^2$$

where:

- (h, k) is the center of the circle,

- r is the radius of the circle.

This equation represents all the points (x,y) that are equidistant from the center (h,k) by a distance of r.

It is the standard equation of a circle.

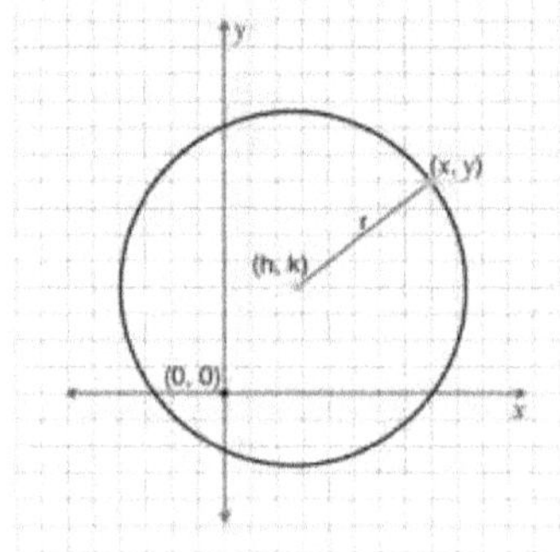

General Form of the circle : The general form of the equation is $x^2 + y^2 + Ax + By + C = 0$, where A, B, and C are constants.

- **Identify the Center and Radius:**

    - Once the equation is in standard form, the center (h, k) is given by $\left(-\dfrac{A}{2}, -\dfrac{B}{2}\right)$, and the radius r is given by $h^2 + k^2 - C$.

$$(x - h)^2 + (y - k)^2 = r^2$$

In this standard form, (h, k) is the center of the circle, and r is the radius.

Example 7: On the unit circle with a radius of 1, consider an obtuse central angle of 120^0. Find the coordinates of the point on the unit circle corresponding to th

Solution:

Given:

- Unit circle with radius = 1

- Obtuse angle = 120 degrees

To find:

- Coordinates of the point on the circle corresponding to the 120-degree angle

Steps:

- Angle 120 degrees is in quadrant II of the coordinate plane

- The reference angle is 180 - 120 = 60 degrees

- On the unit circle:

    - x-coordinate = cos(angle)

    - y-coordinate = sin(angle)

- For the reference angle 60 degrees:

    - $\cos(60) = \frac{1}{2}$

    - $\sin(60) = \frac{\sqrt{3}}{2}$

Therefore, the coordinates of the point on the unit circle corresponding to a 120 degree angle are: $\left(\frac{1}{2}, \frac{\sqrt{3}}{2}\right)$

Example 8: Given the equation $x^2 + y^2 - 6x - 4y + 3 = 0$, find the center and radius.

Solution:

1. Complete the square for both x and y: $(x^2 - 6x) + (y^2 - 4y) + 3 = 0$

To complete the square for x: $(x^2 - 6x + 9) + (y^2 - 4y) + 3 - 9 = 0$

To complete the square for y: $(x^2 - 6x + 9) + (y^2 - 4y + 4) + 3 - 9 - 4 = 0$

Combine the perfect squares: $(x - 3)^2 + (y - 2)^2 - 10 = 0$

2. Now, identify the center and radius:

    - The center is $(3,2)$ (from (h, k)).

    - The radius is $r=10$ (from the coefficient of the completed square term).

So, the equation $(x - 3)^2 + (y - 2)^2 = 10$ represents a circle with center $(3,2)$ and radius $\sqrt{10}$.

Practice question:

1. Convert between radian and degree measure
   (a) Convert $20°$ to radians.
   (b) Convert $60°$ to radians.
   (c) Convert $\frac{2}{3}\pi$ to degrees.
   (d) Convert $\frac{13}{18}\pi$ to degrees.
   (e) Convert $200°$ to radians.
   (f) Convert $\frac{11}{12}\pi$ to degrees.

2. Find the area and circumference of each circle. Round the answer to two decimal places. (use $\pi=3.14$)

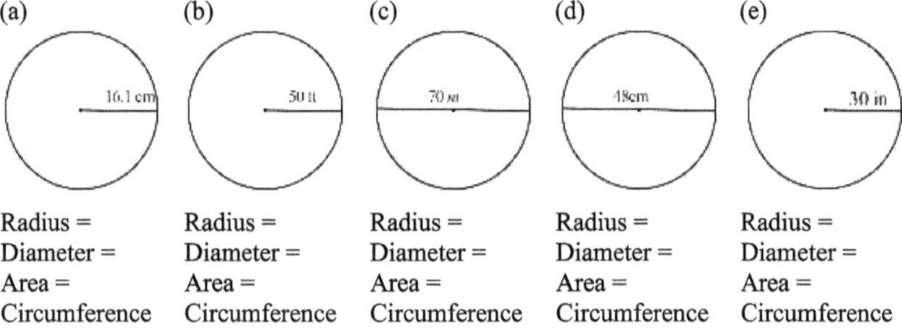

(a)	(b)	(c)	(d)	(e)
Radius =	Radius =	Radius =	Radius =	Radius =
Diameter =	Diameter =	Diameter =	Diameter =	Diameter =
Area =	Area =	Area =	Area =	Area =
Circumference =	Circumference =	Circumference =	Circumference =	Circumference =

3. Find the length of the arc and area of the shaded region. Round the answer to two decimal places. (use $\pi = 3.14$).

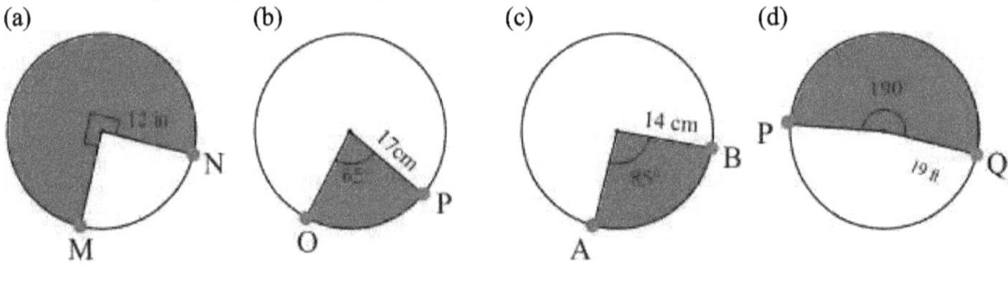

Length of the arc MN =	Length of the arc OP =	Length of the arc AB =	Length of the arc PQ =
Area of a sector =	Area of a sector =	Area of a sector =	Area of a sector =

4. Find the value x

(a)

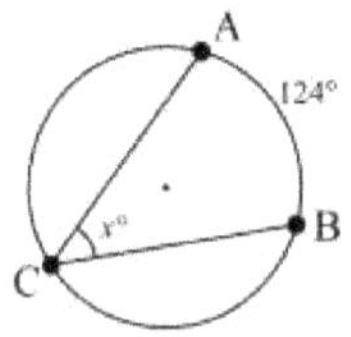

(b)

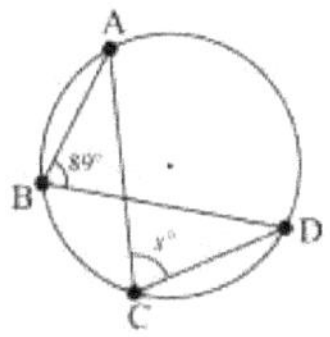

(c)

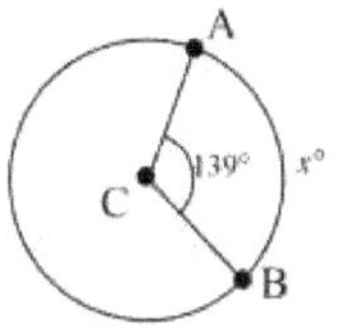

(d)

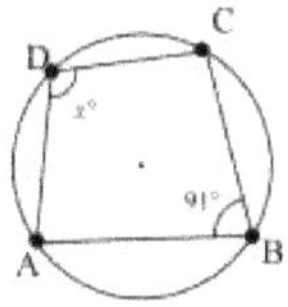

(e)

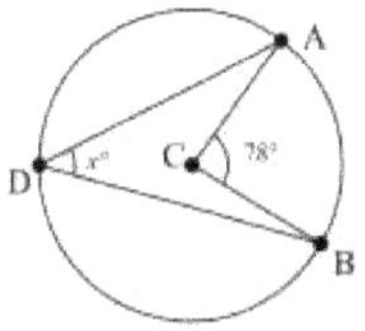

(f)

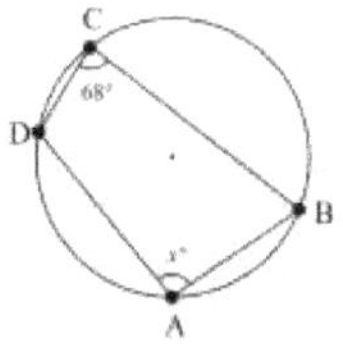

(g)

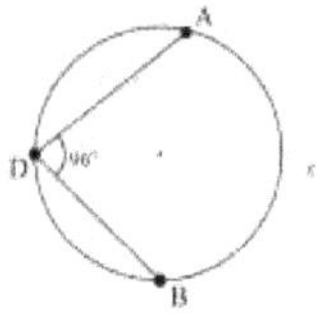

(h)

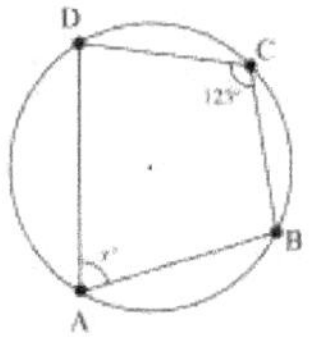

(i)

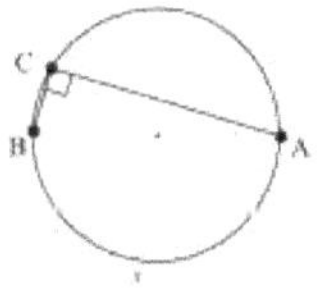

(j)

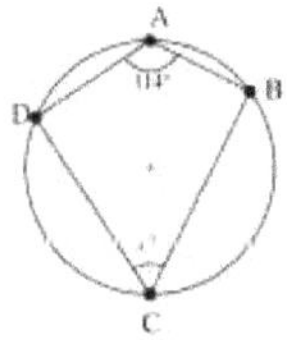

(k)

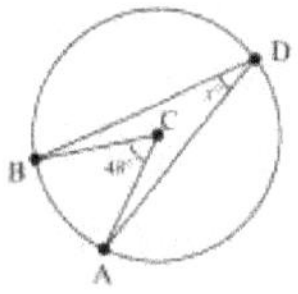

(l)

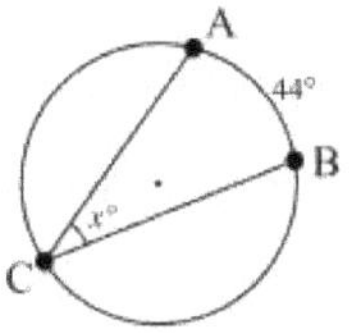

(m)   (n)

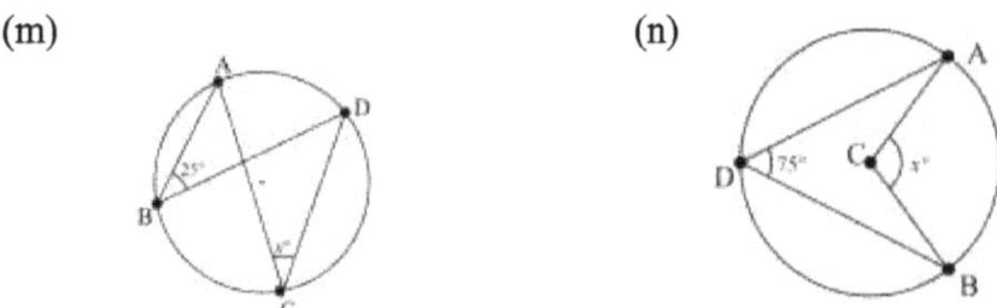

5. What is the area of a circle, one-quarter of the circumference of which is 5.5 inches?

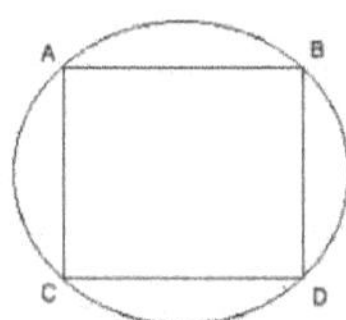

6. In the diagram above, square ABCD is inscribed in the circle. If the area of the square is 9, what is the area of the circle?
7. If a circular garden with a radius of 3 ft. is bordered by a circular sidewalk that is 2 ft. wide, what is the area of the sidewalk?
8. If the equation of a circle is $(x - 7)^2 + (y + 1)^2 = 81$, what is the area of the circle?
9. A circle with a diameter of 6" sits inside a circle with a radius of 8". What is the area of the interstitial space between the two circles?
10. If the radius of Circle A is three times the radius of Circle B, what is the ratio of the area of Circle A to the area of Circle B?
11. A circle has center O and radius 10 cm. The central angle of a shaded sector measures 120°. What fraction of the circle's area is shaded?
12. A sector of a circle of radius 8 m has an arc length of 12π m. If the entire circle has circumference 25π m, what fraction of the circle's area is the sector?
13. A sector of a circle with a radius '18cm' has a central angle '120°'. Find the area of the sector.$(\pi = 3.14)$
14. Validate if the point $P\left[\frac{1}{2}, \frac{\sqrt{3}}{2}\right]$ lies on the unit circle.
15. A sector of a circle of radius 6 ft has an area of 18π ft2. If the central angle of the sector is 135°, what is the area of the entire circle?
16. Write the equation of a circle with a center at (2, 3) and a radius of 5.
17. Given the equation of a circle: $(x^2 + y^2 - 6x + 4y - 12 = 0)$, find the center and the radius of the circle.
18. A circle has the equation $((x - 1)^2 + (y + 4)^2 = 25)$. What is the center and the radius of the circle?
19. Write the equation of a circle with a center at (5, -3) and passing through the point (1, 2).
20. A circle has its center at (2, -1) and passes through the point (6, 5). What is the equation of the circle?

21. Does the point (1, -2) lie inside, outside or on the circle with equation $x^2 + y^2 - 4x - 8y + 12 = 0$?
22. Find the point(s) of intersection of the circles $x^2 + y^2 = 25$ and $x^2 + y^2 = 16$.
23. The endpoints of a diameter of a circle are (-4, 1) and (2, -3). Write the equation of the circle.
24. Find the exact value of tan 210° using the unit circle.
25. Find the value of sin 900° using unit circle.
26. The diameter of a circle has endpoints at points (2, 10) and (–8, –14). Which of the following points does NOT lie on the circle?

27. A circle exists entirely in the first quadrant such that it intersects the y-axis at y=6. If the circle intersects the x-axis in at least one point, what is the area of the circle?

28. We have a square with length 2 sitting in the first quadrant with one corner touching the origin. If the square is inscribed inside a circle, find the equation of the circle.
29. What is the radius of a circle with the equation $x(x - 8) + y(y - 6) = 24$?
30. If the central angle of a circle is 82.4° and the arc length formed is 23 cm then find out the radius of the circle.
31. In right $\Delta PQR,\ m\angle R\ =\ 90^{\circ}, \cos P\ =\frac{2}{11},\ What\ is \sin Q$?
32. In a right triangle, given that $sin\ (y\ +\ 50)\ =\ cos\ (9y\ +\ 20)$ for the 2 acute angles, find the number of degrees in the acute angles.
33. In right $\Delta ABC,\ m\angle C\ =\ 90^{\circ}$. Simplify the following expression: $SinA\ -\ CosB$
34. In right $\Delta ABC,\ m\angle C\ =\ 90^{\circ}$ and $m\angle A$ does not equal the $m\angle B$.
If $sin\ A\ =\ x\ and\ \cos A\ =\ y, find\ \cos B\ +\ \sin B$
$(a)\ x - y,\ (b)\ 90 - (x + y), (c)\ y - x, (d)\ x\ +\ y$

Answer:

1. (a) π/9 (b) π/3 (c) 120° (d) 130° (e) $\frac{10}{9}\pi$ (f) 165°
2. (a) Radius = 16.1 cm Diameter = 32.2 cm Area =813.92 cm^2 Circumference =101.11 cm
    (b) Radius = 50 ft Diameter = 100 ft Area =7850 ft^2 Circumference =314 ft
    (c) Radius = 35 m Diameter = 70 m Area =3846.5 m^2 Circumference =219.8 m
    (d) Radius = 24 cm Diameter = 48 cm Area =1808.6cm^2 Circumference =150.7 cm
    (e) Radius = 30 in Diameter = 60 in Area =2826 in^2 Circumference =188.4 in

3. (a) Length of the arc MN = 56.52 in, Area of a sector = 339.12 in^2
    (b) Length of the arc OP = 19.28 cm, Area of a sector = 163.85 cm^2
    (c) Length of the arc AB = 20.76 cm, Area of a sector = 145.31 cm^2
    (d) Length of the arc PQ = 62.97 ft , Area of a sector = 598.26 ft^2
4.

(a) 62^0	(b) 89^0
(c) 139^0	(d) 89^0
(e) 39^0	(f) 112^0
(g) 192^0	(h) 57^0
(i) 180^0	(j) 39^0
(k) 24^0	(l) 22^0
(m) 25^0	(n) 150^0

5. 121/π
6. 4.5π
7. 16π
8. 81π
9. 55π in^2
10. 9
11. 1/3
12. 3/5
13. 339.12 cm^2
14. Yes
15. $36\pi\ ft^2$.
16. $(x - 2)^2 + (y - 3)^2 = 25$.
17. center (3, -2) and radius 5.
18. center (1, -4) and radius 5.
19. $(x - 5)^2 + (y + 3)^2 = 25$
20. $(x - 2)^2 + (y + 1)^2 = 52$
21. the point lies outside the circle.
22. the intersection points of the two circles are (4, 0) and (-4, 0).
23. $(x + 1)^2 + (y + 1)^2 = 25$
24. 1/√3
25. 0
26. (−8,−12)

27. 36π

28. $(x - 1)^2 + (y - 1)^2 = 2$

29. 7

30. r = 16 cm

31. 2/11

32. (y = 2), 52 deg, 38 deg

33. 0

34. d

<u>Math Formula/ Key Notes</u>

1. A linear equation of one variable is $ax + b = c$

2. A linear equation in two variables is $ax + by = c$

3. Linear equations can be written in function notation as $y = mx + c$, where m is the slope and c is the y-intercept.

4. Calculating Slope from Two Points

$$m = \frac{(y_2 - y_1)}{(x_2 - x_1)}$$

5. Given a slope and a point on the line, you can write the equation in point slope form.

$$(y - y_1) = m(x - x_1)$$

6. Parallel lines have the same slope and never intersect.

7. Perpendicular lines have negative reciprocal slopes and intersect at a right angle.

8. Parallel lines have equations with the same slope but different y-intercepts.
9. If No solution => Lines are parallel and have same slopes
10. Perpendicular lines have equations with negative reciprocal slopes and different y-intercepts.
    $(m1 = -1/m2)$
11. If Infinite solutions => Lines are same or multiples, and therefor coefficients are always in proportion
12. Speed = Distance/time. Let "s" be the speed, "d" be the distance, "t" be the time. $s = \frac{d}{t}$

13. A linear inequality in one variable can be expressed as: $ax + b < c$

14. A linear inequality in two variables can be expressed as: $ax + by < c$

15. Quadratic Equation: $ax^2 + bx + c = 0$

16. Quadratic Formula to find out the roots

$$x = \frac{-b \pm \sqrt{b^2 - 4ac}}{2a}$$

Sum of the roots $(x_1 + x_2) := -\frac{b}{a}$

Product of the roots $(x_1 * x_2) := \frac{c}{a}$

17. $|x - a| < b = (x - a) < b \text{ AND } (x - a) > -b$

18. $|x - a| > b = (x - a) > b$ OR $(x - a) < -b$

19. 3 step process to change from inequality to abs value form
$$a < x < b = |x - (a + b)/2| < b - (a + b)/2$$

20. Basic Properties:
   Symmetry: $| x |=| -x |$
   Non-Negativity: $|x| \geq 0$ for all values of x.
   Identity: $| x |= x \ if \ x \geq 0, and \ | x |= -x \ if \ x < 0.$
   Triangle Inequality: $| x + y | \leq | x | + | y |$

21. Rational Equations is $\frac{P(x)}{Q(x)} = 0$, where P(x) and Q(x) are polynomials.

22. Exponential Equations: $a^x = b$

23. Properties of Exponents:
   - $a^m \cdot a^n = a^{m+n}$
   - $a^m \div a^n = a^{m-n}$
   - $(a^m)^n = a^{mn}$
   - $a^0 = 1$
   - $a^{-n} = \frac{1}{a^n}$
   - $(ab)^m = a^m * b^m.$

   - $\left(\frac{a}{b}\right)^m = \frac{a^m}{b^m.} = a^m b^{-m}$
   - $a^{\frac{m}{n}} = \sqrt[n]{(a^m)}$

24. Polynomial Remainder Theorem: The Polynomial Remainder Theorem is a useful concept in algebra that relates polynomial division to remainders. It states that if a polynomial $P(x)$ is divided by $x-c$, then the remainder is $P(c)$.
   For radical equation, the need to plug back and check for extraneous solutions.

25. Linear growth equation $y = mx + b$, where m = linear rate of change, and b = Fixed Cost / Y-Intercept / Starting Point

26. Exponential Growth equation: y = a.b power x, where a = Fixed Cost / Y-Intercept / Starting Point, and b = exponential rate of change / multiplier

27. Vertex Form: $f(x) = a(x - h)^2 + k$
   To convert from standard form to vertex form, we use the following formulas:
   $$h = -\frac{b}{2a},$$
   k = f(h), where f(h) is the value of the quadratic function at x = h.

28. Intercept Form: $f(x) = a(x - r)(x - s),$ where a, r, and s are real numbers and $a \neq 0$

29.   Ratios: a: b

30.   Inverse proportion $x \cdot y = k$ where k is a constant.

31.   Average speed $= \frac{\text{Total Distance}}{\text{Total Time}}$

32.   Calculating percentages: $Percentage = \left(\frac{Part}{Whole}\right) * 100.$

33.   Net Price Calculation: The formula for calculating the net price, considering a discount applied before tax, is:

$$\text{Net Price} = \text{Price} \times \left(1 - \frac{\text{Discount Rate}}{100}\right) \times \left(1 + \frac{\text{Tax Rate}}{100}\right)$$

$$\text{Net Price} = \text{P} \times \left(1 - \frac{\text{D}}{100}\right) \times \left(1 + \frac{\text{T}}{100}\right)$$

34. $\text{Probability} = \frac{\text{Number of favorable outcomes}}{\text{Total number of equally likely outcomes}}$

35.
$$\text{Mean} = \frac{\text{Sum of all values}}{\text{Number of values}}$$

36.   Calculation: Range = Maximum Value − Minimum Value

37.   Calculation: IQR = Q3 − Q1

38.   Calculation: Variance

$$(\sigma^2) = \frac{\sum_{i=1}^{n}(x_i - \bar{x})^2}{N}$$

39.   Standard Deviation$(\sigma) = \sqrt{\text{Variance}}$

40.   Estimate = Sample proportion * Population

41.   Range = Estimate $\pm$ Margin of Error

42. Relation between Sample size / Cluster / Standard Deviation / Margin of Error / Outliers :
    Increase in Sample Size => Decrease in Margin of Error
    Increase in Clustering => Decrease in Standard Deviation => Decrease in Margin of Error
    Outliers have little impact on median, some impact on mean, larger impact on standard deviation

43.   Coefficient of Variation (CV)

$$CV = \left(\frac{\sigma}{\mu}\right) \times 100$$

44.

 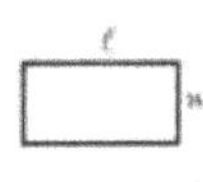 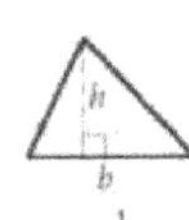 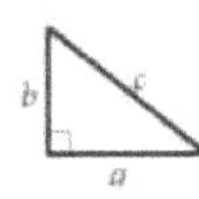 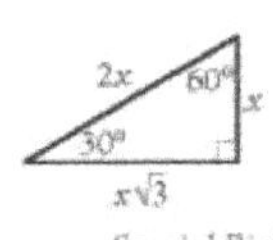 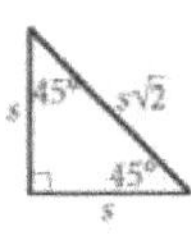

$$A = \pi r^2 \qquad A = \ell w \qquad A = \frac{1}{2}bh \qquad c^2 = a^2 + b^2 \qquad \text{Special Right Triangles}$$
$$C = 2\pi r$$

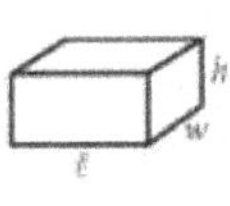 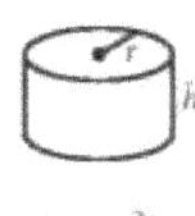  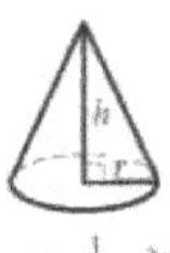 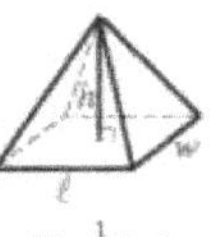

$$V = \ell w h \qquad V = \pi r^2 h \qquad V = \frac{4}{3}\pi r^3 \qquad V = \frac{1}{3}\pi r^2 h \qquad V = \frac{1}{3}\ell w h$$

45.   Pythagorean Theorem: $c^2 = a^2 + b^2$.

46.   Common triplets (3-4-5, 5-12-13)

47.   30-60-90 Triangle: The sides are in the ratio $1 : \sqrt{3} : 2$

48.   45-45-90 Triangle: The sides are in the ratio $1 : 1 : \sqrt{2}$

49.   Sine (sin): $\sin(\theta) = \dfrac{\text{Opposite}}{\text{Hypotenuse}}$

        Cosine (cos): $\cos(\theta) = \dfrac{\text{Adjacent}}{\text{Hypotenuse}}$

        Tangent (tan): $\tan(\theta) = \dfrac{\text{Opposite}}{\text{Adjacent}}$

50.   Sin A = Cos (90-A)

51.

θ (deg.)	θ (rad.)	sin θ		cos θ		tan θ
0	0	0	$\frac{\sqrt{0}}{2}$	1	$\frac{\sqrt{4}}{2}$	0
30°	$\frac{\pi}{6}$	$\frac{1}{2}$	$\frac{\sqrt{1}}{2}$	$\frac{\sqrt{3}}{2}$	$\frac{\sqrt{3}}{2}$	$\frac{\sqrt{3}}{3}$
45°	$\frac{\pi}{4}$	$\frac{\sqrt{2}}{2}$	$\frac{\sqrt{2}}{2}$	$\frac{\sqrt{2}}{2}$	$\frac{\sqrt{2}}{2}$	1
60°	$\frac{\pi}{3}$	$\frac{\sqrt{3}}{2}$	$\frac{\sqrt{3}}{2}$	$\frac{1}{2}$	$\frac{\sqrt{1}}{2}$	$\sqrt{3}$
90°	$\frac{\pi}{2}$	1	$\frac{\sqrt{4}}{2}$	0	$\frac{\sqrt{0}}{2}$	∞
120°	$\frac{2\pi}{3}$	$\frac{\sqrt{3}}{2}$	$\frac{\sqrt{3}}{2}$	$-\frac{1}{2}$	$-\frac{\sqrt{1}}{2}$	$-\sqrt{3}$
135°	$\frac{3\pi}{4}$	$\frac{\sqrt{2}}{2}$	$\frac{\sqrt{2}}{2}$	$-\frac{\sqrt{2}}{2}$	$-\frac{\sqrt{2}}{2}$	-1
150°	$\frac{5\pi}{6}$	$\frac{1}{2}$	$\frac{\sqrt{1}}{2}$	$-\frac{\sqrt{3}}{2}$	$-\frac{\sqrt{3}}{2}$	$-\frac{\sqrt{3}}{3}$
180°	π	0	$\frac{\sqrt{0}}{2}$	-1	$-\frac{\sqrt{4}}{2}$	0

52. Area: $A = \pi r^2$

53. Circumference: $C = 2\pi r$

54. Equations of Circles: The equation of a circle in the Cartesian coordinate system is given by:

$$(x - h)^2 + (y - k)^2 = r^2$$

where:

- (h, k) is the center of the circle?
- r is the radius of the circle.

55. Central Angle $= \dfrac{\text{Length of the Arc}}{\text{Radius}}$

56. Central Angle = 2 time Inscribed Angle

57.

Angles In A Circle	
Inscribed angles subtended by the same arc are equal.	
Angles subtended by the diameter (or semi-circle) is 90°.	
Central angle is twice any inscribed angle subtended by the same arc.	

58. Converting between Degrees and Radians

To convert from degrees to radians: $\text{radians} = \left(\frac{\text{degrees}}{180}\right) \times \pi$

To convert from radians to degrees: $\text{degrees} = \left(\frac{\text{radians}}{\pi}\right) \times 180^0$

Proportional relationship to convert between radian and degree measures

$$\frac{\text{radian measures}}{\pi} = \frac{\text{degree measures}}{180^0}$$

59. Calculating Arc Lengths and Sector Areas:

$$\frac{\text{central angle}}{2\pi} = \frac{\text{arc length}}{\text{circumference}} = \frac{\text{sector area}}{\text{circle area}}$$

- **Arc Length::** $s = r \times \theta$

- **Sector Area:** $A = \frac{1}{2}r^2\theta$

60. $\text{Radians} = \left(\frac{\text{Degrees}}{180}\right) \times \pi$

Author Biography:

Dr. Summiya Parveen is an esteemed educator currently serving as an Assistant Professor at COER University. With over 18 years of teaching experience, Dr. Parveen specializes in mathematics education, with a focus on Numerical Analysis and Image Processing.

She earned her PhD in Mathematics from HNB Garhwal University in Srinagar, India, where her research explored innovative applications of numerical analysis and image processing techniques. Dr. Parveen's expertise in these areas has led to the publication of several research papers in esteemed national and international journals and conferences.

As an educator, Dr. Parveen is known for her dedication to student success and her commitment to fostering a deeper understanding of mathematical concepts. Her innovative teaching methods and passion for mathematics have inspired countless students to excel in their academic pursuits.

Driven by a desire to make high-quality education accessible to all students, Dr. Parveen is excited to share her expertise through her latest publication, "Crack the SAT Math Code: Proven Techniques and Exercises." This comprehensive guide is a testament to Dr. Parveen's commitment to empowering students and helping them achieve their academic goals.

www.ingramcontent.com/pod-product-compliance
Lightning Source LLC
Chambersburg PA
CBHW041557160726
48006CB00042B/1999